Suburban Erasure

Suburban Erasure

How the Suburbs Ended the Civil Rights Movement in New Jersey

Walter David Greason

FAIRLEIGH DICKINSON UNIVERSITY PRESS
Madison • Teaneck

Published by Fairleigh Dickinson University Press
Co-published with The Rowman & Littlefield Publishing Group, Inc.
4501 Forbes Boulevard, Suite 200, Lanham, Maryland 20706
www.rowman.com

16 Carlisle Street, London W1D 3BT, United Kingdom

British Library Cataloguing in Publication Information Available

Library of Congress Cataloging-in-Publication Data

Greason, Walter
Suburban erasure : how the suburbs ended the civil rights movement in New Jersey / Walter Greason
pages cm
Includes bibliographical references.
1. African Americans—Civil rights—New Jersey—History—20th century. 2. Civil rights movements—New Jersey—History—20th century. 3. African American civil rights workers—New Jersey—History—20th century. 4. Suburbs—New Jersey—History—20th century. 5. Segregation—
New Jersey—History—20th century. 6. New Jersey—Race relations—History—20th century. I. Title.
E185.93.N54G74 2012
323.1196'0730749—dc23
2012038912

ISBN: 978-1-61147-570-8 (cloth : alk. paper)
ISBN: 978-1-61147-729-0 (pbk. : alk. paper)
ISBN: 978-1-61147-571-5 (electronic)

Printed in the United States of America

Contents

Acknowledgments

It began as a simple project. At the beginning, I just wanted to know why I was going to school. My mother's reply was that I should get a good education, and because she earned her master's degree, I had to do better than she did. I asked what was better than a master's degree. She said, "You're going to get your PhD." I was five years old.

Given the knowledge of my goal, I never questioned much about the process of achieving it. This naivete was especially true when my parents were injured in a car accident, and I spoke with my dissertation advisor about changing my project from racial violence in South Africa to suburban development in New Jersey. Three years into the dissertation process, I realized how few and fragmented the primary sources about New Jersey's rural communities are. Four years later, my dissertation was complete, and I faced the challenge of revising it into a publishable manuscript. As one of my graduate student colleagues laughed, "No one wants to read about 'Mon-Mouth' County, New Jersey!" Thankfully, thousands of people have disagreed over the intervening years.

Suburbs, and, more specifically, metropolitan growth has become one of the hottest topics for academic work over the last two decades. This interest is the product of a reality that became an emphasis in the popular media after 1990. Millions of people around the world moved out of cities into the surrounding residential suburbs in the second half of the twentieth century. We will spend most of next few decades deciphering the causes and consequences of this massive global migration. *Suburban Erasure* is just one piece of an emerging puzzle that explores the intersection of work, leisure, family, and politics as a result of the changing technologies and ideologies that comprise the process we call "globalization." I could not have accomplished this interdisciplinary analysis of African American and urban history without the support of dozens of advisors, supporters, friends, and family members over the last fifteen years.

The extraordinary faculty at Temple University guided the early stages of my work. Kenneth Kusmer, Wilbert Jenkins, Teshale Tibebu, Peter Gran, and Bettye Collier-Thomas all made invaluable contributions to my first efforts to understand the process of migration. Clement Price, V. P. Franklin, Mary Sies, Andrew Wiese, and Myra Armstead all added important insights that helped me add nuance to my initial conclusions. Recently, colleagues like Maghan Keita, William Carrigan, Emily Blanck, Richardson Dilworth, Julian Chambliss, and John McCarthy challenged my reading of the evidence and helped me improve the conclusions you will find here. The New Jersey Historical Commission generously supported me with multiple grants to find new primary source material in dozens of local libraries. The list of librarians, archivists, and independent scholars who shared the resources they gathered over their lifetimes is much too long to list here, but, as a professionally trained historian, I am humbled and profoundly appreciative of these public historians' efforts to preserve the stories of our past that could easily be destroyed and forgotten.

The last few years of work coincided with my teaching at Ursinus College. College President John Strassburger and Vice President for Academic Affairs Judith Levy were unwavering in their support for my academic career. My departmental colleagues—Ross Doughty, Hugh Clark, Richard King, Dallett Hemphill, and Susanna Throop—are the best team I have worked with as a professional. Additionally, an interdisciplinary collaboration with environmental scientists (Rich Wallace, Leah Joseph, and Patrick Hurley), philosophers and theologians (Kelly Sorensen, Nathan Rein, Roger Florka, and Charles Rice), sociologists (Maggie Ussery, Regina Oboler, and Jane Jones), musicians (Holly Gaines), educators (John Spencer), art historians (Matt Shoaf and Deborah Barkun), and literary analysts (Nzadi Keita, Patti Schroeder, Meredith Goldsmith, Rebecca Jaroff, Greg Weight, and Erec Smith) enriched my approach to this work in ways that could only occur at a small, liberal arts college. I am deeply indebted to all of them.

Mostly, however, this work reflects my upbringing among the tomato and potato farms of rural New Jersey. To Mom, Dad, Wilma Diana, Cousin William, Shaylah, and all of my aunts, uncles, cousins, nieces, and nephews who know all the details I could not manage to squeeze into this book, thank you for your love, patience, and support on this long journey. To Janiece, you are the reason I celebrate every day and pray that I get to see another sunrise in the morning. To my sons, the Greason brothers, I hope that one day you both will read this book and be reminded that justice is always within your grasp, and it is your responsibility to never surrender in its pursuit. Nas once wrote, "If Heaven was a mile away / would I pack up my bags and leave this world behind?" He meant paradise is always with all of us in our hearts, if we just choose to see it. If you're reading this sentence, you are seeing one of the moments when I got another glimpse of Heaven in my life. Thank you for sharing it with me.

Introduction

George Henry White's "Defense of the Negro Race" in 1901 opened the twentieth century with an appeal to the national interest of all Americans in promoting the improved social status of African Americans. "Obliterate race hatred, party prejudice, and help us to achieve nobler ends, greater results, and become more satisfactory citizens to our brother in white. . . . These parting words are in behalf of an outraged, heart-broken, bruised, and bleeding, but God-fearing people, faithful, industrious, loyal people—rising people, full of potential force."[1] After he departed as the last elected African American congressional representative for nearly three decades, White began a project that year to create a self-sustaining African American community in southern New Jersey. His Afro-American Equitable Association pursued a vision of black dignity, industry, and ownership that inspired thousands of African American migrants to follow White's example.[2] White worked to provide a physical space for African Americans—both southern migrants and those born in New Jersey—to demonstrate their commitment to a new vision of American equality that ignored the artificial boundaries of white supremacy. Black rural communities like Whitesboro promoted the reconstruction of democracy in the Garden State.

More than half a century later, Ollievita Williams continued the pursuit of a racially inclusive democracy. Her life in Glassboro emphasized education as the path to social status and success for all people. As a career educator, Williams opened doors for children from elementary school through college in an effort to create a body of engaged citizens who accepted the reality of a racially integrated society. She represented the culmination of the work White began at the start of the twentieth century. Williams also revealed obstacles to the continuing progress on civil rights that were not anticipated before 1965. The urgency of the Black Freedom Movement waned after the accomplishment of legislative desegregation in New Jersey between 1950 and 1970.[3] As new opportunities in education and employment emerged, few community leaders noticed the reinforcement of economic barriers in residential segregation and wealth accumulation.

George White faced violent terrorism coupled with political repression that transformed coastal North Carolina at the turn of the twentieth century. His movement north foreshadowed the Great Migration and created opportunities for African Americans to build new churches,

schools, and civil rights organizations dedicated to eliminating the legitimacy of racial intimidation in American democracy. White's success in
rural New Jersey laid the foundation for Ollievita Williams's career as an
educator in New Jersey's racially integrated school system. Her efforts to
transform the legislative victories of the mid-twentieth century into
greater opportunities for economic equality in the twenty-first century
reflected the transformation of the Black Freedom Movement across the
state and the nation. The African American experience in the rural parts
of the Garden State illustrates the intersection of family values, community politics, state legislation, and economic development between 1900
and 2000. Communication within black families laid the foundation for
community activism and leadership, which became local and state policy
regarding civil rights and racial integration within the context of sprawl-
ing residential growth and global service economic development from
the start of the twentieth century to its end.

This work examines the roles of African Americans in transforming
the culture, politics, and economics of rural New Jersey in the twentieth
century. After surviving both slavery and gradual emancipation in small
towns throughout the state during the nineteenth century, African
Americans moved into towns and neighborhoods outside of the major
urban centers as southern migrants attempted to preserve aspects of folk
life from Virginia, North Carolina, South Carolina, and Georgia. These
black communities coalesced around the families who reinvented their
ideas of work, recreation, and home ownership as they explored the
meanings of freedom within a segregated society. Often without running
water or electricity in their homes, migrant laborers became permanent
residents who built churches, schools, and businesses with the pennies
they saved on jobs as ditch diggers or maids. Local white authorities'
paternalism often provided the only opportunity to transform the lives of
their children and grandchildren. The cost of this assistance was frequently silence as the barriers of discrimination and segregation grew
more rigid through the first two decades of the twentieth century. Booker
T. Washington's prescription for self-reliance was the only consistent
foundation for black success in those early years, yet it fostered a commitment to racial equality in politics modeled on W. E. B. Du Bois's agenda
after 1920.[4] The Black Freedom Movement took root in rural New Jersey
and small towns throughout the North in ways similar to how it took
root in communities in the rural South and the urban North. African
American activism within these towns shaped the legislative and political transformation of the United States that became the civil rights movement after 1950. Their ideas, agency, and organizations redefined the
meaning of freedom and equality as the end of the twentieth century
approached. However, the political orientation of the movement did not
engage the economic aspects of white supremacy. This missing element
led to the continuation of racial assumptions in the consolidation of sub-

urban poverty and the metropolitan growth of suburbs in the Garden State after 1970. As both the state and the nation grappled with continuing inequalities between racial groups in terms of wealth, income, education, residence, and occupation, a better understanding of the ways the Black Freedom Movement transformed race relations in some of the most intransigent rural communities provides crucial knowledge for the revitalization of American democracy in the twenty-first century.

New Jersey's transformation from an agricultural economy to one based on the residential and commercial growth of suburbs allows this study to consider the African American experience in areas where there were few industrial jobs. The different economic context was only one facet of the need for a new historical analysis. Local histories of rural communities rarely engaged questions about race relations in the twentieth century. Sociological studies of the suburbs most often focused on the period after 1940. Increasing the scope of this work to cover the entire twentieth century and integrating the coverage of rural counties provides new foundations for both the chronology and geography of New Jersey's history. Balancing the examination of African American families and communities with the evidence of local and state economic forces permits new arguments about the ways race, class, and gender intersected in the process of metropolitan growth beyond the urban fringe. The resulting history is simultaneously local and regional, cultural and political, economic and social.

The evidence used in this analysis comes from a wide range of sources. Small towns in rural New Jersey frequently possess fragmented public records about the official histories of their communities. The case of African American history expands this limitation. Some of the records were found at Rutgers University, Temple University, Princeton University, the University of Pennsylvania, the Schomburg Center for Research, the New Jersey State Archives, the Newark Public Library, and the Library of Congress. More information was available through the library systems in the county libraries. However, the most recent oral histories and family records came from intensive engagement with African American families of the small towns. Microfilms of the *New Jersey Afro-American* and the *Asbury Park Press* also provided valuable clues about black life and race relations outside of the larger cities. The statistical data on many municipalities came from local and county planning boards and their professional libraries. Combining the cultural histories from the families with the social data from the research libraries and planning boards created a historical narrative that illustrated the complex relationships between institutional power and personal action. This historical method owes a significant debt to the interdisciplinary discourse of urban studies that has generated a new library of research about metropolitan growth over the last twenty years. The inclusion of the countryside as part of the megapolitan connected small, black communities in the rural North to global patterns of suburbanization.

New Jersey's "rural corridor" defines the spatial and geographic identity of the counties providing the most evidence to this book. Gloucester, Camden, Burlington, Monmouth, Middlesex, Somerset, and Morris counties formed a contiguous zone of agricultural production through the first half of the twentieth century. Thousands of African Americans established settlements outside of the state's major cities between 1890 and 1960—the period of the Great Migration from the South. Many scholars have retained a broadly conceptual understanding of New Jersey as two geographic clusters—North (Monmouth County and above) and South (Bergen County and below). The division reflects Benjamin Franklin's famous characterization of New Jersey as a keg tapped at both ends. With Philadelphia metropolitan influences shaping southern Jersey and New York's effects on northern Jersey, the continuing perception is understandable. However, as the state's population grew in its suburbs, New Jersey no longer lost resources to the major cities—it attracted new people and businesses from both New York and Pennsylvania. The garden became the suburb. Franklin's keg became a vacuum, inhaling at both ends. Gloucester, Camden, and Burlington counties attracted disenchanted Philadelphians, while Morris, Somerset, and Middlesex counties drew thousands of commuting New Yorkers. Monmouth County experienced more rapid growth from northern-oriented suburbanites, but also seduced thousands of former Philadelphians. This rural corridor provides a crucial point of spatial reorientation for the study of metropolitan development because it begins with the countryside rather than the city center. Sprawl from this perspective is not expansive. Instead, it is an ominous advance that contracts the available spaces for the slower pace of rural life.

This book attempts to answer several questions. Why did African American migrants choose to settle in rural New Jersey? How did these decisions change their families' opportunities for education, employment, and civic engagement? What was the role of historical memory in these families and communities? How did this role change over time? Why did civil rights organizations form in these towns? Did the size of the populations have any impact on the function of these groups? How did the politics of race change at the local and state levels in response to the success of civil rights laws? What happened to small, black communities as these changes unfolded? Why did racial integration fail to improve education, employment, income, and wealth in many of these towns? How did the absence of black elected officials in rural New Jersey contribute to racial inequalities at the end of the twentieth century? The examination of family life, community politics, state policy, and metropolitan economics will illustrate the ways race and class allowed some new opportunities for African Americans and reinforced other barriers against racial equality.

This book connects two bodies of scholarly literature in the history of New Jersey. Marion Thompson Wright's *The Education of Negroes in New Jersey*, Clement Price's *Freedom Not Far Distant*, Giles Wright's *Afro-Americans in New Jersey*, and Graham Russell Hodges's *Slavery and Freedom in the Rural North* provided a foundation for understanding the variety of African American experiences in the Garden State.[5] Marion Wright presented the dignity of African Americans as part of New Jersey's history within a larger argument about the illegal maintenance of racially segregated school facilities. She blazed the trail that other scholars would follow after 1960. Clement Price and Giles Wright expanded on her work by undertaking the careful reconstruction of African American history, document by document and town by town. Their emphasis on the larger cities reflected the available documents through the first decade following the achievement of federal civil rights. Hodges advanced the understanding of African American life in New Jersey by expanding the geography to include rural areas, especially in the colonial and antebellum periods. Black history included every aspect of the state's past, and its inclusion required a broad reinterpretation of the state's identity. Their collective historiographical tradition stretched from making the argument that African Americans were an important part of history to correcting assumptions about the homogeneity of African American life and culture in both the nineteenth century and the twentieth century.

Urban scholars studied New Jersey as an example of both urban and suburban development with books from Charles Stansfield (*A Geography of New Jersey*); David Kirp, John Dwyer, and Larry Rosenthal (*Our Town*); Howard Gillette (*Camden after the Fall*); Lizabeth Cohen (*A Consumer's Republic*); and Bryant Simon (*Boardwalk of Dreams*).[6] All of these books retain a sense of the urban center as the starting point for metropolitan growth that drives the discussion of African American involvement in the larger narrative. Gillette and Cohen argue for the significance of New Jersey in the national history of suburban development and consumer culture, respectively. They also weave the narrative of the African American experience into the larger context of the social trends at the heart of their research. Combining the spatial frame of historical analysis with the insights of African American history allows the reader to understand a new perspective on metropolitan change—a view that begins in the unexplored rural North of the twentieth century from the marginalized positions of migrant African American families.

This approach contributes to the expanding national literature on suburbanization, metropolitan regions, and uneven development from Myron Orfield's *American Metropolitics*, Andrew Wiese's *A Place of Their Own*, David Freund's *Colored Property*, and Thomas Sugrue's *Sweet Land of Liberty*. Orfield demonstrates the social and economic developments of megapolitans across the United States that shape the global financial landscape without permitting democratic accountability at the local level. Wiese illustrates the variety of African American residential communities around the country in the late nineteenth and early twentieth centuries. Freund shows that white political leaders changed their rhetoric justifying residential segregation from racial arguments to economic arguments in response to federal civil rights legislation. Sugrue presents the difficult and evolving struggle to end racial discrimination and segregation in the northern United States.[7] Bringing the voices of rural African Americans into the historical narrative about spatial, political, and economic change over time in the twentieth century constitutes a significant step towards the understanding of the metropolitan past.

The practices within African American homes and communities enabled generations of black people in New Jersey to develop a functional model of multiracial democracy that transformed the state in the second half of the twentieth century. However, macroeconomic forces of suburbanization and globalization enabled white political and economic authorities in these small towns to limit the effects of the conceptual shift in the meaning of equality during the consolidation of the Boston–Washington megapolitan. Civil rights organizations, churches, and schools dedicated to the uplift of African American social and political engagement in New Jersey became civic antiques, unable to mobilize mass political action against the criminalization of black youth activism and increasing unemployment among the rural working class. This work offers a coherent narrative of black families, communities, and organizations that overcame the racial barriers in small towns, only to encounter spatial and cultural displacement within a massive, metropolitan context beyond the accountability of local, state, and national government.

The analysis emphasizes four key concepts: agency, infrapolitics, residential segregation, and uneven development. African Americans as freed people in the southern United States began their lives as citizens with virtually none of the tools to access political authority and almost all of the obstacles to prevent their attaining real citizenship. Even moving North afforded only a few (if significant) improvements in this status, especially if a family chose to relocate to rural New Jersey. Where movement was the primary form of agency individual African Americans could exercise to escape lynching and de jure segregation, infrapolitics became the strategies and tactics black families employed across the United States to negotiate better opportunities within spatial contexts dominated by white authorities. Black Americans used these two concepts to attain more freedom in their daily lives between 1870 and 1920. Their children internalized these lessons through church and school experiences and established civil rights groups throughout rural New Jersey between 1920 and 1970. The civil rights groups embodied the transformation of the hidden transcript into a public discourse on white supremacy and its incompatibility with democracy. Residential segregation was the most resilient form of white supremacist public policy. Its political adherents in the United States, including New Jersey, transformed the racial foundation for segregation into an economic justification—uneven development. The politics of uneven development buttressed the illegitimate barriers of racism through the end of the twentieth century within the rhetoric of color-blind fairness. The individual agency, community interactions, and organizational power pressed against the class ceiling of residential segregation, global uneven development, and systemic adaptation at the start of the twenty-first century.

Michel Foucault's idea that power constituted a relationship between the oppressor and oppressed recognizes an inherent "agency" within all human beings.[8] No one enjoys absolute authority or suffers permanent alienation in society. The connections between individuals, groups, societies, and humanity are relational, constantly in flux, as language and political economy shift from moment to moment. The episteme, man, was simultaneously subject and object. Power became fluid and mercurial. James Scott defined infrapolitics as the knowing negotiation of changing power relations.[9] People could use their oppressors' perceptions of authority and alienation against those same oppressors to secure more space and time for greater exercise of their individual will without the awareness of their oppressor. Contextual knowledge reveals these hidden transcripts where ostensible victims articulate multiple meanings simultaneously to various audiences. African Americans in rural New Jersey used the language of self-reliance to appear to support the barriers of racial segregation, while gaining access to financial and political resources to create civil rights groups dedicated to eliminating the legislative foundations of those barriers.

As white authorities throughout the rural corridor in New Jersey witnessed the reversal of longstanding laws and policies that permitted or ignored the existence of racial discrimination and segregation, they mobilized the financial infrastructure of private equity to maintain the spatial isolation and economic marginalization of African Americans through the second half of the twentieth century. Douglas Massey and Nancy Denton explained segregation as five distinct dimensions of geographic variation—unevenness, isolation, clustering, concentration, and centralization.[10] Within the small towns of the rural corridor, each of the five dimensions shifted, but persisted, as the region became more populous and connected to metropolitan growth in the northeast. As John Logan and Harvey Molotch described it, uneven development—the declining access to education, employment, and wealth—became a metropolitan phenomenon rather than an urban one.[11] Impoverished suburbs became common in each county in rural New Jersey after 1970. The overall prosperity of the region made it a residential hub for commuting workers who traveled daily as far away as Boston and Washington, D.C. The systemic authority of white conglomerates and political institutions remained intact despite the success of black community organizations in removing the overtly racist language from public legislation and culture.

How did the emergence of the global service economy flummox the organized leadership of black community organizations in rural New Jersey? The chapters in this book present a methodical answer that relies on thematic emphases. Family life among African Americans in the rural corridor is the starting point for the first chapter. Oral testimonies about the lifestyles, habits, culture, and structure of the home reveal evidence about the discipline of black life in small towns between 1870 and 1930. Moral piety and civic reform formed the pillars of the lessons taught from parent to child through extended family networks in the lives of Lenora Walker, Ada Bryan, Marion Russell, Lillie Hendry, and Alice Archibald. Chapter 2 considers the influence of historical memory in the communication of these lessons from the home to the church. Florence Spearing Randolph, Marion Thompson Wright, Lenora Walker McKay, and Madonna Carter Jackson offer four cases of women historians preserving evidence of black history to instruct and inspire future generations. The consistency of their admonitions to maintain personal discipline and accountability shows that African Americans built their communities around a resilient sense of dignity and history. Chapter 3 explores the ways that individual African American leaders—often ministers, doctors, or teachers—motivated people to create new institutions and organizations dedicated to ending de facto segregation. The responsibilities of black leadership created new expectations for African Americans to meet as engaged citizens. Chapter 4 investigates the function of the church as the core institution committed to the survival of the fledgling black communities in rural New Jersey. The measure of the churches' success in these towns was the education of young people about their spiritual worth. However, the churches also transformed local segregated schools from symbols of racial inferiority into bastions of scholastic achievement. Chapters 5 and 6 argue that civil rights organizations emerged from the foundation provided by black churches and schools between 1920 and 1970. In chapter 5, African Americans in communities like Red Bank and Long Branch began to use negotiations with local authorities and lawsuits at the state level to overturn previously unchallenged policies of racial segregation. However, in chapter 6, their success after 1970 suffered dramatically as increasing incarceration rates for young black people removed the constituency that pushed for the most dramatic legislative reforms. These chapters document the transformation of the internal forces shaping rural African American communities through the twentieth century.

The difference between white supremacy and white privilege forms the theme for chapter 7. As the public discourse founded on the assumptions of the former concept lost support in New Jersey after 1950, the rhetoric of color-blindness became a consistent refrain in denying the legitimacy of African American opinions. White privilege constituted the subconscious denial of any advantages white Americans continued to enjoy, despite the adoption of civil rights laws to eliminate racial discrimination. Access to better housing and more assets remained one of the most profound manifestations of these advantages between 1970 and 2000 in the rural corridor. Chapter 7 explores how the rhetoric of color blindness combined with white financial advantages to reinforce limitations on black educational and occupational achievement within the context of the global service economy. The citizen consumer relied on the absence of African American social challenges to enjoy the benefits of metropolitan development and commerce. Chapter 8 explains the emergence of a black middle class within the geographic context of suburbanization in New Jersey. Greater physical and occupational mobility offered opportunities for higher income and more conspicuous consumption than in any previous generation of African Americans in the region. However, few black professionals attained elective offices in these suburbs. Chapter 9 demonstrates the impact of uneven development in the suburbs on the earlier black settlements in the rural corridor. Higher rates of unemployment, poverty, drug addiction, and crime created isolated and destitute suburban communities after 1970. Places like Red Bank, Long Branch, and Asbury Park contrasted sharply against the larger regional patterns of suburban affluence. Chapter 10 considers the intersection of white privilege with the economics of uneven development as three rural communities became desirable suburban communities after 1970. Rampant duplication of municipal services under the guise of "home rule" threatened to bankrupt municipalities and the entire state because these patterns went unchallenged at the end of the twentieth century. Chapter 11 concludes with an examination of local and state planning organizations and their collaborations with civil rights organizations through the second half of the twentieth century. These chapters inquire about the impact of external forces of suburban politics and metropolitan economics on black communities in New Jersey's rural corridor.

African Americans took the initiative in sustaining a long-term vision of democratic reform in the United States between 1900 and 2000. When George White left the Congress, he had every reason to sound a pessimistic note about the return of racial oppression and promise of freedom denied by ignorance and violence. He chose another path. His words led him to new partnerships and ideas that reshaped the physical and cultural geography of the Garden State. The African American commitment to a brighter day survived and thrived to produce generations of leaders who were determined to end racial restrictions on human achievement. Ollievita Williams and hundreds of other leaders seized these opportunities between 1920 and 1970, making changes to the political and economic structure of the state that allowed millions of young people to reimagine the idea of American excellence. The collective achievement merits celebration and analysis, but it is only half of the story.

As African Americans implemented their vision of democracy at both the state and federal levels, other communities of interest adapted their agendas to take new initiative based on the changed social context. The movement to the rhetoric of color blindness and the establishment of the global economy both used the language of racial equality to justify their existence and growth. Metropolitan development resisted the strategies and tactics of African American community civil rights activism in the late twentieth century. In the first decade of the next century, black communities and organizations faced new challenges involving the exercise of political authority and the effective use of private equity for commercial development. The lessons of previous attempts may help create new efforts to take the initiative again.

NOTES

1. George Henry White, "Defense of the Negro Race, 1901," http://docsouth.unc.edu/nc/whitegh/whitegh.html, 9 April 2008.

2. Benjamin R. Justesen, *George Henry White: An Even Chance in the Race for Life* (Baton Rouge: Louisiana State University Press, 2001), 356–84.

3. Unpublished typed transcript, "Ollievita Williams with Jane O'Donnell," 1 May 2002, Color Line Project Papers, Rowan University, Glassboro, NJ, 5–12.

4. Michelle R. Boyd, *Jim Crow Nostalgia: Reconstructing Race in Bronzeville* (Minneapolis: University of Minnesota Press, 2008), 11–24.

5. Clement Alexander Price, ed., *Freedom Not Far Distant: A Documentary History of African Americans in New Jersey* (Trenton: New Jersey Historical Commission, 1980), 226; Giles Wright, *Afro-Americans in New Jersey* (Trenton: New Jersey Historical Commission, 1988), 13–16; Graham Russell Hodges, *Slavery and Freedom in the Rural North* (New York: Madison House Publishers, 1997), xi.

6. Charles Stansfield, *A Geography of New Jersey: The City in the Garden* (New Brunswick, NJ: Rutgers University Press, 1998), 128–34; David Kirp, John Dwyer, and Larry Rosenthal, *Our Town: Race, Housing, and the Soul of Suburbia* (New Brunswick, NJ: Rutgers University Press, 1997), 15–34; Howard Gillette, *Camden after the Fall: Decline and Renewal in a Post-Industrial City* (Philadelphia: University of Pennsylvania Press, 2005), 95–120; Lizabeth Cohen, *A Consumer's Republic: The Politics of Mass Consumption in Postwar America* (New York: Knopf, 2003), 12–13; Bryant Simon, *Boardwalk of Dreams: Atlantic City and the Fate of Urban America* (New Brunswick, NJ: Rutgers University Press, 2006), 63–82.

7. Myron Orfield, *American Metropolitics: The New Suburban Reality* (Washington, DC: Brookings Institution, 2002), 23–27; Andrew Wiese, *Places of Their Own: African American Suburbanization in the Twentieth Century* (Chicago: University of Chicago Press, 2004), 125–29; David M. P. Freund, *Colored Property: State Policy and White Racial Politics in Suburban America* (Chicago: University of Chicago Press, 2007), 14–18; Thomas J. Sugrue, *Sweet Land of Liberty: The Forgotten Struggle for Civil Rights in the North* (New York: Random House, 2008), 493–531.

8. Michel Foucault, *The History of Sexuality: An Introduction*, vol. 1 (New York: Vintage Books, Inc., 1978), 99–100.

9. James C. Scott, *Domination and the Arts of Resistance* (New Haven, CT: Yale University Press, 1992), 183–84.

10. Douglas S. Massey and Nancy A. Denton, *American Apartheid: Segregation and the Making of the Underclass* (Cambridge, MA: Harvard University Press, 1993), 74.

11. John R. Logan and Harvey L. Molotch, *Urban Fortunes: The Political Economy of Place* (Los Angeles: University of California Press, 1988), 50–98.

ONE

Family Life

Race relations were one of the most important changes in the United States during the twentieth century. African Americans had begun to migrate to the major cities of the northeast as soon as the Civil War concluded. The attraction of better pay, nicer homes, and larger black communities motivated five generations of African American families as they traveled up the Atlantic coast. The difficulties of racial contact took a multitude of forms during the early decades, ranging from evenings in speakeasies to open violence in the streets. At times, it appeared that segregation would be the only way to maintain American democracy. This continuity would come at the expense of the promise in the Declaration of Independence that all human beings enjoyed the equal endowments of their Creator. Material wealth remained beyond the grasp of black families because of local, state, and national commitments to white supremacy and Jim Crow segregation. Instead, African Americans pursued the possibilities of sharing in the promise of political equality. Sharecroppers became day laborers and nursemaids became live-in domestics as African Americans moved north into New Jersey, especially in the rural corridor of the state that stretched from Morristown to Long Branch to Willingboro. By 1900, these families had built churches throughout these small towns. By 1920, they began to use their collective wages to start challenging the legal barriers against their prosperity by founding civil rights organizations. Where white and European immigrant families built their hopes on the foundation of political enfranchisement and entrepreneurship, African American families used churches as political organizing centers and nurtured their dreams of equality with small, steady advancements through the court system. By 1950, black children glimpsed the first signs of democracy, as it applied to them. School desegregation unfolded throughout the state. Women were crucial actors in all of these struggles, maintaining family, farm, and resort life in New Jersey by relying on the cult of true womanhood, moral piety, and civic reform to provide a cultural shelter within a raging gale of technological and economic change.

Stability was the hallmark of family life in the Garden State's rural corridor during the first half of the twentieth century. From the resorts like Asbury Park to the farming towns like Freehold to college towns like New Brunswick, African American migrant families fed, clothed, educated, and inspired the children of the state to grasp the promises of equality. Lenora Walker McKay and Ada Bryan's respective stories show the possibilities and limitations of the pursuit of civil rights. Marion Russell and her sister Lillie Hendry provide insights into the ways family life shaped their emphasis on community empowerment. Alice Archibald adds detail about the opportunities children gained through kinship networks. Taken together, these testimonies about the ways black families overcame barriers show that diligent sacrifices laid the foundation for their children's knowledge of history and society.

LENORA WALKER MCKAY

Lenora Walker McKay's autobiographical recollection of her childhood, *Mama and Papa*, describes professional and lower-middle-class life for African Americans in Asbury Park. Her portrait of her parents, friends, school, and social life provides an invaluable insight into black life at the Jersey shore in the first half of the twentieth century. In an era when the overwhelming majority of African Americans worked as domestic servants and factory laborers, Walker's family resembled an earlier incarnation of Bill Cosby's television family. Lenora's mother, Mrs. C. H. Walker, attended the Manassas Training School in Virginia and taught school in Asbury Park for over twenty years. Lenora's father, Reverend C. J. H. Walker, was a Virginia native who graduated from Lincoln University with a divinity degree, yet he still had to deliver newspapers during the week to make ends meet. The family enjoyed their own home with fruit trees and a chicken coop in the backyard. The Walkers owned an oak dining set, a china closet, a chandelier, brass beds, and wall-to-wall carpeting. Most African American families in Asbury Park relied upon at least two incomes from jobs: cook, laundress, domestic, and laborer. Many of their residences were overcrowded or shared duplexes for multiple families.[1] Clearly, this family lived more comfortably than most urban African Americans in 1920 due to their postsecondary education.[2] The Walker family experience demonstrates that, despite rampant segregation and racism, some African Americans in Asbury Park could achieve a degree of economic and social comfort in the period prior to World War II.

Figure 1.1.   Labor Housing (Walter David Greason, 1987) African American farm workers in Manalapan lived in these two-bedroom, one-bathroom buildings at the intersection of Tennent and Millhurst Roads in 1987.

In the Asbury Park of McKay's childhood, the whole family worked to help maintain their standard of living. The men sold copies of the *Asbury Park Press* on the street, while the women worked in local laundries or resort hotels. The latter jobs generally paid one dollar a day plus tips. Children were expected to contribute whatever money they could to help the family. McKay's father's primary occupation was as an associate minister at Mount Pisgah Baptist Church under Reverend E. D. Cawley. He was a Lincoln Republican, a Mason, and a member of Marcus Garvey's Universal Negro Improvement Association (UNIA), the National Association for the Advancement of Colored People (NAACP), and the National Urban League. When Garvey spoke in Asbury Park in 1924, the Walker family attended in support.[3]

Reverend Walker and his wife typify the pillars of the black community in New Jersey at the start of the twentieth century. Their commitments to education and the church reflected the values of the families that formed throughout the state. Families reinforced these ideas on a daily basis through frequent interactions. Lenora McKay's belief in the importance of history and community leadership was the fruit of her mother and father's experiences at the start of the century. She wrote, "Despite [African Americans] being a people oft maligned, oft scorned, and oft misunderstood, I owe much that follows to family—from which emanated support, strength, encouragement, and inspiration to overcome."[4] None of the achievements of civil rights and democratic equality would have been possible absent these building blocks. As McKay concluded, "This [story] projects the feeling that we lived the most wonderful life of all generations—recollections of our parents and their inimitable style of parenting; our schools and the teacher's excellence; [and] the strength of church leaders that enabled us to press on."[5]

The senior Walkers' journey began in 1916 on the eve of the First World War. Most newcomers to New Jersey's rural black communities during this period were from Virginia and North Carolina; Lenora's parents were from Virginia. They were also more educated and younger than the majority of migrants. It was the strong character of young African Americans in the southern United States that pushed them to seek new opportunities in both the urban and rural North between 1880 and 1930. W. A. Wheeler, one of the migrants in this generation, said, "In the South, you could get by as long as you stayed a boy . . . but I wanted to be a man for a long time."[6] Reverend Walker's Pennsylvania education enabled the couple to seek work among the shore resorts as opposed to the larger urban industrial centers like Newark and Camden. While both farm and factory labor were physically demanding, work at the resorts relied on bursts of effort and energy that left time for individual reflection and creativity.[7] These early choices in favor of a rural setting revealed important aspects of the Walkers' thinking. Smaller churches at the core of relatively prosperous and conservative black communities were likely attractive to them. The presence of African American home owners provided role models for their children. Even the possibility of deciding when to challenge and when to accept the barriers of racial segregation in public facilities with white community leaders would likely contribute to the attraction of a town like Asbury Park for black migrants. The persistence of romantic and paternal ideas about African Americans allowed greater discussion to occur in New Jersey's small towns than in the urban North or the rural South.[8] The perceptions and ideas about a different life in the North reaffirmed the core values of African American families from the South.[9]

The work ethic in the Walker household reflected and supported their core values. In the African American tradition, work is evidence of human worth. Even facing the reality of severe underemployment due to the restrictions of Jim Crow in the North, Reverend and Mrs. Walker showed their children that dignity was not out of reach. McKay's understanding of the opportunities that resulted from diligent effort was a direct product of her parents' determination. The responsibilities of freedom go too often unspoken, even in the twenty-first century, but African

Americans in New Jersey grounded their lives in the acceptance of these responsibilities. In a world with few civil rights for African Americans, the practice of civil responsibility became the platform for social activism and human freedom. The celebration of the Emancipation Proclamation in small towns like Asbury Park showed how churches promoted community leaders who delivered messages of racial equality. On January 1, 1935, Reverend Walker delivered an address titled "What Can the Negro Do to Better His Economic and Social Condition in this Country?" His speech came first and led to five additional messages by Lorenzo Harris, E. D. Cawley, J. S. Brown, J. H. Ashby, and J. D. Mitchell, who explored the relationship between churches, schools, and civil rights organizations in the fight against inequality. [10]

Local black churches through the rural counties of the Garden State benefited significantly from the influx of new congregants. The growth of the black churches swelled the number of community leaders to a degree that commanded the formation of secular organizations to complement the churches' efforts to challenge northern Jim Crow. Delivering newspapers around town built dozens of important relationships for Reverend Walker. As a school teacher, Mrs. Walker was one of the most respected voices in the black community at Asbury Park for decades. The combination of their secular work during the course of the week with their sacred calling to serve on Sundays embodied many African Americans' commitment to free life in small towns throughout New Jersey. Rural black communities, known for their passivity and subservience in the nineteenth century, became fertile soil for the growth of civil rights leaders by 1920. [11] The Walkers were important public influences in Asbury Park. They established local civil rights organizations and won early victories for racial equality, as shown in chapters 3 and 5. However, in the early decades of the twentieth century, they remained exceptions to the rule of the African American experience in rural New Jersey because most of their neighbors lacked both the education and the economic security to engage in civil rights work on a regular basis.

ADA BRYAN

Most African Americans in Asbury Park were members of the working class. Ada Bryan moved to this shoreline black community as a preteen after 1920. Her family relied upon her ability to earn a supplemental income, especially during the peak times of summer tourism. Access to education and travel was much more limited for Ada than for Lenora Walker. Bryan's description of economic opportunities for African Americans shows how families sacrificed time and recreation together to make daily living easier. "My father happened to make a good living for us because he had contracts to paint the outsides of three hotels in the summertime and he did the inside of the hotels during the winter months when they were closed. My mother used to be a cook. People would call her up and say they were going to have a dinner party and . . . and my mother would say 'Yes.'" [12]

Bryan explained that manual labor (whether cooking or painting) was crucial to her family's ability to make money. These jobs were better than those many African Americans had as ditch diggers and nannies, as the latter only paid on a daily basis. [13] The nearly total dependence on white employers for opportunities in these resorts cannot be overstated. Local workers relied on these jobs to heat their homes and feed their families. Much of the unity that brought black workers together resulted from the shared reality of racial discrimination in the resort environments and households. "Domestic employment was just about the only kind of employment people of color could get at that time. One particular hotel would not hire anyone of color except as cleaning people. [African Americans] were not hired for jobs that were paying well." [14] Bryan's father may have taken the risk of working dozens of feet off the ground to avoid the frequent social contact with his employers that would remind him of his subordinate status. In the winter, his job also allowed more privacy than most because the spaces he painted were mostly empty. [15] Ada's mother, however, likely suffered through a very different set of experiences. Culinary work in the household meant increased supervision from the white family's matriarch. In this scrutinized setting, Bryan mother's position as a temporary cook was not as economically stable as her husband's. She had little control over discussions about the domestic work she performed. [16] By working with one family and then moving to another, not remaining in a single household for years, Bryan's mother created a social network of employers who used her services but had fewer chances to become unappreciative of her efforts. [17] As a result of their choices, Bryan's parents attained some of the same insulation against racism on their jobs that the Walker family enjoyed by virtue of their education. More importantly, the increased amount of time these working parents had with their family as a result of their decisions about education and employment laid a foundation of high expectations for their children and of community engagement for themselves.

NICY MARION HAM RUSSELL

These families defied the prevailing assumptions about black inferiority in these small towns by growing the congregations of nineteenth-century churches as well as building new churches in these communities. [18] Local efforts brought families together and created new social networks that expanded the local black community. In farming villages like Freehold, these networks began to form after 1920. (See Figure 1.1.) Seasonal migration was a dominant factor in the area, and year-round black residents were few as compared to the resort towns. Familiar seasonal work patterns and the beauty of the rural environment drew many families who wanted to escape the lynchings and race riots of the South but did not enjoy the accelerated life of larger cities like New York and Philadelphia. Between 1882 and 1902, over one hundred African Americans were lynched each year in the South. By 1906, racial incidents in Atlanta, Georgia, and Brownsville, Texas, raised the urgency among many African Americans to find new lives in the North.[19] Freehold and many other hamlets offered attractive opportunities. Canning factories used black male labor in the fields throughout the year and inside the plants during the harvest.[20] Black women most often found jobs as maids, cooks, housekeepers, or laundresses in the borough. These patterns were consistent with the national concentration of black women in unskilled and domestic service work.[21] Even boys and girls, sometimes as young as seven or eight years old, worked as domestic servants. Nicy Marion Ham Russell, born in 1913, commented, "When I was nine years old, I got my first job. I [took] care of J. Halerin Conover's daughter, Anne. I was supposed to be, what they called, a mother's helper. While she took her nap, I had to dust the furniture, peel the potatoes, wash the dishes, and back out to play. After Mr. Conover would come in from his work and have their dinner, I had to wash the dishes, and then I could go home. All for $3 a week. That was my salary."[22]

The economic success of the black family hinged on the ability of every family member to contribute something to the greater whole, as Bryan's family showed at the shore. The experience of being a caregiver and contributor to the family economy was formative for children like Marion. The sense of common responsibility based on children's work, the importance of public accountability in the form of extended kinship networks, and the pride of wage-earning achievement all contributed to a general sense of character at very early ages for African American children in the rural North. "My thoughts of Asbury Park are of deep-rooted families, a loving and caring community, a thriving community, and an abundance of positive role models, segregation and overcoming the obstacles it presented, available employment, an Entertainment Mecca, and a real estate jewel by the sea."[23] These opportunities certainly reflected the paternalism of white employers towards their black workers. Ideas about the racial nature of domestic and manual labor drove affluent white families to view black servants as indicators of their material security. Moreover, white acceptance of black children as domestic servants reassured the segregated society that the next generation of African Americans would know their place.

LILLIE HAM HENDRY

For African Americans themselves, financial stability was a measure of a family's commitment to work at whatever jobs became available. Russell's parents routinely instructed their nine children to study beyond the requirements of their segregated schooling and to listen carefully to the speech and knowledge of white families like the Conovers (for whom Marion worked) to learn the secrets to social success. Marion internalized these lessons quickly and became one of the first black children to enroll in the local high school, in 1926. Marion and Lillie Ham Hendry, her sister, were part of the Ham family, who moved to Freehold from North Carolina in 1922. Their experiences reveal the presence of racism in the area as well as the determination and pride exhibited by the local black community in transcending the limitations assumed by white residents. Hendry earned a Fulbright teaching scholarship after graduating from Trenton State College, receiving support to teach English in London in 1956.[24] Russell remembered the challenges of segregated schooling. She recalled the fights she and her sister often faced when returning from school. Local students from the nearby whites-only elementary school would ambush them and try to chase them home. Russell said, "They used to pick fights and throw things. I learned to fight with my lunch-box. . . . Mom bought us a tin lunchbox. That thing had more dents in it because my sister Kate was always getting into something, and I was defending her."[25] In her time at Court Street School in Freehold (the elementary school for black children), there were two teachers for nine grades and the supplies they received were always outdated. She said, "I often felt it was unfair because the kids at the segregated white schools didn't have to use old books that were passed down to [us]."[26]

Figure 1.2.   Last Garden (Walter David Greason, 2001) Arianna Harris, her sister Pearl, and her son, William, moved into the house (on the left) in 1960 and used the field in the foreground for subsistence agriculture (pole beans, corn, pump-kins, watermelons, tomatoes, peas, and spinach) as late as 1980.

Hendry's recollections discussed more of the racial atmosphere in high school, college, and the employment world during the years surrounding the Second World War that show at every level how assumptions of black inferiority colored the judgments and opinions of white administrators and functionaries, obstructing her path to high achievement. Her religious background, family support, and individual determination carried her through all of these trials. In one confrontation in 1943, Hendry's parents had to defend her right to take college preparatory courses. She said, "My class advisor said to me, 'Your parents have [nine] children. You'll probably have to work after high school to help with the family.' Mother and Daddy explained to her that the teachers had no right to tell their child what the future was going to be."[27] Hendry continued to confront racial assumptions as a college student. At Trenton State College (now the College of New Jersey), an entry interview shook her confidence when the interviewer questioned Hendry's segregated educational experiences. Hendry explained, "[The interviewer] said, 'I think you are peculiar.' I always remember how my heart sank! I could live with being called a failure or a success with getting into college, but peculiar? That's somewhere out there that you don't know what you are!"[28]

Hendry also discussed the importance of mentoring in her success at the college level. Marian Vanderveer, an older graduate of the local segregated school in Freehold, served as Hendry's Big Sister during her sophomore year of college. It was this friend's presence that gave Hendry an example of black success in higher education. She noted, "I was the only Afro-American in [my first] class. When I went for orientation with a girl from my hometown, I was thrilled. Her name was Marian Vanderveer. There were sixty-two students to begin with. I graduated from Trenton State with fifteen!"[29] Hendry's parents' conviction about the importance of education provided her with the necessary determination to pursue her high school diploma and college degree. Her reliance on her family and community's support translated into her affinity for the Big Sister/Little Sister community in college. She said, "I could always come home to my church for encouragement. You got through college and the hard times because of the black community that surrounded you with love, acceptance, and support."[30] Russell and Hendry's experiences illuminate the perseverance and courage necessary for success under the circumstances of racial segregation in a rural northern community.

The unrelenting indignity of segregated schooling—South and North—shaped Russell's commitment to her education. Facing verbal and physical harassment both going to and coming from the segregated elementary school on Court Street, two girls under the age of ten marched together. Russell defended her younger sister, Kate, with a lunchbox. The transformation of this common item into a multipurpose weapon represents the resilience of these children as they faced harassment and violence from their white peers.[31] Family bonds were the foundation of this common defense. Every day, black schoolchildren faced down their antagonists, learning increasingly complicated coping mechanisms—including swinging a lunchbox—to maintain their personal and collective self-esteem.

Inside the schools, the facilities and resources marked the larger conceit of the local, all-white school boards in New Jersey. With the smallest school building and the oldest workbooks, Court Street School relied on the excellence of its elementary teachers and the determination of its students to transcend the boundaries of white supremacy. Russell recognized the shame of this conscientious neglect in her reflection about the disparities between the white and black schools. She said, "I didn't think it was fair to have to use old books—the books that were outdated and that they were no longer using with the white kids were passed down to Court St. school. We had dedicated Black teachers and they would take their own money and buy two and three and sometimes only one book—up to date—and give them to us to read. You had better not thumb it down, turn down the edges, or spill anything on it because that was the only book."[32] Her distress in response to institutional discrimination did not carry the same defiant tone she voiced in describing neighborhood fights against local white bullies. Russell witnessed the powerlessness of her teachers and principals in addition to her own vulnerability. There was no recourse to correct this oppression in the moment. Any attempt to question or to eliminate these practices would be dismissed as ridiculous by the school board at best, or led to her family's loss of employment and return to migrant labor at worst. Even these consequences were mild in comparison to the harassment civil rights activists faced in the South between 1915 and 1955. The beating of NAACP Executive Secretary John Shillady in Texas in 1919 and the murders by bombing of Harry and Harriette Moore in Florida in 1951 made the consequences for African American defiance of white authority clear.[33] In this way, the Ham family was part of an extended family among African Americans in rural New Jersey. The silence forced on them in accepting subordinate status in school, in town, and on the job fostered a culture of resilience. (See Figure 1.2.) The common experiences and understanding of injustice created a political solidarity that provided the foundation for correcting institutional discrimination over the next three generations.

The effects of a resilient family culture among African Americans in New Jersey became more apparent as Lillie Hendry followed her sister, Marion Russell, through the school system. Hendry faced less harassment and ridicule from white students through elementary and middle school, while the tradition of excellence inside Court Street School had proven its strength in propelling black students into secondary education in increasing numbers. Although Hendry faced continuing frustration and opposition from teachers and guidance counselors in high school,

with her parents' support, she moved on to college and eventually received her master of arts degree in educational counseling in 1955. The
presence of familiar faces and their consistent support of her ambition
made the difference in her achievements. Combined, Russell's and Hendry's stories about New Jersey education reaffirm the implications of
Walker's and Bryant's narratives. African American migrants before 1930
made their children's education the top priority in pursuing the vision of
an egalitarian America; their children recognized the sacrifices and hard
work that their parents made and matched those efforts with daily engagement against both personal and institutional racism; the home was
the essential cauldron for the formation and promotion of a distinctly
African American definition of democratic society.

ALICE JENNINGS ARCHIBALD

Alice Archibald's story of family and community illustrates the ways
values taught in the home became the foundation of public customs and
community expectations about educational success and social activism.
Her parents struggled to support her as an infant, so her extended family
took her in and raised her. "[They didn't adopt me because of my father's
wishes, but] they raised me and they really were like my second parents."[34] The connections between her birth family and her adoptive family remained strong throughout her life. In New Jersey during the first
half of the twentieth century, these informal kinship networks were crucial to providing a sense of stability and safety to African American children, who often encountered derision and hostility from white neighbors
and authorities. "Since I was with my aunt and uncle all of the time, I
grew up like an only child. I knew my siblings looked forward for me
coming over in a trolley car on holiday times because I always brought
gifts."[35] The class distinctions implied in her statement reflected the roots
of the formative black middle class, even before 1930, in the rural North.
Her adoptive family enjoyed the professional status and home ownership
common among African American elites dating back to the early nineteenth century in the Mid-Atlantic states.[36]

Archibald's conjugal family grew out of the connections her adoptive
parents provided for her through the teenage years. "[My aunt] was not
one of these mothers who are great kissers and huggers. She was a no-
nonsense person. She loved me, but she could see that I had possibilities."[37] Church socials and networking through regional religious networks provided ample opportunities to learn the niceties of dating and
the judgment for potential suitors. However, education and professional
commitments postponed Archibald's prospects for marriage until later
life. Her story about marrying her husband focused on the ambivalence
of his previous partner. "We met while World War II was going on, when

he had been engaged to a teacher who had been teaching in Atlantic City, but he asked her one time 'what do you think of me?' And she said 'oh you'll do!' So that ended it right there and on the rebound he met me and we courted for a year and got married.[38] Archibald recognized a good catch when she saw him. There were also lingering social tensions between native-born African Americans and immigrant West Indians that persisted into the late twentieth century.[39]

Archibald reproduced the lessons she learned from her adoptive family in both her conjugal family and the surrounding community in New Brunswick. "I have always been an enabler, trying to push someone else on to go try that to see what you can do. Don't try to be like someone else, be yourself and see what you can do."[40] At the core of these lessons was a recurring thesis that Archibald framed as her mission as a Christian and a human being. She said, "My earliest childhood recollection was that I was striving to do my best, whatever the task might be. Another basic value that became a part of me was that of trying to keep a level head when confronted with the grief, disappoints, injustices, humiliations, and troubles of this world." Archibald measured her best efforts by continuously striving for a better world. Archibald credited her aunt with the development of her creativity and dedication in support of human rights. The determination to make an impact, not just be heard as an advocate, led her to a life fulfilling the promise of extended family and community uplift through her work in the Urban League and Mount Zion AME Church. "Each of us can make this world a better place by loving humanity, by caring what happens to our fellow man, and then believing that what you are is God's gift to you."[41] The combination of faith, patience, accountability, and interdependence illustrated in Archibald's experiences in church and community leadership demonstrates how many African American women like Lenora Walker McKay, Ada Bryan, Marion Russell, Lillie Hendry, and Alice Archibald adapted their childhood memories into life lessons in the twentieth century.

As New Jersey's economy became increasingly industrial and less agricultural between 1900 and 1950, African American families relied on the values of interdependence, faith, and diligence to resist the prevailing racism. Migrant families transformed the horizons of their economic success by moving from the nineteenth-century context of sharecropping to the twentieth-century framework of home ownership, resort town employment, and secondary education. The daily praxis of thrift, sacrifice, and selfless love taught millions of children the importance of a community beyond their households. Walker, Bryan, Russell, Hendry, and Archibald's narratives connect scholars to historic communities. They all valued autonomy, communication, and interdependence. Unlike the dominant history of suburban sprawl and the pursuit of individuality within a broader context of conformity, the story of African American life in the rural North teaches lessons about the balance among ideologies that is necessary for effective civic engagement. The metropolitan development of the Garden State could also balance the maintenance of farm production with its suburban service economy and a light manufacturing base. Examining Walker's legacy of community uplift and collaborative leadership yields a more efficient use of a community's resources. Bryan's recognition of the balance between work, education, and play provides a guide to wellness and success. Russell and Hendry's examples of religious engagement and educational excellence explain how families unite to generate a culture that changes their material circumstances. Taken together, these histories address the human need for individuality, family, community, and nation in ways that balance and complete each facet of life. The process of transmitting this knowledge remains less clear. How do the lessons of family become the politics of community? Historiography provides one explanation.

NOTES

1. New Jersey Bureau of the Census (NJBC), *New Jersey State Census—1915* (ms.) (Manalapan, NJ), schedule 1.

2. Lenora W. McKay, *Mama and Papa: The Blacks of Monmouth County, Volume 2* (privately published, 1984), 6, 15, 27. McKay's work receives additional analysis in the context of local historiography in chapter 2.

3. Ibid., 52, 63, 94, 110.

4. Ibid., 4.

5. Ibid.

6. Andrew Wiese, "Interview with W. A. Wheeler," 16 June 1989, in *Places of Their Own: African American Suburbanization in the Twentieth Century* (Chicago: University of Chicago Press, 2004), 38.

7. Myra B. Young Armstead, *"Lord, Please Don't Take Me in August": African Americans in Newport and Sarasota Springs, 1870–1930* (Chicago: University of Illinois Press, 1999), 4.

8. George M. Fredrickson, *The Black Image in the White Mind: The Debate on Afro-American Character and Destiny, 1817–1914* (Hanover, NH: Wesleyan University Press, 1971), 101–2.

9. Thomas J. Sugrue, *Sweet Land of Liberty: The Forgotten Struggle for Civil Rights in the North* (New York: Random House, 2008), 3–31. The discussion of Anna Arnold Hedgeman in this chapter reveals the complexity of personal growth when a southern migrant's ideals about northern life ran afoul of the segregated realities that persisted through the first half of the twentieth century.

10. Lenora Walker McKay, *Mama and Papa*, 46.

11. Graham Russell Hodges, *Slavery and Freedom in the Rural North: African Americans in Monmouth County, New Jersey* (New York: Madison House, 1997), 208.

12. June West, "Interview with Ada Bryan," in *Remembering the Twentieth Century: An Oral History of Monmouth County*, ed. Flora T. Higgins, accessed 11 December 2000, http://www.shore.co.monmouth.nj.us/oralhistory/bios/BryanAda.html, 3.

13. McKay, *Mama and Papa*, 63.

14. West, "Interview with Ada Bryan," 3.

15. Ibid., 2–4. The tone and diction of Bryan's comment reveal her ideas about her family's discomfort with their proximity to white authority both on the job and in the town more generally. Her discussion of racial disparities in pay, occupation, and housing is most pronounced on the second page of the transcript.

16. Fannie Barrier Williams, "The Problem of Employment for Negro Women," *Southern Workman* 32 (1903): 432–37.

17. West, "Interview with Ada Bryan," 3.

18. John P. Jackson Jr. and Nadine M. Weidman, *Race, Racism, and Science: Social Impact and Interaction* (New Brunswick, NJ: Rutgers University Press, 2004), 107–9.

19. Stewart E. Tolnay and E. M. Beck, *A Festival of Violence: An Analysis of Southern Lynchings, 1882–1930* (Chicago: University of Illinois Press, 1995), 17–27; Paul A. Gilje, *Rioting in America* (Bloomington: Indiana University Press, 1996), 87–115. Racial violence was the primary mechanism for the enforcement of slavery, segregation, and discrimination against Africans and African Americans in North America between 1529 and 1965. Lynchings and riots as specific forms of this violence reasserted the authority of white Americans over black Americans at the end of the nineteenth century. No part of the United States was immune to these forms of racial terrorism. However, small communities in the North where African Americans did not present a demographic threat to white authority experienced fewer incidences between 1890 and 1910.

20. Lee Ellen Griffith, *Images of America: Freehold, Volume II* (Charleston, SC: Arcadia Publishing, 1999), 54–57.

21. Hebert G. Gutman, *The Black Family in Slavery and Freedom, 1750–1925* (New York: Pantheon Books, 1976), 443.

22. Nicy M. H. Russell, interview transcript, 8 January 1998. European immigrants also faced the need for their children to work at an early age, but African American families had to sustain children's labor continually in places like Freehold in ways that local immigrant families did not experience.

23. Madonna Carter Jackson, *Asbury Park: A West Side Story* (Denver, CO: Outskirts Press, 2007), 194.

24. "The Queen Greets American Teacher," *Philadelphia Inquirer* photo, 24 July 1957.

25. Ibid.

26. Ibid.

27. Connie Paul, "Interview with Lillie Hendry and Marion Russell," 28 August 2000, in *Remembering the Twentieth Century: An Oral History of Monmouth County*, ed. Flora T. Higgins, http://www.visitmonmouth.com/oralhistory/bios/Hendry-Russell.htm.

28. Ibid.

29. Ibid.

30. Ibid.

31. Robin D. G. Kelley, *Race Rebels: Culture, Politics, and the Black Working Class* (New York: Free Press, 1994), 18–21; David R. Roediger, *Colored White: Transcending the Racial Past* (Berkeley: University of California Press, 2002), 52–54. Kelley writes about the ways African American women subverted their employers in the workplace, while Roediger addresses the subtle ways white authority continues to assert itself over black lives and images.

32. Marion Nicy Ham Russell, interview transcript, 8 January 1998.

33. Philip Dray, *At the Hands of Persons Unknown: The Lynching of Black America* (New York: Random House, 2002), 248–50, 411–12.

34. Alice J. Archibald, interview transcript, 9 January 1998.

35. Ibid.

36. Wilma A. Dunaway, *The African American Family in Slavery and Emancipation* (New York: Cambridge University Press, 2003), 268–88; Becky Nicolaides and Andrew Wiese, eds. *The Suburb Reader* (New York: Routledge, 2006), 207; Julie Winch, *Philadelphia's Black Elite: Activism, Accommodation, and the Struggle for Autonomy, 1787–1848* (Philadelphia: Temple University Press, 1993), 152–66.

37. Archibald, transcript, 9 January 1998.

38. Ibid.

39. Ibid.

40. Ibid.

41. Ibid.

TWO

Black Women's Historiography

Because the writing of history has tended to be a male-dominated profession, women—and African American women in particular, as a "double minority"—have been treated as historically insignificant. The absence of women's voices limits a reader's historical insights in a number of ways. What did it mean to work? Who constituted family? Where were public and private values taught? When did church and school overlap as social arenas? How did people articulate public identity to diminish patriarchy and white supremacy? Without attention to women's perspectives and the ways their perspectives reshaped the understanding of history, the writing of new history about Americans in the twentieth century is flawed.

African American women in New Jersey created and used a variety of resources documenting the forgotten events and processes of democratic revitalization since the beginning of the republic. Primary documents tracing the lives of important female leaders of the black community reveal numerous lessons about how family life laid the foundation for social organization in churches and schools. Values taught in segregated black institutions inspired generations of African American youth to embrace the ideologies of racial uplift espoused by Mary Church Terrell, Booker T. Washington, Ida Wells Barnett, and William E. B. Du Bois through the first half of the last century. These young people formed the body of the Black Freedom Movement between 1920 and 1990, winning battle after battle for racial equality in American politics throughout their lives.[1] Stories of the abolition of white supremacy continued to emerge as the first decade of the twenty-first century came to an end.[2] It is in this context that the study of African American women's historiography in rural New Jersey becomes necessary.

In her book *Black Feminist Thought*, sociologist Patricia Hill Collins addresses the issue of women's voices in academic work: "Reclaiming black women's ideas involves discovering, reinterpreting, and analyzing for the first time the works of individual U.S. Black women thinkers who were so extraordinary that they did manage to have their ideas preserved. In some cases this process involves locating unrecognized and unheralded works, scattered and long out of print."[3] The record of the Garden State's black women historians fits Collins's description well. Focusing on New Jersey reveals a "hidden transcript" that lay in plain sight and belies the simplicity of Whig history in the story of American race relations.[4] Gradual emancipation in the North instigated de facto segregation in neighborhoods, public accommodations, and education from the earliest years of the nineteenth century.[5] The northern forms of white supremacy in public and private life shaped a different range of responses from black families and organizations between 1790 and 1950. Free blacks in the middle of the nineteenth century understood the resilience of Chief Justice Roger Taney's pronouncements in the *Dred Scott* decision: "[The blacks] had no rights which the white man was bound to respect."[6] Taney's reasoning justified slavery by reinforcing an eternal sense of racial prejudice. It was a declaration of inequality as a permanent facet of American society. African Americans' understanding that black bondage was only more extreme in the South, not absent in the North, shaped the careers of Florence Spearing Randolph, Marion Thompson Wright, Lenora Walker McKay, and Madonna Carter Jackson. Reflecting on the courage and intelligence of these historians reveals the historiographical power of their voices in crafting public memory of the twentieth century. Not only were they central actors in the historical processes of societal maintenance and adaptation, but they were the final arbiters of familial knowledge about the past across multiple generations.[7]

At the end of the nineteenth century, black women developed local and state organizations to promote literacy and Christian values in their homes and communities. The National Association for Colored Women understood that wide-ranging reform of Jim Crow segregation required a patient, gradual approach. However, their strategic successes opened the door for the first generation of successful black politicians after 1930. Access to federal officials through groups like the National Council of Negro Women forced grudging progress on race relations in the North and the Midwest. Even without stable relationships with white women organizers and historians, African Americans like Florence Randolph and Marion Wright preserved the dignity and integrity of black people nationwide.

Historian Patricia Morton states: "[Many African American men] warned that the women's movement was an anti-male movement that would turn the black woman against her man."[8] Patriarchal expectations among black men in the leadership of northern civil rights programs and organizations fueled their rhetoric more than any historical reality about their exploitation of black women. The complexity of gender relations among African Americans in New Jersey in the twentieth century deserves more attention than the straightforward analysis of men's writing can sustain.[9] Contextualizing these statements with biographical data offers some additional insight, but the conversation among all black leaders must be the foundation of a clear understanding about the tensions and joys men and women shared as they struggled for equality. Women were simultaneously daughters, sisters, and mothers to the men who were sons, brothers, and fathers in their lives.[10] The overlapping relationships affected the ideologies about family, community, and historical memory that shaped Randolph, Wright, Walker, and Jackson's visions of the past.

All four women carried similar complicated connections to the larger American feminist movement over the last century. Having to choose between gender and race was the constant dilemma for black women activists through the history of the United States.[11] While contact with white women was common in early-twentieth-century New Jersey, many of these relationships suffered from misunderstandings and grievances across the color line. Black women's uncompromising stance that equality applied to all Americans contradicted a frequent feminist assertion that illiteracy and criminality disqualified many black men from inclusion in the body politic. African American men, on the other hand, rarely called for the maintenance of white women's disenfranchisement. As Randolph and Wright negotiated this delicate debate, the ideological integrity of full enfranchisement drew them further away from the overtly segregationist positions many white feminists embraced. In choosing their allies, white women discriminated more forcefully against people based on race than black men did against all women. Engaging in programs for civil rights education on both fronts, African American women were the leaders who defined the logic and praxis of racial equality throughout the twentieth century.[12]

While black men debated the ideas and appeared in the black newspapers of the era, women did the unrecognized labor of canvassing, fundraising, and curriculum design. In addition, many African American women worked one or two full-time jobs to provide the pennies and nickels that built churches and bought books for their children.[13] Doing both the paid work and the volunteer organizing, they created the foundation for family life in the rural communities of New Jersey. Without the progressive ideas about femininity, piety, and civic reform that emerged from these experiences, historians like Randolph, Wright, Walker, and Jackson could not have guided the transformation of family values into organizational policy.

There were essentially two different types of African American women in the minds of white racist thinkers. The first was the Mammy. The Mammy was the cartoonlike image of a fat dark-skinned woman dressed in an apron with a handkerchief around her head. She was a slave who was jolly, perfectly happy to work for her master, and even happier to raise and rear his children at the cost of neglecting her own. The other stereotype was the Jezebel. She was the opposite of the Mammy, thin and light-skinned. This woman was a sexual creature with an insatiable sex drive, luring white men into her bed. These images of slave women ignore their strength and perseverance. They say nothing about the way they brought their communities together. They overlook the commitments of these women to nurture and to educate the people around them. They suppress any information about how they formed schools and churches over the last century and a half. Accounts of the African American women who fought for women's suffrage, who formed the National Association of Colored Women and the National Council of Negro Women, and who fought during the civil rights movement find little expression in the formal history of this country.

Patricia Hill Collins breaks African American female leadership down into two different categories. The first group fights for the survival of all African Americans in the late nineteenth and early twentieth centuries. The second group of women fights for institutional transformation in the twentieth century. The first group builds organizations from the grassroots like churches, schools, and literacy clubs. Their leadership and sacrifices defy ordinary historical scrutiny because few archivists have collected their records in the most distinguished libraries and museums. She was the woman down the street who organized Sunday school. She was the woman that helped to bring the members of the community together through prayer in times of need. Her life promoted unity. She provided validation for faith that can help get the African American community through the hardships that they faced before and after Jim Crow. She was the woman who ran day care centers that offered affordable and trustworthy childcare for working mothers. She was the woman who started the children of the neighborhood on the path to education. She was the teacher at the high school who pushed her students to do their best and showed them that a good education will provide them with a better life. She prepared them for interviews. These were the women whose leadership many professional historians have ignored. They remain, however, some of the most important leaders in the history of the United States.

Hill Collins defined the second category of black women's leadership: "[Their] activism consists of struggles for institutional transformation— namely, those efforts to change discriminatory policies and procedures of government, schools, the workplace, the media, stores and other social institutions."[14] These women fought publicly for what they wanted from elected officials and business leaders. They battled the system as a whole and did not wait for change. Black women who chose this path risked condemnation as dangerous because they threatened established social hierarchies. These women took beatings at rallies and protests. They were the women who refused to sit back as assistant pastors simply because of their gender.

FLORENCE SPEARING RANDOLPH

Reverend Dr. Florence Spearing Randolph was born in 1866 in South Carolina. She migrated to New Jersey in 1885 and began work as a dressmaker in Jersey City. She married her husband, Hugh, the next year. Her activist work began in 1892 as a member of the Women's Christian Temperance Union (WCTU), and she became a leading missionary known for her intelligence and moral authority. Randolph's childhood introduced her to the African Methodist Episcopal Zion Church. After a few years of missionary work, she successfully applied for a license to preach—despite the objections of male deacons in the church hierarchy. Between 1897 and 1903, Randolph advanced from the office of exhorter to deacon to church elder. Her promotion to church elder occurred just before she received her first assignment to pastor a church in New Jersey. She worked without salary for more than a decade at small, mission churches in the New York metropolitan area. Randolph founded the New Jersey State Federation of Colored Women's Clubs (NJFCWC) in 1915 and worked on the executive committee of the New Jersey Suffrage Association. Over the next decade, she became one of the most prominent black women in the state. Wallace Chapel AME Zion in Summit, New Jersey, welcomed Randolph as its pastor in 1925. She expanded its membership and annual budget dramatically during her twenty-one-year tenure. Randolph continued to lead her congregation in using the suffrage rights gained by the Nineteenth Amendment, sending students to college, and, by 1946, eliminating all debt that the church held. [15]

Randolph's insight into the African American experience in rural New Jersey grew out of her experience as a migrant from South Carolina in the late nineteenth century. Dirt roads, searing heat, and virulent white supremacy in the South drove her to find new opportunity in New Jersey. The church nurtured her through the difficult transition to a new life in the North. [16] Randolph sought freedom in the North in the wake of its denial for the first generation of African Americans in the South after the abolition of slavery. She made better wages as a dressmaker in New Jersey than she did in South Carolina. Every day her words made a difference in churches that barely existed in the state where she was born. During her speech in accepting the leadership of the New Jersey Colored Republican Women's organization, she said, "We are 70,000 strong in this state. . . . Now we are asking no special favors, no Negro rights, but human rights and justice." [17] Randolph, and the black women historians who followed her in New Jersey, understood the value and immediacy of the opportunities they possessed, even in the face of northern racial seg-

regation and oppression. The power of her emotion and her intellect
drove black congregants to find new ways to challenge the discrimination they faced. Randolph modeled praxis for racial uplift that shaped
civil rights organizations at the local level through the Garden State.[18]

Randolph's faith was the foundation for the women's club movement
in New Jersey. Black women's clubs were crucial organizations bridging
the legacy of nineteenth-century abolitionism and women's suffrage with
the twentieth-century civil rights activism of the NAACP and National
Council of Negro Women.[19] She emphasized the lived experience of
Christianity in ways few American theologians had done in the nineteenth century. Salvation through faith was more than a personal matter
for Randolph. It was the foundation of a blessed society. Christians who
organized social and political organization brought a better world into
existence for their children and grandchildren. Women guided the development of the Christian world through their roles as wives and mothers
but, more importantly, through their public love of God and their service
to his will outside of the home. "As hopeful for the spiritual, we should
also be hopeful for the temporal; for life while it reaches throughout all
eternity, begins in this world."[20] Transformative salvation of one's self,
one's family, or one's nation only occurred when people chose the difficult path of hard work and diligent sacrifice. Divinity was the inspiration
for strategies to overcome segregation and white supremacy, but individual determination was the key to achieving Randolph's vision of human
dignity.

Florence Randolph represents the transition from slavery to freedom
for African Americans in New Jersey and across the United States. In the
aftermath of the most sustained and debilitating oppression ever conceived and executed, faith was the bedrock for the organized effort to
redefine civilization.[21] Randolph's experience encompassed the black
church and its secular product, the club movement. Her success in organizing at the local and state levels provided a social and political structure for the aspirations of her generation to address racial equality to
national and international audiences. Randolph and hundreds of women
leaders like her developed literacy programs, childcare facilities, and employment networks for African American women throughout the United
States.[22] The confluence of her religious conviction and her secular activism forged a new path of democracy.

MARION THOMPSON WRIGHT

Marion Thompson Wright carried this legacy into New Jersey's public
school system between 1927 and 1940. In black communities nationwide,
schools became the arena for the expression of "New Negro" ideals about
racial uplift in the first half of the twentieth century.[23] Wright's excellence

as a teacher, scholar, and researcher embodied the range of new possibilities for the second generation of African Americans born after slavery.
Without the persistence of Randolph's generation, the achievements of
Wright's generation would have been impossible. Marion Wright continued the ethic of "lifting as she climbed" that Randolph espoused in the
late nineteenth century.[24] Marion Thompson Wright was born in 1902
and was graduated from Barringer High School in Newark, New Jersey,
in 1923. Her parents were Moses and Minnie Thompson. She bore two
children, Thelma and James, for her husband, William Moss, in 1919 and
1920, respectively. She earned both her baccalaureate degree and her
master's degree from Howard University, in 1927 and 1928. Wright continued her studies as a doctoral student at Columbia University, graduating in 1941 with a dissertation titled "The Education of Blacks in New
Jersey." Wright's work analyzed the transformation of education for
African Americans in three parts. It is most comprehensive in the presentation of information about the eighteenth and nineteenth centuries in
part 1. She then focused on the consequences of Reconstruction in part 2.
Part 3 addressed the early twentieth century and made recommendations
for the future. Her work earned her one of the first positions for a woman
as a professor at Howard University, where she published new research
on race, education, and history until her death in 1962.[25]

Wright practiced the political history of her era while applying it to
the questions of civil rights and racial equality raised by her predecessors
in the Black Freedom Movement.[26] Placing these questions within the
national context of the federal New Deal programs gave legitimacy to the
debate over expanding governmental programs that many contemporary
professional historians would have rejected without a second thought.[27]
The prevailing assumption of black inferiority prevented any serious engagement with ideas and practices designed to diminish the barriers to
educational achievement placed on black communities governed by
white school boards and state departments of education. Wright developed a research agenda that used the rhetoric, methodologies, and techniques of the established academic hierarchy to attack the evils of Jim
Crow segregation in the halls of institutional power. Earlier black women
leaders founded the club movement to improve conditions in African
American communities from the bottom up. Wright used the lessons she
learned in Barringer High School to redefine the core assumptions about
American education with her work at Columbia University. Her efforts
reflected the national strategies developed and implemented by Mary
McLeod Bethune, Nannie Helen Burroughs, and Charlotte Hawkins
Brown.[28] The combination of the two approaches—institutional reform
through government and community improvement through activism—
yielded the infrastructure for expanded political engagement in the form
of a civil rights movement between 1948 and 1972.[29]

The combination of secular and religious elements to generate community activism carried the efforts to develop local and state organizations through the first two decades of the twentieth century. Wright's scholarship reveals another ideological factor that proved decisive in the creation of institutional political power: nationalism. Wright creates a framework for understanding federal education reform in "The Education of Blacks in New Jersey." Nearly all of the themes she develops have antecedents in the documents crafted by women's clubs over the previous fifty years.[30] When Wright emphasizes the importance of citizenship education, she crafts a specific appeal to northern white politicians who have an interest in shaping the direction of black voting patterns.[31] Appeals to health, activism, recreation, and home life contradict common assumptions about the nature of black families and communities. The revelation of citizen responsibilities provides a practical link to the political careers of superintendents, judges, legislators, mayors, and governors. Combining the rhetoric of racial equality with the basic, patriotic nationalism of citizenship moves Wright's scholarship beyond the theoretical and idealistic claims of radical liberals of the previous generation.[32] Her words connect the urgency of reform in northern segregated schools to the maintenance and promotion of state pride and national identity. "If children are to be trained in the schools in accordance with the ideals of democratic thinking and practices, the educators of New Jersey and America will be called upon to assume roles of leadership in purposive planning instead of allowing themselves merely to reflect the sentiments, ideas, and practices of social groups of which they are members."[33] The compelling power of faith, reason, and patriotism held the potential to override the base hatred of white supremacy as civil rights organizations gained political leverage through the middle decades of the twentieth century.

Marion Wright understood the legacy of Florence Randolph's efforts to transform the lives of African Americans in New Jersey. Where Randolph laid a foundation for black women's ideas to be heard and respected within the black community, Wright carried those voices to the universities and state legislatures. The lesson of these achievements is not the significance of one over the other, but the interdependence of these women's work across generations. From the grassroots with Alice Archibald to the halls of Congress with Mary Bethune, the persistence and consistency of Randolph and Wright as scholars and activists engaged black families and communities with new senses of purpose toward the goal of ending white supremacy.[34] The national transformation shaped by the civil rights movement between 1948 and 1972 drew its force directly from the work black women historians undertook in the first half of the twentieth century. After the successes of the Civil Rights Act of 1964, the Voting Rights Act of 1965, and the Fair Housing Act of 1968, a new generation of New Jersey's black women activists and historians faced unprecedented challenges in determining the meaning of these victories and assessing the threats posed by a resurgent white conservatism powered by the segregationists' mass conversion to the Republican Party.[35]

LENORA WALKER MCKAY

Lenora Walker McKay looked to craft a new vision of New Jersey's past in order to guide a generation in an uncharted territory of politics absent the signposts of Jim Crow. The same principles of faith, reason, and patriotism fueled her passion to interpret the past for the benefit of her children. In her writings, McKay stretched the reach of Wright's historiography to include black communities forgotten by the waves of the Great Migration and the industrialization of New Jersey's larger cities. McKay emphasized the difficult challenges of home ownership and middle-class aspirations within northern Jim Crow alongside the grassroots and institutional politics of the NAACP, Urban League, and Universal Negro Improvement Association. The achievement of legislative civil rights guaranteed none of the economic access to jobs and business ownership that northern white paternalism allowed the previous two generations. McKay's histories of black communities in New Jersey heralded a new starting point for African Americans experiencing the first sustained measures of political equality in American history.

As mentioned in chapter 1, Lenora McKay was born in 1917 and was graduated from Asbury Park High School between 1933 and 1935, but did not attend college. She never completed any collegiate work. Her parents (Reverend C. J. H. Walker and Mrs. C. H. Walker) both attended the Manassas Training School in Virginia in the first decade of the twentieth century. Reverend Walker received his divinity degree from Lincoln University in 1910. McKay followed in her mother's footsteps as a homemaker and church missionary through her adult life. The first of her two histories, *The Blacks of Monmouth County*, shed new light on race issues in the rural communities of the Garden State in 1976. In 1984, McKay published *Mama and Papa*, a collection of historical documents and a recollection of her childhood.[36] Her explicit purpose in both works was to examine the African American community in greater detail. McKay understood that the best histories offered the most complete interpretations, even if they created contradictions in a grand mythology. She transformed the achievements of Randolph's theology and Wright's historicism about the black community into an accessible public memory for everyone.

The Blacks of Monmouth County presented a detailed chronology of African Americans in the heart of New Jersey's farming communities dating back to the colonial period. Graham Hodges added depth and drama to the story of slavery in the state, but McKay opened the door for future analysis by expanding Marion Wright's challenge to the rhetoric of black inferiority.[37] However, McKay crafted this argument from the bottom up rather than the top down. Wright applied the values that Randolph pioneered in her effort to redesign New Jersey education for equal opportunity. McKay seized the principles of faith, reason, and patriotism to inspire black children by reading her work to become community activists. Her systematic study of the organizations, institutions, and individuals who survived and overcame the barriers of northern Jim Crow segregation offered strategies for young people looking for direction and purpose within a society claiming to accept racial integration. Careful attention to the grassroots application of these precepts of black women in New Jersey as leaders—not just activists—led to the expansion of black political and economic opportunity in the state at the end of the twentieth century.[38]

The shift from spiritual elites (Randolph) to a corps of educated leaders (Wright) to a generation of organic intellectuals (McKay) reveals a determination across time that explains the success of the Black Freedom Movement in the twentieth-century United States. McKay's work represents the radical vision of the movement, achieved by redefining the scope of black activism from its roots. *Mama and Papa*, McKay's memoir, acts to inspire young people who might not otherwise realize the opportunities open to them. Using detailed recollections about the material culture of black life within segregated towns, McKay shows how the ability of African American families and communities can dismantle whatever obstacles they encounter from white authorities and institutions. McKay incorporates dozens of documents ranging from birth certificates to newspaper advertisements to school report cards to illustrate the historical changes in record keeping over her lifetime. In her discussion of education, she provided a copy of an early classroom evaluation from the Neptune Township public schools. Parents received these report cards every two months, and the district required them to sign and return the cards. O. J. Moulton encouraged parents to visit the school and explained the district's reasoning for cooperation between the parents and teachers. "'Upon these depend the future of democracy and the stability of government.' In this training, we recognize that the school shares the responsibility with the home." Students received comments in two categories—citizenship and scholarship. Categories like courtesy, reliability, promptness, cheerful cooperation, initiative, effort, cleanliness, and attendance informed the evaluation of citizenship. Scholarship criteria included reading (silent and oral), English expression (language, composition, and spelling), arithmetic, social studies (geography, history, and hygiene), domestic science (cooking, sewing, and homemaking), manual training, penmanship, music, art and handwork, and health education.[39] These documents illustrate the terms of engagement for African American families in transforming the values of the larger society.

McKay restrained her writing in telling her family story, but opened the door for later scholars to interpret the primary source material she provided. The balance of autobiographical analysis with documentation compels the reader to engage the process of actively interpreting the past.[40] McKay's books offer a new intellectual beginning for African Americans looking to maximize their opportunities for success in a world that offers less overt hostility and more neglectful ambivalence.[41] By inscribing the family and community with renewed meaning, McKay empowers young African Americans to visualize an American dream of integrity, wealth, and leadership.

MADONNA CARTER JACKSON

Madonna Carter Jackson expanded on this historical endeavor in the first decade of the twenty-first century. Against a narrative of the decay and decline of black leadership following the civil rights movement, Jackson created a public history of African American excellence. She interpreted a range of photographs her father took, documenting the transformation of New Jersey's black communities between 1940 and 1980. Her collection demonstrates the dignity of African Americans in everyday life as it celebrates their political and economic achievements. Ultimately, Jackson completes the circle of African American women's historiography in New Jersey by illustrating the rewards (integrity, wealth, and leadership) of the values (faith, reason, and patriotism) underlying black activism.

Born in 1948, Madonna Carter Jackson witnessed the ways black women historians' lived experiences shaped the transformation of the United States in the second half of the twentieth century. Her mother and father—Joseph and Lenora Carter—lived in Asbury Park, New Jersey, between 1920 and 1980. Jackson worked as a secretary and office assistant for most of her adult life after graduating from Asbury Park High School in 1967.[42] In 1981, after her father's death, she became the first black woman to publish a magazine focusing on black culture and history in rural New Jersey, *Exposure*. The stories and photographs she collected for *Exposure* carried the banner of African American activism and leadership that Lenora McKay promoted over the previous decade. Jackson compiled her father's photographs and her own historical documents in her book *Asbury Park: A West Side Story* in 2007. In one photo dating back before 1950, Jackson's father (Joseph Carter) took a photo of his cousin, Doris Niblack-Wynn, posing near a jukebox at the Carver Hotel in Neptune. He took many event photographs as famous performers like Ray Charles visited the Convention Hall in Asbury Park between 1951 and 1963. By 1972, however, Carter's images documented the declining residential and commercial real estate in the wake of white flight and race riots.[43] Jackson's presentation of these images conveyed the profound sense of loss she experienced when she returned to her community and saw that living conditions had worsened, despite the victories of the Black Freedom Movement. *Asbury Park* corrects much of the historical revisionism about the impact of the Civil Rights Movement in New Jersey after 1950. By revealing the tensions beneath the legislative and political transformation of state that persisted through 1990, Jackson reaffirms the dignity and determination African Americans sustained through the resegregation of New Jersey's school districts and municipalities. "Even though discrimination was still ravaging the South, it was at another level in the North. We grew up in a society that made my father feel that we had to embrace the diversity of our world, and understand the cultures and religions outside of our own." [44] Her work simultaneously inspires young people by revealing the family and community accountability of civil rights leaders and debunks the mythology of disco and hiphop entertainment cultures that betrayed the promise of racial integration. "It has been our feeling that the news media considers Black news good news only when it is negative and therefore covers very few positive achievements of individuals and groups in the community." [45]

Asbury Park relies on a chronological structure to demonstrate the changes in the African American community between 1940 and 1980, with a particular emphasis on the later decades. Professionals featured in the earlier photographs held advanced degrees in scientific fields, reflecting the technological orientation that became a crucial part of the shore economy starting with World War I. [46] Politicians, police officers, and businesspeople became more common subjects of Carter's photographs after 1970. While a select group of college-educated African Americans could excel in New Jersey's private sector before 1950, the black middle class in the second half of the twentieth century relied on public employment at the county and state levels. With more public employees, civil rights enforcement became more vigorous. However, the transformation of the private sector stagnated as African Americans found few opportunities at the senior executive level before 1995. [47] This shift reveals the increased political separation between whites and blacks in New Jersey's small towns as civil rights enforcement at the federal level became more vigorous. [48] Jackson's use of her father's images indicates a crucial shift in the historiography black women developed at the end of the twentieth century. The boundaries of professional historiography that circumscribed the inquiries Marion Wright developed fell away completely for Jackson's public exhibitions of the black experience. Jackson takes another step beyond the cultural preservation McKay showcased in her works by encouraging readers to add their own notes and recollections on nearly every page of her book. *Asbury Park* stands as an interactive text, where each copy becomes its own unique historical document through the reader's written responses to the text and images. The mass reproduction of this praxis upholds the black public sphere as the ultimate judge of historicity and relevance in ways Randolph could only imagine when she first received her license to preach in 1897.

Jackson lived the achievement of the Black Freedom Movement in witnessing and documenting the transformation of black middle-class occupations like waiters and teachers to career technicians and engineers. She envisioned communities where African Americans could own their own businesses with financing from national banks and customers from every part of the world. Yet the realities of continuing racial restrictions in an era of legislative integration frustrated this vision after 1980. Her work on *Exposure* magazine and the thesis of *Asbury Park* revealed her determination to continue the Black Freedom Movement, despite these persistent obstacles to racial uplift. "God protected me as a child and is still protecting me today. All because my parents made us keep an open mind about faith."[49] The consistency of black women historians' collective commitment to human equality across time contributed greatly to the expansion of American democracy as an international phenomenon in the twentieth century.

The life and work of two of Jackson's contemporaries are further testimony to the prevalence of the values embedded in her work. Lila Stevenson helped to shape the evolution of the black church in rural communities and to bridge the gap between family and community life. Helen Elliott served the state as a community educator at Brookdale Community College in Lincroft. Disentangling the influences from the church to the school to the council room or legislature misses the larger point about the relationships among these entities across the history of the Black Freedom Movement. Jackson's lessons of interactive accountability drew on the legacy of the black church and its adaptability as shown in Stevenson's life. They also shaped the ways Elliott's commitment to higher education sustained the legacy of legislative integration. Together, the three women's work illustrates how black communities redefined the economics of equality in New Jersey by the start of the twenty-first century.

Lila Stevenson moved to Manalapan Township during the Great Depression. She briefly described the difficulty in finding employment and housing: "When I first came here, it was hard to find a house. I did mostly farm work and worked in chicken factories. My husband went into the army, and I saved money to buy two houses on Pension Road."[50] Her ability to confront employment discrimination and still secure housing for her family revealed the creativity and determination many black women displayed in the mid-twentieth century. Stevenson emphasized the central importance of the church community in her life. She said, "I started [a] church here from my home with prayer meetings and Sunday school around 1945 or 1946. The church was a tremendous help for our community. We bought food for needy families and we added two rooms to the church for everyday children's recreation."[51] Since the earlier black churches no longer operated on a consistent basis, Stevenson's actions served to energize the new black community which evolved in the area after the Second World War. The regular church, Sunday school, and Bible study meetings provided social outlets that laid the foundation for black working-class community in the second half of the twentieth century. Stevenson also recalled details about racism that highlighted its prevalence and economic impact. She noted, "We were raised up under [racism]. It was the way things were. It was very hard to get a house here. If you were black, you couldn't go and borrow money from the bank."[52] Yet African Americans remained trapped at the bottom of the agricultural economy and could not transform their racial identity in the same ways that the local Jewish community did after 1950.[53] Still, the prospects for consistent, but limited, employment attracted sufficient new residents between 1930 and 1960 for the black community to grow.

Helen Elliott spent her entire life living and working in the Asbury Park community. Elliott's insights help us to understand the lines of residential segregation that existed in this town as late as the 1950s. She also sheds a light on the importance of community among African Americans in the area through the mid-twentieth century. "The west side of Asbury Park [had] middle-class African Americans moving in. Dr. Hayes, Dr. Robinson (a dentist and general practitioner), and Dr. Carter all had practices and lived on the west side. Most teachers at Bangs Avenue School lived on the west side as well as police officers. Professionals lived next to domestic and manual laborers. There was a sense of community economy."[54]

The southwest corner of Asbury Park, known as the west side, was the largest African American community in Monmouth County in the first half of the twentieth century. Elliott's commentary reveals how clearly defined ethnic neighborhoods were there before 1960—a characteristic Asbury Park shared with large cities across the country. Another common characteristic—born of racial segregation nationally—was the economic and social heterogeneity of the black community.[55] Elliott herself became a professional educator along the central Jersey shore. Elliott closed her description of her childhood by contrasting her memories of the west side with common stereotypes about late-twentieth-century black neighborhoods. Safety, intraracial class integration, and residential segregation stand as hallmarks of life in this rural resort. Although nostalgia may play some part in her memories, her experiences as a social worker and employment counselor add some objectivity to her understanding of how her hometown changed during the twentieth century.

The intersection of patriarchy and white supremacy defined the conditions, limitations, and opportunities black women historians encountered in New Jersey and throughout the United States.[56] The core assumptions of white, male intellectuals defined the social realities women like Florence Randolph, Marion Wright, Lenora McKay, and Madonna Jackson encountered throughout their lives. For generations, white men taught each other that African American women were property. Despite the weight of this general proscription, some women managed to undertake leadership roles within the African American community. Women elders, in particular, supported, encouraged, and protected their communities. They were the women who built and maintained the Black Freedom Movement from 1870 through 2000. "Later, when civil rights workers testified to the source of their commitment, or to the strength that enabled them to hold fast in the face of overwhelming opposition, many of them would allude to the image of the black working woman (in some cases their own mother); her back, bent over a washboard or a cotton patch, seemed broad enough to support the cares of the world."[57]

In the fight for equality, there is nothing more fundamentally important than the survival of the group which is trying to gain equality. Struggling against an institution is futile if everyone dies. These survival tactics included education to protect against prejudice. African American women accomplished the transformation of American democracy using these tactics. Their successes indicated that no one was more important to the movement than the women and mothers who kept their families and their communities moving towards racial equality. Their sacrifices and leadership deserve the attention and respect of the historical profession. Although many black women never gained state or national elective office, black women historians' collective body of work constitutes the foundation for one of the most inclusive definitions of political equality in American history.

NOTES

1. Barbara Ransby, *Ella Baker and the Black Freedom Movement: A Radical Democratic Vision* (Chapel Hill: University of North Carolina Press, 2005), 90–91.

2. Bettye Collier-Thomas and V. P. Franklin, eds., *Sisters in the Struggle: African American Women in the Civil Rights-Black Power Movement* (New York: New York University Press, 2001), 1–8; Matthew Countryman, *Up South: Civil Rights and Black Power in Philadelphia* (Philadelphia: University of Pennsylvania Press, 2007), 1–12; Thomas J. Sugrue, *Sweet Land of Liberty: The Forgotten Struggle for Civil Rights in the North* (New York: Random House, 2008), xxvii–xxviii.

3. Patricia Hill Collins, *Black Feminist Thought: Knowledge, Consciousness, and the Politics of Empowerment* (New York: Routledge, 1990), 13.

4. James C. Scott, *Domination and the Arts of Resistance: Hidden Transcripts* (New Haven, CT: Yale University Press, 1992), 45–69.

5. Winthrop Jordan, *White over Black: American Attitudes toward the Negro, 1550–1815* (Chapel Hill: University of North Carolina Press, 1968), 414–21; Julie Winch, *Philadelphia's Black Elite: Activism, Accommodation, and the Struggle for Autonomy, 1787–1848* (Philadelphia: Temple University Press, 1993), 4–25.

6. Dred Scott v. Sandford, 60 U.S. (19 How.) 393 (1857).

7. William D. Carrigan, *The Making of a Lynching Culture: Violence and Vigilantism in Central Texas, 1836–1916* (Chicago: University of Illinois, 2006), 206–8.

8. Patricia Morton, *Disfigured Images: The Historical Assault on Afro-American Women* (Westport, CT: Praeger Publishers, 1991), 114.

9. Hill Collins, *Black Feminist Thought*, 7; Julie Des Jardins, *Women and the Historical Enterprise in America: Gender, Race, and the Politics of Memory, 1880–1945* (Chapel Hill: University of North Carolina Press, 2002), 40.

10. bell hooks, *Feminism Is for Everybody* (Boston: South End Press, 2000), 67–71.

11. Jacqueline Jones, *Labor of Love, Labor of Sorrow* (New York: Vintage, 1986), 3–10.

12. Morton, *Disfigured Images*, 114.

13. Paula Giddings, *When and Where I Enter: The Impact of Black Women on Race and Sex in America* (New York: Perennial, 1984), 329.

14. Hill Collins, *Black Feminist Thought*, 8.

15. Bettye Collier-Thomas, *Daughters of Thunder: Black Women Preachers and Their Sermons, 1850–1979* (San Francisco: Jossey-Bass Publishers, 1998), 102–6.

16. Ibid., 107.

17. Bettye Collier-Thomas, *Jesus, Jobs, and Justice: African American Women and Religion* (Knopf: New York, 2010), 302.

18. V. P. Franklin and Bettye Collier-Thomas, "For the Race in General and Black Women in Particular: The Civil Rights Activities of African American Women's Organizations, 1915–1950," in *Sisters in the Struggle*, 23.

19. Paula Giddings, *When and Where I Enter: The Impact of Black Women on Race and Sex in America* (New York: Bantam Books, 1988), 83, 93.

20. Collier-Thomas, *Daughters of Thunder*, 107.

21. Vincent Harding, *There Is a River: The Black Struggle for Freedom* (Orlando, FL: Harcourt, Brace, and Company, 1981), 46, 48, 166–68; Orlando Patterson, *Slavery and Social Death: A Comparative Study* (Cambridge, MA: Harvard University Press, 1982), 33–34. Patterson equivocates on the question of racial slavery in the Americas, but Harding's persuasive point is that the confluence of the political rhetoric of liberty, the capitalist economies of tobacco, rice, sugar, and cotton, and the ideology of white European Christian supremacy combined to produce the most alienating form of chattel slavery ever conceived.

22. Giddings, *When and Where I Enter*, 95–97.

23. Alain Locke popularized the term "New Negro" to describe his generation of African Americans who would no longer accept white violence and assumptions of black people's racial inferiority in 1925. His ideas represented the surge of racial pride in black urban neighborhoods across the country, but most famously remembered in New York City as the Harlem Renaissance.

24. Ibid., 153–82. Women's clubs in the black community coined the phrase "lifting as we climb" at the start of the twentieth century. The phrase captured the priorities and strategies of racial uplift that pervaded black women's activism in the civil rights movement.

25. "Marion Thompson Wright biography," http://65.36.189.169/ (7 March 2008).

26. Peter Novick, *That Noble Dream: The "Objectivity Question" and the American Historical Association* (Cambridge: Cambridge University Press, 1995), 96–98; Ransby, *Ella Baker and the Black Freedom Movement*, 1–12; Julie Des Jardins, *Women and the Historical Enterprise in America: Gender, Race, and the Politics of Memory, 1880–1945* (Chapel Hill: University of North Carolina Press, 2003), 118–42. At the start of the twentieth century, politics and ideology were the primary lenses that professional historians used to understand the past. Gradually, economics and culture became accepted within the profession to interpret human activity. The role of black women librarians, archivists, and researchers played a crucial role in this transformation.

27. Ibid., 231.

28. Darlene Clark Hine, Elsa Barkley Brown, and Rosalyn Terborg-Penn, eds., *Black Women in America: An Historical Encyclopedia*, vols. 1 and 2 (Bloomington: Indiana University Press, 1993), 113–27, 172–74, 201–5.

29. Sundiata Keita Cha-Jua and Clarence Lang, "The 'Long Movement' as Vampire: Temporal and Spatial Fallacies in Recent Black Freedom Studies," *Journal of African American History* 92, no. 2 (Spring 2007): 265–88. The debate at the start of the twenty-first century about what constitutes the civil rights movement as opposed to the Black

Power Movement or the Black Freedom Movement emphasizes the discontinuities across space and time rather than the continuities. Both approaches are valuable and ultimately must engage in a process of synthesis to develop a plausible historical narrative in service to the values for which the leaders and activists themselves died.

30. Giddings, *When and Where I Enter*, 153–82.

31. Kevin K. Gaines, *Uplifting the Race: Black Leadership, Politics, and Culture in the Twentieth Century* (Chapel Hill: University of North Carolina Press, 1996), 259; Adolph Reed Jr., *Stirring in the Jug: Black Politics in the Post-Segregation Era* (Minneapolis: University of Minnesota Press, 1999), 79–115. The heart of the Republican Party had been the northeastern and midwestern United States from the beginning of the organization. As more African Americans migrated to northern cities between 1910 and 1930, tensions between black migrants and white northerners' visions of the Republican agenda clashed frequently. Northern Democrats struggled for a generation to pull African Americans into their party before finally having success in the federal elections in 1932 and 1936.

32. Eric Foner, *Reconstruction: America's Unfinished Revolution, 1863–1877* (New York: Harper Perennial, 2002), 60–76; Kevin Mumford, *Newark: A History of Race, Rights, and Riots in America* (New York: New York University Press, 2007), 32–49.

33. Marion Thompson Wright, *The Education of Negroes in New Jersey* (New York: Columbia University, 1941), 211.

34. Giddings, *When and Where I Enter*, 199–230. Bethune embodied a singular vision of racial uplift and integration through the intervention of the federal government in the states that defined the strategy of the Black Freedom Movement in the twentieth century.

35. Jonathan Birnbaum and Clarence Taylor, eds., *Civil Rights since 1787* (New York: New York University Press, 2000), 725–30.

36. Lenora Walker McKay, *The Blacks of Monmouth County* (privately published, 1976), 2; Lenora Walker McKay, *Mama and Papa* (privately published, 1984), 4.

37. Graham Russell Hodges, *Slavery and Freedom in the Rural North: African Americans in Monmouth County, New Jersey* (New York: Madison House, 1997), xiv–xv.

38. Clement A. Price, *Freedom Not Far Distant: A Documentary History of African Americans in New Jersey* (Trenton: New Jersey Historical Commission, 1980), 290.

39. McKay, *Mama and Papa*, 84.

40. Ibid., 114–66.

41. Charles M. Lamb, *Housing Segregation in Suburban America since 1960: Presidential and Judicial Politics* (New York: Cambridge University Press, 2005), 139.

42. Madonna Carter Jackson, *Asbury Park: A West Side Story* (Denver: Outskirts Press, 2007), 190.

43. Ibid., 27, 115, 200.

44. Ibid., 243.

45. Ibid., 229.

46. Ibid., 25, 41.

47. Michael B. Katz, Mark J. Stern, and Jamie J. Fader, "The New African American Inequality," *Journal of American History* 92, no. 1 (June 2005): 88–92.

48. Sugrue, *Sweet Land of Liberty*, 59–84.

49. Jackson, *Asbury Park*, 217.

50. Lila Stevenson, interview, 17 June 2001.

51. Ibid.

52. Ibid.

53. Karen Brodkin, *How Jews Became White Folks: And What That Says about Race in America* (New Brunswick, NJ: Rutgers University Press, 1998), 150, 156–58. Jewish Americans continued to face discrimination in New Jersey and the United States after 1950; however, the degree of racial segregation that transformed the African American experience in major cities in the second half of the twentieth century did not continue to affect Jewish families and communities.

54. Helen Elliott, interview, 18 December 2000.

55. Douglas S. Massey and Nancy A. Denton, *American Apartheid: Segregation and the Making of the Underclass* (Cambridge, MA: Harvard University Press, 1993), 45–55.

56. Jordan, *White over Black*, 91–99; George Fredrickson, *The Black Image in the White Mind: The Debate over Afro-American Character and Destiny, 1817–1914* (Middletown, CT: Wesleyan Press, 1987), 198–227; Michael Omi and Howard Winant, *Racial Formation in the United States: From the 1960s to the 1990s* (New York: Routledge, 1994), 77–93; Maghan Keita, *Race and the Writing of History: Riddling the Sphinx* (London: Oxford University Press, 2000), 15–26; Margaret Marsh, *Suburban Lives* (New Brunswick, NJ: Rutgers University Press, 1990), 1–19.

57. Jacqueline Jones, *Labor of Love, Labor of Sorrow* (New York: Basic Books, 1985), 286.

THREE

Leadership

Leadership is the example of individual character given public display. It can occur in a moment. It can unfold over an entire lifetime. Leadership must be both given and taken, in many instances simultaneously. It is a combination of thought, speech, and activity. A leader without character is both ineffective and unproductive. A person of good character without public audience will never be a leader. Leaders take the next step beyond good character into compassionate negotiation. Listening, forgiveness, delegation, and inspiration are the core leadership skills. Many scholars believe that decisive action is the crucial aspect of leadership. This is merely a facet of good character. Leadership involves shaping the moments, days, and years that produce moments of decision. The thankless task of listening to multitudes and valuing the lessons their lives offer provides the wisdom of varied experience. Forgiving those who inflict pain and suffering is the first step to healing and spiritual renewal. Delegation utilizes the skills, knowledge, and expertise of a community to build institutions greater than anyone could do alone. Inspiration is the ability to motivate people, to generate public belief in programs and ideas that most consider impossible. The mere notion of challenging white supremacy stretches each of these leadership skills to their limits. The prospect of victory over white supremacy—the renewal of the spirit of humanity—renews leaders to continue working toward success.

Heroism is leadership under pressure. When there is adversity, the ability of good leaders to succeed makes them heroes. Often the idea of a hero is limited to those who triumph in the face of violence—police, firefighters, doctors, and soldiers. This definition is not without merit. Courage, despite the possibility of death or injury, deserves commendation. Yet, by privileging the victory over physical adversity, success against social, cultural, economic, and psychological problems is minimized. Businesspeople, lawyers, teachers, planners, secretaries, and engineers all perform heroic tasks against daunting odds every day around the world. Building roads, debating laws, managing commerce, and shaping education are the bedrocks of civilization. Heroism is also the defense and advancement of civil society. White supremacy (along with poverty, homophobia, patriarchy, and ableism) erodes the possibility of realizing an effective democratic republic. The daily battles against disease, intolerance, and bureaucracy require more persistence than the dramatic, instantaneous challenges of physical harm. There is no hierarchy of heroism. Yet the contributions of those who fought (and fight) white supremacy receive little public acclaim. Masculine assumptions about the function of the public arena shaped the idea of political citizenship in New Jersey. From traditional electoral and policy debates through the silent, but effective, infrapolitics among the disenfranchised, the values taught and nurtured through families shaped the moment-to-moment, day-to-day reformulation of American democracy from the bottom up.

Some scholars have taken some note of the importance of understanding these three categories (character, leadership, and heroism). Political scientist Adolph Reed Jr.'s recent work still succumbs to an urban myopia regarding African American leadership.[1] By ignoring the rural dimensions of black leadership in the early twentieth century and the suburban aspects in the late twentieth century, an oversimplified perception of black organizations and political strategies emerges. More nuanced accounts of African American character and heroism appear in historians Kevin Gaines and Nikhil Pal Singh's respective works. Singh does more than merely caution scholars away from simplicity in discussing black activism. He identifies the coincidence and contradictions of positing a long-standing tension between nationalism and integrationism among African Americans.[2] The recognition of how these categories overlapped resulted from the application of multiple organizational identities in small, rural communities throughout the United States. The academy is only beginning to recognize how these blurred categories shaped racial organization in urban centers during the "New Negro" era after World War I. Gaines, on the other hand, reveals the importance of applying political, cultural, and intellectual strategies persistently at the grassroots level. Too often, middle-class African Americans contented themselves with lawsuits and subsequent proclamations of victory without paying any heed to the continuing structural inequalities that faced the masses of black people.[3] These New Jersey experiences in the twentieth century reflect the broader ideology and methodology of African social and intellectual engagement to transform the material conditions of oppression and exploitation.

THE NATIONAL ASSOCIATION FOR THE ADVANCEMENT OF COLORED PEOPLE

Leaders from across the African diaspora understood that sustained social transformation is only the result of continuous organization across all social barriers. They graphically illustrated the evolution of character to leadership, and leadership to heroism. Lenora Walker McKay documented her family's involvement in the National Association for the Advancement of Colored People (NAACP), the National Urban League (NUL), and the Universal Negro Improvement Association (UNIA). At the national level, these organizations espoused three different ideologies for the liberation and uplift of African Americans. The NAACP stood for racial integration and the abolition of Jim Crow society through the application of the law. The NUL focused on the development of economic self-sufficiency among African Americans as the best path to prosperity and racial integration in the United States. The UNIA organized the masses of black workers under the banner of Pan-African nationalism in ambitious business ventures such as the Black Star shipping line and *Negro World* newspaper. In New Jersey's resort communities, these ideological divisions held little weight. Small black communities shared resources and leadership across these philosophical differences. Walker's father led local chapters of all three organizations.[4] By using his titles with several different organizations, Reverend Walker attracted a wide range of civil rights activists to his small town. Multiple group identities also allowed rural leaders like Walker to attract the maximum number of supporters. Even when the functions at various events differed between entertainment, education, and engagement, the agenda for activism in the community remained the same. Walker was also able to position himself as a spokesperson for the region to all of the major racial uplift organizations. His ability to connect with the knowledge and resources of these three groups increased the variety of programs he could offer and the perceptions of local members that their work was important. The two sets of organizational credentials—credibility locally and nationally—established Walker as a "race leader" in the eyes of both black and white New Jerseyans. In negotiations about the operation of Jim Crow in the North, Walker's voice shaped the compromises to black dignity that white authorities allowed. Finally, the coalition of local black organizations reflected the growth of leadership outside the boundaries of the ministry. While Walker himself was a minister, local doctors, dentists, and funeral directors also took active roles in organizing and promoting the local UNIA, NUL, and NAACP. The development of multiple group identities to advance the freedom struggle against racial segregation in the rural North is evidence of both creative judgment and good character.

THE YOUNG MEN AND WOMEN'S CHRISTIAN ASSOCIATION

White supremacy in the rural North faced a continual assault between 1920 and 1950. Black leaders published newspapers, organized political advocacy groups, and sponsored cultural education programs. The United Colored Republican Clubs of Monmouth County coordinated their political campaigns from their headquarters in F. Leon Harris's funeral home.[5] A community betterment club sponsored a Negro History Week, also held at Harris's establishment in 1946. [6] However, the local Young Men's Christian Association (YMCA)—although segregated—was the main location for black activism during this period throughout the rural corridor. Dr. James Parker Sr. and Mrs. Marie Parker took leadership on race matters in Red Bank, New Jersey. Dr. Parker enjoyed the respect of both black and white residents in Red Bank because he represented dignity and accomplishment for African Americans without angrily challenging the lines of de facto segregation. The Parkers led a coalition of local African Americans in establishing the YMCA branch for residents on Red Bank's segregated west side in 1931. The committee of management for the project included Thomas E. Taylor (retired executive secretary of the Harlem branch of the New York YMCA), Isaac Foreman, Bernard Mason, Sprague Williams, Dr. M. C. Dabney, L. G. Handy, P. L. Jones, William Lyons, and Walter Greer. Marie Parker coordinated the volunteer staff for the Westside Y. Mae Westbrook, Nancy Fields, and Dorothy Flax gave their time, knowledge, and skills as well. These individuals were the secular, black, middle-class leaders in Red Bank, operating out of the AME Zion church at the intersection of Shrewsbury and West Bergen avenues. The YMCA brought Count Basie and Billie Holiday and the Renaissance Five basketball team to Red Bank in 1938 to help with fund-raising.[7] The combined efforts of these leaders resembled similar strategies applied by African Americans in larger urban centers throughout the United States in the first half of the twentieth century.[8]

In 1946, the national YMCA disallowed segregated branches, but the well-organized Westside Y persisted until 1958 because the local black middle class supported it. The Parkers created an enduring fund-raising and cultural pride event through the YMCA in 1950 when (under the guidance of Lillian Sharp Hunter of the *Amsterdam News*) they developed a debutante cotillion. The event was a celebration of youth, beauty, parenting, and scholarship. Twenty-eight debutantes appeared at the first cotillion, and the number increased steadily through the next decade. Count Basie even agreed to come back to his hometown and play for the event in 1952 and 1956, adding prestige to the festivities.[9] James Sr. and Marie Parker continued and developed the tradition of black leadership in Red Bank that persisted through the 1960s.

Dr. James Parker Jr. followed in his parents' footsteps in becoming a notable role model for local African Americans in the late twentieth century. His recollections are testimony to the persistence of racial discrimination in this town. As a Red Bank native, he combined grassroots knowledge with his parents' leadership skills in assessing the transformation of the town between 1920 and 1950. He spoke about racial discrimination in housing during the Great Depression. Parker said, "I really remember the Depression; some of the white people bought homes around here cheaply and sold them to black families at a profit."[10] Discrimination in the housing market maintained the segregation of Red Bank's west side and built wealth among the local white community. Racial discrimination affected the town's theaters. Parker said, "The Carlton Theater (now the Count Basie) was segregated, and I had to sit in the balcony. The black section in the Strand Theater was 10 rows back on the right. The Strand restaurant wouldn't let black people in."[11]

Parker's portrait of black middle-class success within this context of racial discrimination demonstrates the importance of organizations like the Westside YMCA for small African American communities. The Parker family embodied the generational leadership against white supremacy in a small, resort community in New Jersey. Their efforts did not revolve around crises and confrontations with discriminatory practices and racist officials. Weekly programs addressing cultural pride, physical hygiene, political action, and a commitment to education formed the basis of a thirty-year effort to achieve racial equality. The Parkers were responsive to the dreams and aspirations of their neighbors, not just their fears and complaints. Entertainment was a crucial part of their leadership. Without the voices of Holiday and Basie, there would have been far fewer people in attendance at local fund-raisers like the debutante cotillion. The organized appeal to both black and white citizens for support formed the persistent waves of pressure that eventually eroded the local commitment to segregation.

THE WAR ON POVERTY

Leadership and organization remained the key to adapting to changing social and economic circumstances through the second half of the twentieth century. Reverend Caleb Oates became the pastor of Bethany Baptist Church in Howell in 1948 and remained the spiritual leader for the congregation through the 1990s. Oates's 1954 sermon on "The Key to Living" exemplified his connection between spiritual and political-economic life in this changing rural area. He said, "Most of our difficulties are fairly simple; the job, the people with whom we work, the children, the wife or husband, our needs to be loved, to feel important, to be a part of things. Why then are so many people leading lives of quiet desperation? . . . Faith alone never helped any man. It is what we do with it that makes the difference."[12] Placing religion at the center of all life, Oates emphasized the importance of individual action to realize the gift of faith. This world-view translated into an activist agenda for self- and community improvement for black congregants experiencing economic upheaval. Oates's ability to take effective action based upon his ideas earned him statewide recognition through the early 1950s. In 1953, Bethany Baptist received a grant from the Kiwanis Club to operate a snack bar for two hundred customers.[13] Oates used sermons on faith like "The Key to Living" to earn recognition for his church and its activities, such as the snack bar.

In the summer of 1966, Oates worked to address poverty within the local black community, using federal funding. As a member of the Monmouth Community Action Program (MCAP) Board of Directors, he oversaw the distribution of federal antipoverty funds to every black community in the county. MCAP was a result of the federal government's War on Poverty during Lyndon Johnson's presidency. Oates organized the local branch through Bethany Baptist and marshaled the local newspapers to pressure county and federal officials to include poor and working-class African Americans in the decision-making processes. Oates's efforts helped to create separate childcare facilities in Farmingdale, Englishtown, Red Bank, Long Branch, Neptune, and Asbury Park. Federal money from the Office of Economic Opportunity never materialized because administrative salaries consumed the funds. Oates persisted and was able to locate alternative funding. It arrived through the 1965 Elementary and Secondary Education Act and in the form of support from the Farmers Home Administration Office.[14] Oates continued his efforts that summer by developing a federal credit union within the church. Citing abuses of the credit system by local businesses at the expense of working-class blacks, Oates devised a strategy to provide cash loans to his congregation. He said, "Jewish landlords abused black migrant laborers, who numbered less than 700 in the area at the time. Banks wouldn't let blacks have money to buy homes and insurance. Howell Township put a moratorium on house building around 1949 or 1950. That discouraged working blacks from staying in town."[15] The credit union immediately attracted over one hundred members who paid five dollars to open their accounts and deposited between twenty-five and fifty cents each month thereafter. Account holders could then borrow up to seven hundred dollars at 1 percent annual interest.[16] The immediate effect of this program was the stabilization of several black households who worshipped at Bethany Baptist Church. Oates's successes helped farm workers create small savings accounts between 1967 and 1970 to withstand the weeks when local farms did not pay their laborers. Over time, however, the small size of the credit union loans (and the delays in federal antipoverty aid) limited the borrowers' ability to sustain themselves and their families in the face of the massive suburbanization and the expansion of the local, nonfarming, service economy.

Oates's leadership was tested in the face of deindustrialization and metropolitan growth. However, it was no longer the local racism that threatened his work. Like many black churches after 1980, Bethany Baptist confronted a more skeptical and materialistic group of worshippers with more financial resources than his previous congregations.[17] As a result of the greater degree of affluence enjoyed by the new black residents, the African American community in suburban central New Jersey became much more individualized and less connected as a group. Oates noted this distinct change in the local black working class. He said, "When I came along, we had pride—no one walked over us. Now, blacks are addicted to dope, in and out of prison. [Members of the Five Percent Nation—an offshoot of the Nation of Islam] threatened to burn me out, and I told them I'd blow their brains out. . . . I go to the black neighborhood, and there were prostitutes approaching my car on Sunday morning."[18]

Oates's comments begin with nostalgia for the black community of his youth, but they also illustrate important changes in the issues facing African Americans. The massive drug and crime epidemics that afflicted larger urban centers also affected these developing suburbs after 1970. These crises drove a wedge between civil rights activists like Oates and the new generation of poor and working-class blacks. The militancy of the Five Percent Nation merged with rampant apathy among black people (and youth, in particular) to undermine Oates's accomplishments in Howell and Farmingdale.[19] The Five Percenters were no longer a local presence after 1980, and they left no records to explain their opposition to Oates and his work. The decentralization of this community through the 1980s stymied the formation of cultural organizations and institutions. Oates's ability to maintain a small mission church in the face of this transformation is a testament to his heroism. It is also clear evidence that white supremacy is not always promoted and defended by white Americans. Some of the most dangerous white supremacists are African Americans and other minorities who undermine the strategies and tactics of racial uplift.

SEGREGATED SCHOOLS

The operation of the Freehold (New Jersey) Colored Young Men's Christian Association (YMCA) is a tale of continuing heroism throughout the entire twentieth century.[20] Reverend W. J. Wilson of Bethel AME Church, Reverend L. B. Brooks of Second Baptist Church, and U. S. Young, an early principal of the Court Street School in Freehold, all contributed to promoting the YMCA's message of sobriety, spirituality, and empowerment for the local African Americans, starting in 1916.[21] In the course of one year, the YMCA closed the local gambling establishment, hosted twenty-four lectures on educational topics, provided temporary food and shelter for those without any, and created a sense of racial solidarity among the new black residents.[22] By providing political education and demonstrating the power of collective organization, the Y taught the black population lessons about their potential influence in their new home. With the support of local black churches and educators, this organization solidified the foundation of the local African American community as it rapidly expanded through the 1920s.

The other major black institution to rise between 1920 and 1950 was the Court Street School. African American children attended the segregated elementary school until 1947, although few went on to the regional high school before the 1950s. African American families often needed a young adult's income in the 1930s and 1940s, often ending black students' pursuits of higher education. U. S. Young, William Reid, and George I. Reed all served as teachers and principals for the black students at Court Street School during this period.[23] These men were representative of the outstanding quality of black teachers and administrators in the first half of the twentieth century. Ferdinand G. Fenderson was the trailblazing leader of the Court Street School. Originally from New Haven, Connecticut, he was a graduate of Yale University. Fenderson took charge of the school in 1912 and became determined to enroll some of his eighth-grade students at the high-school level, despite the prevailing misconceptions about black academic inability. Combining state exam preparation with a focus on black history, Fenderson guided three students into the high school the following fall—Lucy Brown, George Winston, and Geraldine Neal. Winston and Neal continued to college at Lincoln and Howard universities, respectively. Although his leadership and educational credentials were never in doubt, Fenderson was sometimes forced to take dishwashing jobs in local restaurants because his services in education and law were unappreciated in early-twentieth-century New Jersey.[24] Persistence and sacrifice distinguished Fenderson's career in central New Jersey. He instilled a sense of pride in his students, despite racial segregation, and several of the Court Street students went on to college over the coming decades.[25]

Ferdinand Fenderson continued his activism after 1940 with his efforts to build a local chapter of the NAACP. In February 1942, Freehold Borough police beat James Lee Wilder, a young African American, in the street, an incident that pushed Fenderson into action. Police brutality against young black men was a continuation of the violence of the slave plantation's overseers to guarantee the productivity of black labor by any means necessary. Across the nation, police forces had established clear policies permitting the abuse of young black people to defend the national Jim Crow color lines. After the Wilder beating, Fenderson fought back by hosting a meeting of the Freehold Colored Civic Group to register community outrage. He also asked for advice and guidance from Lorenzo Harris of the Asbury Park NAACP.[26] By May 1942, Fenderson wrote an official charter for the Freehold NAACP with the support of a full executive board and fourteen charter members.[27] The next year, Fenderson led campaigns to open the two largest local factories—Karagheusian's rug mill and Eisner's uniform plant—to black workers. The Freehold NAACP received written agreements to interview, hire, and promote local African Americans in January 1943.[28] Local activity slowed through the remainder of the year, but Fenderson continued his push by seeking an office space for the local NAACP. The national office discouraged him from pursuing any economic activities, but Fenderson's response captured the essence of black heroism in western Monmouth County. Fenderson said, "In small communities in New Jersey, colored groups are associated in all the projects. Freehold is a rural farming community and the economic opportunities for the colored citizenry are restricted because farming is the chief industry."[29] Fenderson recognized the historical pattern of black leadership in small communities using multiple approaches to civil rights activism. In this way, each individual leader performed dozens of roles under several different organizational titles to create the appearance of a larger movement. These efforts were essential in a farming area because so many of the rank-and-file membership worked twelve- and fifteen-hour days for different farm owners. Activists in this tradition emulated their counterparts in large cities and southern towns, but had less support and recognition to sustain them in the face of adversity.

By August 1943, a grand jury dismissed Wilder's accusations of police misconduct. His case moved into civil court. Fenderson believed that justice would be done. His attitude changed in January 1944 when Wilder and his mother testified poorly in the civil case (the police officers were subsequently found "not liable"). Around the same time, bootleggers attacked Fenderson on Main Street for criticizing their activities.[30] Fenderson left the area in 1946, having established an NAACP chapter, but it had little direction going forward. Through the late 1940s and early 1950s, NAACP programs became more associated with Second Baptist Church on Throckmorton Street and leadership changes were frequent.[31] Chapter secretary Adah Williams wrote to the national office, "There are two churches and three fraternal lodges [in the area], but they are just not interested in [civil rights] work."[32] By September 1953, the Freehold NAACP no longer held regular meetings and the legacy of Ferdinand Fenderson faded away.

While Fenderson's heroism was almost completely forgotten, Marion Russell and Lillie Hendry (whose family lives appeared in chapter 1) returned from their educational endeavors to Freehold and committed themselves to instilling their values in the next generation of young people by working in Bethel AME Church and the public school system. Russell recalled her experiences at Sunday school, at various church trips, and through efforts to increase youth attendance at weekly services. "I would go on Saturday and help those people comb those kids' hair, polish their shoes, and get them ready so that on Sunday morning all the mother had to do was wash their faces and hands and dress them."[33] Russell's activities were indicative of the responsibilities local residents assumed on a daily basis in order to teach the value of community. Between 1930 and 1960, the formal principles of dignity and propriety shaped African American perceptions about self-worth and community pride. Russell stood in the place of working mothers and fathers who could not always care for their children in preparation for church on Sunday. As a role model for both the parents and the children, she demonstrated the behaviors and appearance of an American citizen with full, equal rights. However, her work also continued within the church's walls. She said, "We started a junior church. It wasn't just children setting up the junior church—we had our own boards like the Trustee Board and the Stewards Board. It was fun. We also started the junior choir."[34] Marion Russell, who devoted her life to serving her church, said, "With the Sunday school, I worked with them—I was one of the teachers and one of the people who helped with the younger children. I would take them if we went on a picnic, and your parents couldn't go with you—picnics were going to Asbury Park, Long Branch, Keansburg, and then we started going north to places like Coney Island."[35] Church activities such as these helped instill the value of leadership, organizational management, and self-esteem in young people.

Hendry discussed her work as a guidance counselor and teacher in the borough's middle and high schools after 1960. "Every eighth grader who left that school had to come to my classroom [in the high school]. I made sure that they had what the high school needed, as well as the life skills that I had been taught in Court Street School. I had a group of youngsters for whom I was almost a second parent."[36] Hendry's experience of institutional racism was gradual. She slowly realized that because of her skin color, she was treated as inferior. "Also, I didn't think it was fair to have to use old books—the books that were outdated and that they were no longer using with the white kids in the other classes, they were passed down to Court Street school. We had dedicated Black teachers and they would take their own money and buy two and three (and sometimes only one [recent]) books and give them to use to read."[37] When Hendry moved from the middle school to the high school, Russell took the job as middle school counselor. Russell described the continuity she and Hendry provided for young people after 1970. She said, "When I caught one of the kids doing something he shouldn't, he said, 'Miss Russell, you know I'm going to high school next year.' And I told him he needed to meet my sister. Sure enough, one day [the next year] he was flying down the hall at the high school and bumped into Lillie. And Lillie let him know who she was."[38]

The value of these sisters' efforts must have reverberated widely through the corridor's student population. Hendry and Russell's contributions reflected the spiritual values they were taught at home, in Bethel AME Church, and through the years at Court Street School. Their diligence in teaching young people the value of consistent attendance at (and proper attire for) church and the unwavering affection with which they engaged rambunctious students on a daily basis for over twenty years was testimony to their character and leadership qualities. Their careers forged a foundation for the possibility of a skilled, educated, black middle class in rural New Jersey by the end of the twentieth century. Without this kind of careful tutelage, few people could expect to achieve more than their parents and grandparents had.

CONCLUSION

New Jersey's civil rights leaders broadened the possibilities of political involvement for the entire state between 1920 and 1980. The infrapolitics—the quiet strategies of resistance—became the core assumptions of policy making by the end of the twentieth century. Oppression against African Americans provided an opportunity for civil rights leaders to become new archetypes of heroism around the world. People like Dr. James Parker Sr., Dr. James Parker Jr., Marion Russell, and Lillie Hendry blazed new trails of civil participation for all Americans. Their quiet efforts to dismantle white supremacy advanced democracy because the process was incremental and persistent. The instantaneous shock of violent revolt carries less transformative power than the force of lives sustained in pursuit of justice. These lives yield a praxis of equality, despite the relative anonymity of their efforts.

Service formed the foundation for this heroic leadership. It was both immediate and perpetual. The race leaders in New Jersey understood the holistic achievement of creating both personal and social excellence simultaneously. Oates did not just speak to his congregation. He also listened. Fenderson's effectiveness relied on his negotiation skills and willingness to delegate responsibility. Both men's visions expanded the perception of American community in rural New Jersey. Their decisions in pursuit of those visions crafted new realities based on the new perception. The race leaders discussed in this chapter applied the skills to listen, to forgive, to delegate, and to inspire their communities based on the values and historiographies developed by earlier generations in the Garden State. Each of them possessed the character necessary to make a leap of faith for a dream their lived experiences told them might lie beyond their ability. The cost of this sacrifice was their lives, but the reward was the perpetuation of hope for their children.

Teaching students to embrace a new historical narrative requires institutions to convey the essential ideas. As the assumptions and organizations that supported white supremacy crumbled, race leaders built their own venues to communicate their visions of a racially inclusive democracy. New Jersey's segregated public schools and churches allowed African Americans the private spaces they needed to develop the ideologies of racial equality. From Franklin Township to Willingboro, from Hamilton to Long Branch, black communities gathered in churches and financed educational programs that promoted intellectual excellence for their children. Schools and churches became the training grounds for new leaders who would promote multiracial democracy, feminism, and economic opportunity into the twenty-first century. James Parker, Caleb Oates, Ferdinand Fenderson, Marion Russell, and Lillie Hendry led a group of leaders that redeemed the promise of America.

NOTES

1. Adolph Reed Jr., *Stirring in the Jug: Black Politics in the Post-Segregation Era* (Minneapolis: University of Minnesota Press, 1999), 79–115.

2. Nikhal Pal Singh, *Black Is a Country: Race and the Unfinished Struggle for Democracy* (Cambridge, MA: Harvard University Press, 2004), 49.

3. Kevin K. Gaines, *Uplifting the Race: Black Leadership, Politics, and Culture in the Twentieth Century* (Chapel Hill: University of North Carolina Press, 1996), 259.

4. Lenora W. McKay, *Mama and Papa*, 52, 63, 94, 110.

5. "Annual Barbeque of Colored Republicans," *Red Bank Register*, 27 July 1944, 1.

6. "Observes Negro History Week," *Red Bank Register*, 28 February 1946, 2.

7. Karen L. Schnitzspahn, *A Strong Legacy: 125 Years of the Community YMCA* (Red Bank: Community YMCA Publications, 1999), 54–62; McKay, *The Blacks of Monmouth County*, 47.

8. Kenneth L. Kusmer, *A Ghetto Takes Shape: Black Cleveland, 1870–1930* (Urbana: University of Illinois Press, 1976), 265–66.

9. Schnitzspahn, *A Strong Legacy*, 54–62.

10. Dr. James Parker Jr., interview, 22 June 2001.

11. Ibid.

12. "A Spiritual Message," *Howell Booster*, 2 April 1954, 3.

13. "Honor Roll," *New Jersey Afro-American*, 1 March 1953, 6.

14. "Neighborhood Groups See Many Promises Not Kept," *Asbury Park Press*, 28 June 1966, 1, 33.

15. Reverend Caleb E. Oates, interview, 27 July 2000.

16. "U.S. Embraces Shore Pastor's Anti-Poverty Formula," *Asbury Park Sunday Press*, 14 August 1966, 4.

17. C. Eric Lincoln and Lawrence H. Mamiya, *The Black Church in the African American Experience* (Durham, NC: Duke University Press, 1990), 394–95.

18. Oates, interview, 27 July 2000.

19. Jeff Chang, *Can't Stop, Won't Stop: A History of the Hip Hop Generation* (New York: Picador, 2005), 258–59. The Five Percent Nation is an offshoot from the Nation of Islam that preaches that they are the five percent of the world population that are destined to teach freedom and civilization to the rest of humanity.

20. YMCA Committee, "Colored YMCA," *Monmouth Democrat*, 30 November 1916, 4.

21. "Colored YMCA," *Monmouth Democrat*, 26 July 1917, 4; "Colored YMCA," *Monmouth Democrat*, date unknown.

22. "Review of YMCA," *Monmouth Democrat*, 4 October 1917.

23. Russell, interview, 8 January 1998; "Colored YMCA," *Monmouth Democrat*, date unknown. Maria Sandoval, "A Family Reunion," *Asbury Park Press*, 1992.

24. M. Geraldine Neal Bledsoe, "Ferdinand G. Ferguson: A Great Humanitarian, A Great American" (privately published, 1976), unpaginated.

25. Lori J. Atkins, "Walking Strong out of Freehold's Colored School," *Asbury Park Press*, 25 February 1993, E1, E3.

26. Frank Reeves to Dr. D. W. Anthony, 5 March 1942, box C: 108, file "Freehold, 1942–1954," group II, NAACP, Library of Congress (LOC); Ferdinand Fenderson to Frank Reeves, 12 March 1942, box C: 108, file "Freehold, 1942–1954," group II, NAACP, LOC; Frank Reeves to F. G. Fenderson, 18 March 1942, box C: 108, file "Freehold, 1942–1954," group II, NAACP, LOC; Reeves to Fenderson, 25 March 1942, box C: 108, file "Freehold, 1942–1954," group II, NAACP, LOC.

27. William Foster to Lucille Black, 6 May 1942, box C: 108, file "Freehold, 1942–1954," group II, NAACP, LOC.

28. Fenderson to NAACP, 13 August 1942, box C: 108, file "Freehold, 1942–1954," group II, NAACP, LOC; Fenderson to NAACP, 12 January 1943, box C: 108, file "Freehold, 1942–1954," group II, NAACP, LOC.

29. Secretary to Fenderson, 25 January 1943, box C: 108, file "Freehold, 1942–1954," group II, NAACP, LOC; Fenderson to NAACP, 11 February 1943, box C: 108, file "Freehold, 1942–1954," group II, NAACP, LOC; Fenderson to NAACP, 5 May 1943, box C: 108, file "Freehold, 1942–1954," group II, NAACP, LOC.

30. Fenderson to NAACP, 6 August 1943, box C: 108, file "Freehold, 1942–1954," group II, NAACP, LOC; Fenderson to NAACP, 29 January 1944, box C: 108, file "Freehold, 1942–1954," group II, NAACP, LOC.

31. "NAACP Hosted 'This Could Happen to You,'" 29 October 1946, box C: 108, file "Freehold, 1942–1954," group II, NAACP, LOC; Adah Williams to Lucille Black, 16 August 1949, box C: 108, file "Freehold, 1942–1954," group II, NAACP, LOC; "Williams to Black" (24 May 1950), box C: 108, file "Freehold, 1942–1954," group II, NAACP, LOC.

32. Williams to Gloster Current, 23 May 1953, box C: 108, file "Freehold, 1942–1954," group II, NAACP, LOC.

33. Russell, interview transcript, 8 January 1998.

34. Ibid.

35. Ibid.

36. Connie Paul, "Interview with Lillie Hendry and Marion Russell," 28 August 2000, in *Remembering the Twentieth Century: An Oral History of Monmouth County*, ed. Flora T. Higgins, http://www.visitmonmouth.com/oralhistory/bios/Hendry-Russell.htm.

37. Ibid.

38. Ibid.

FOUR

Churches and Schools

Countless Sundays begin with children's feet running up church steps. Their voices, laughter, and songs open the morning for expressions of faith that rejuvenate millions of people in the United States and around the world. At church, grandparents, parents, and children came together throughout the twentieth century in New Jersey's rural communities to keep the circle of family, history, and leadership unbroken. The hymns, sermons, and prayers offered within the churches' walls created the emotional power needed to create civil rights organizations and to challenge the perpetuation of white supremacy. Both Baptist and Methodist traditions emphasized the stories of Exodus, Jonah, and Daniel in the African American tradition. Congregations internalized the lessons of pursuing unlikely success against impossible odds. Church instilled purpose in the hearts of its members. It provided the reason for continuing struggle against an unyielding foe.

On Monday mornings, families began their week sending children off to school. Schools formed the center of community pride and optimism, even within segregated systems in New Jersey. Work remained a reality for any youngsters, who labored on farms alongside their parents. However, they attended classes whenever possible to fulfill the promise of their grandparents' sacrifices. In towns as widespread as Gouldtown (Cumberland County), Lawnside (Camden County), Whitesboro (Cape May County), Asbury Park (Monmouth County), Freehold (Monmouth County), and Manalapan (Monmouth County), schools reinforced the lessons taught in church on Sunday. Black public schools also created frameworks for academic achievement in communities where messages of racial inferiority bombarded African American children.[1] Where churches taught purpose, schools taught methods. The strategies of civic engagement and the tactics for occupational excellence grew from the foundation of scholastic accomplishment taught by determined instructors and parents, who often worked in tandem to show young people their visions of a better future.

Together, the function of churches and schools in the black towns of rural New Jersey during the twentieth century formed the core of the ideological machinery that transformed the United States. Black leaders in small communities could not create corporations or exclusive clubs without the threat of legal or extralegal sanctions from both government and private individuals.[2] In that context, segregated churches and schools formed two pillars of support for African American families in their efforts to overcome the barriers to full equality throughout American society. The system of racial uplift and social integration created four generations of human beings who lived lives that contradicted the racist sociology, anthropology, and history that passed as scientific knowledge between 1850 and 1950. Ministers, deacons, and missionaries shaped the community life of these isolated villages, providing regular expressions of autonomy and authority beyond the constraints of the rural South and urban North. Principals, teachers, and visiting speakers charted courses toward secondary education, college attendance, and professional training that created artists by 1920, engineers by 1950, and corporate executives by 1970. In 1870, the unquestioned seat of public authority was the pulpit. Churches initiated the encounters that defined culture, politics, and economics for the small towns in New Jersey's rural corridor. As science and education became the foundation for industrial society in the United States, the racial integration of the state's schools in 1948 represented the transformation of a racist system into attempts at an egalitarian one. African Americans who led the efforts for racial equality emphasized the inclusion of racial minorities in school systems as the paramount achievement of their lives.

CHURCHES

Richard Allen's African Methodist Episcopal Church created the mold of the church as an institution of liberation for African Americans in the late eighteenth century.[3] While Mother Bethel AME Church opened in Philadelphia, Allen's work spread rapidly into New Jersey after 1800. South Jersey residents Reuben Cuffe and Joseph and Jarena Lee carried Allen's legacy as disciples of the African Methodist Episcopal ministry.[4] Mount Zion continued the Methodist connection, while Peter Mott organized the Mount Pisgah Society.[5] Racial discrimination in the early years of the American republic mirrored the divisions of slavery and segregation throughout the entire society. White churches enforced the recognition of European superiority in every aspect of congregational life. As much as the town hall or the marketplace, churches taught white supremacy throughout the nineteenth century. African Americans in New Jersey seized on the legacy of the AME Church to expand Allen's mission to assert the dignity and intellect of black people around the world.

Baptists

New Jersey's black Baptists did not formally organize until southern migrants began moving north in larger numbers. Baptist congregations did not create hierarchies like the Methodists, but instead functioned very independently of each other. Without a larger organizational structure, Baptist communities grew more slowly. Once a Baptist church opened in a town, however, two or three additional places of worship often followed. The first recorded meeting of black Baptists occurred in Camden in 1854. A group met for Sunday worship at Mary Colding's house at 736 Chestnut Street and Kaighn Avenue. In 1863, the congregation built a wooden church at Seventh and Kaighn and dedicated it as Mount Zion Baptist Church.[6]

Baptist churches were the founding institutions of several new black communities in New Jersey. In Glassboro and Mullica Hill there were nearly ten Baptist churches by the start of the twentieth century. Conflicts among the Baptists revolved around theological issues, creating some confusion about the future of these African American communities. In 1908, a group of ministers (representing Saint John's of Camden and Second Baptist of Moorestown, Merchantville, and Atlantic City, along with Saint Paul of East Riverton and Kaighn Avenue of Camden) established the Bethany Baptist Association of Southern New Jersey and elected Reverend J. T. Plenty of Kaighn Avenue Baptist as the first moderator.[7] This consolidation signified the establishment of two major African American theological traditions among the small towns of rural New Jersey.

Theory and Practice

Much of the fundamental, doctrinal debate within the Methodist and Baptist traditions in New Jersey resolved itself through the first two decades of the twentieth century.[8] As the small towns where these churches were seated grew, disagreements over church leadership and social programming became more common. New migrants relied on their faith in the Holy Trinity to support them through the difficult transitions in residence, work, and recreation in an unfamiliar setting. The collision between the social customs of the rural South, the urban North, and the rural North produced some of the most emphatic debates about the formation of an African American cultural identity. Conversations about the proper reference title for former slaves and their children often reflected profound and complex arguments about the future of American freedom.

Choosing a description ("colored," "negro," or "Afro-American") signified an epistemology about the purposes and methodologies of achieving full citizenship rights. Language dictated the creation of new spaces
(black churches) and the discursive boundaries of the social meanings
communicated there (family, history, and leadership).

New Jersey's rural black churches existed at the intersection of faith
and reason between 1870 and 1920. The creation and survival of small
African American communities relied on the ability of the church to
maintain a sense of community for new residents. These churches
brought the ideas and theory of divine will into the realm of material
debate about homes, jobs, and education. Sharecroppers questioned attorneys, and nursemaids interrogated pastors after services. Accountability was the currency of the society, as everyone knew the stakes of success or failure were high. Church leaders articulated a vocabulary of faith
to sustain families against poverty and unemployment. They used scrip-
ture to offer a body of values that opened new opportunities for reason to
the congregation as a whole. Within the context of New Jersey's de facto
racial segregation, black churches formed centers for both worship and
recreation. They allowed mental equanimity and intellectual creativity in
a society that permitted neither. Glassboro resident Bill Myers recalled
that "we did everything at the church," even as late as 1940. The church
became a civic club that catered to African American youth who were
members of the congregation.[9]

The black church in the northern United States helped migrants adjust
to their new homes. In Long Branch, Second Baptist Church, in particular, helped these African American migrants locate jobs, identify prospective homes, and organize social activities. Second Baptist began as a small
collection of individuals meeting in a safe setting to express their shared
faith. Few records about the church's formation survived from this period. William Bloodsaw founded the church in 1877, and Ellen Hill volun-
teered her home on Brook Street as the initial place of worship. Hill's
house soon became overcrowded with weekly worshippers, forcing services to move to Liberty Hall on Broadway. The church continued to
grow, moving first to the public primary school before settling in Layton
Hall on Broadway, where it was officially organized. Bloodsaw was not
an ordained minister, however, despite his effectiveness in attracting
members to the church. Thus, Reverend R. A. Bolden, a minister from
Asbury Park, held the first communion for Second Baptist. Several ordained ministers followed Bloodsaw's tenure, but none stayed with the
church longer than he did. The church's leadership changes did not stop
the members from purchasing land at 93 Liberty Street and beginning
construction of their first edifice. In 1904 the building was completed—a
testament to the determination and commitment of this small black community.[10] Second Baptist was the leading religious organization for black
Long Branch at the turn of the century.

Limits on Agency

Yet there were clear limits on the agency black churches offered to African Americans in rural New Jersey. Pastor Ronald Tucker in Glassboro stated that the black church did not play a major role in the civil rights movement. Organizations like the national office of the NAACP rarely communicated with these institutions.[11] Tensions between churches and civil rights organizations often allowed racial segregation and discrimination to persist in New Jersey, especially before the creation of the state's Division against Discrimination in 1941. Segregation in small towns often escaped legal challenges because the black families did not want to risk losing their jobs or homes. The failure of the black church to organize more effectively at the state level in this period reveals the difficulty of civil rights organizing throughout the twentieth century. The successes of the churches emphasized a more gradual approach to the transformation of the cultural resources available within the African American community.

The black churches in the twentieth century prioritized the safety and survival of African Americans, their culture, and their customs. These institutions remained this way because they resisted white domination from the moment they were created. Churches could not advance the secular idea of integration like the NAACP because their mission was different. However, the political accomplishment of racial integration would have been impossible without the foundation for black creativity and expression provided by the churches. In fact, many of the flaws in the politics of racial integration reflect the absence of the black church's mission in the enforcement of civil rights laws since 1970. The purpose of the African American religious tradition did not survive the process of federally mandated racial integration.

Church Leadership

One of the major shortcomings that left churches vulnerable to social isolation was the acceptance of religious hierarchy as the primary leadership model. Pastors exercised almost exclusive control of policy within the church. The major formal limitation on a pastor's authority was the existence of extensive state, regional, national, and international hierarchies above them. This religious structure stymied efforts to dismantle racial segregation in New Jersey. Community activists required the freedom and creativity to respond to local and state authorities in unexpected ways, if the Black Freedom Movement was to be successful.[12] Centralized leadership structures protect institutions well, but the process of social change occurs more quickly within an open and adaptive organizational system.

Civil rights pioneer Ella Baker represented one approach to national civic engagement through her work with the NAACP and the Student Nonviolent Coordinating Committee between 1940 and 1986.[13] Democratic accountability within these organizations could have bridged the gap between rural New Jersey's black churches and their emerging civil rights groups during the middle decades of the twentieth century. However, the transition between the two leadership models would have been very difficult. Status accrues to central leadership. Democratic accountability requires humility from those leaders in response to the status they receive. The fundamental contradiction between the desire for status and the willingness to remain anonymous yielded frustratingly slow progress against segregation in the small towns throughout the Garden State. Churches instead formed stronger connections with the segregated schools for black children. The church and the school relied on each other for support in the black community between 1900 and 1950. This relationship revealed the commitment of ministers and teachers to the long arc of justice. No transitory gains against racist policies in public accommodations would suffice.

Religious Organizations

In Freehold, the black population increased during the decades leading up to World War II. The African American community consistently numbered around two hundred through 1920, but grew rapidly over the next few decades to nearly 1,100 by 1950.[14] The Great Migration certainly contributed to this increase, but the combination of job opportunities with rural lifestyles probably attracted black migrants to Freehold. The steady growth of this community stimulated the creation and expansion of churches and community organizations, just as urban churches in the South grew during this era in response to migrants from rural, southern towns. Bethel AME Church, founded in 1848, anticipated the growth of the black community in Freehold and moved into a larger building there in 1895.[15] Consequently, its congregation doubled in size. Bethel hosted fund-raising dinners, black history competitions, trips to Sunday school conventions, and sports competitions to foster stronger ties among the new black residents.[16] Also, Second Baptist Church opened its doors to the new African American Baptists in the area.[17] The County Welfare Board established a branch in Freehold to assist black migrants in finding work during the Depression.[18] African American migrants found both decent jobs and a tolerant political atmosphere (compared to the Jim Crow South) in Freehold. Their numbers increased accordingly. However, none of the dominant urban black organizations of the era (NAACP, UNIA, and NUL) formed lasting organizations in Freehold. The small, rural, black community in Freehold could not maintain the financial and organizational resources for these groups to thrive. National organizations also ignored or dismissed calls for assistance from the Freehold area before 1930.

The formation of the Freehold Colored Young Men's Christian Association (YMCA) in 1916 promoted a sense of community because it fostered regular social events and community service.[19] Several local leaders contributed to promoting the YMCA's message of sobriety, spirituality, and empowerment for the local African Americans.[20] In the course of one year, the YMCA closed the local gambling establishment, hosted twenty-four lectures on educational topics, provided temporary food and shelter for those without any, and created a sense of racial solidarity among the new black residents.[21] By providing political education and demonstrating the power of collective organization, the Y taught the black population lessons about their potential influence in their new home. With the support of local black churches and educators, this organization solidified the foundation of the local African American community as it rapidly expanded after 1920.

Freehold experienced one of the more successful applications of the church-led Black Freedom Movement. Marion Russell and Lillie Hendry moved to Freehold from North Carolina in 1922. Their experiences reveal the presence of antiblack racism in the area as well as the determination and pride exhibited by the local black community in countering the stereotypes imposed by white residents. As we saw in chapters 1 and 3, Hendry overcame many obstacles in her life. She earned the title of Fulbright Scholar in 1956. Her participation as one of the earliest African Americans in this program remains inspirational. When Senator William Fulbright initiated the international exchange in 1949, it was meant to improve the perception of the United States around the world. Few African Americans gained access to these opportunities even in the early years of the twenty-first century.[22]

Agricultural workers rarely achieved more than a middle-school education before 1930. They formed the basis of the black community in the first half of the twentieth century. However, in the Manalapan area, southern migrant workers reshaped the black parts of town, overwhelming the local tenant farming population. Local historian James Brown's comment summarizes the transition well. He wrote, "Communities such as Woodsville that had been populated by year-round farm workers [in the nineteenth century], became centers for summer migratory labor living in temporary quarters. Many other farm workers, brought north from southern states by crew chiefs, lived in temporary housing on the farms where they worked."[23] Woodsville was the largest African American community in Manalapan in the early twentieth century, but there were several smaller, unnamed settlements throughout the area. These typically formed and disbanded in response to local demand for temporary farm labor. The Woodsville church held Sunday school for adults and children in addition to regular morning and evening services. However,

Saint James AME Church embodied the importance of the local black community when it began meeting informally in 1836.[24] Lewis I. and Catherine Conover sold land for the construction of a formal edifice in 1843. Through the first half of the twentieth century, Saint James hosted an annual harvest home festival that was widely attended by black and white locals.[25] It was an important event for the African American community in Englishtown and Manalapan, attracting migrant laborers to settle in the area. The festival relied upon the participation of the entire community as children decorated the church grounds, women prepared the food and organized choir and solo vocal performances, and men donated their labor and money. Few political activities grew out of these black communities in the first half of the twentieth century, because the migrant laborers were not permanent residents.

Lila Stevenson specifically emphasized the central importance of the church community in her life. She said, "I started [a] church here from my home with prayer meetings and Sunday school around 1945 or 1946. The church was a tremendous help for our community. We bought food for needy families and we added two rooms to the church for everyday children's recreation."[26] Since the earlier black churches no longer operated on a consistent basis, Stevenson's actions served to energize the new black residents who came to the area after 1940. Even without a harvest festival, the regular church, Sunday school, and Bible study meetings provided social outlets that laid the foundation for black working-class community in the second half of the twentieth century.

SCHOOLS

Schools increasingly became transitional spaces that bridged the gap between the essential religious institutions and the emerging civil rights groups in these small communities. Ministers could unilaterally end discussions about the changing needs of New Jersey's black communities within the church walls. The sanctity and authority their churches epitomized gave them power to remind parishioners about the threats to their freedom and the acceptable risks the church would endure. Schools allowed for greater parental authority in conversation with better educated teachers and principals, who often were also church leaders. The transition from the pious spaces of the church to the secular spaces of the school allowed greater democratic accountability and reduced the centralized power pastors had enjoyed earlier in the twentieth century.

Principals and teachers still lacked the broader political authority to satisfy families' demands for equal treatment in the school system or the community as a whole. Unable to shield their reputations as educators from potential public criticism with the cloak of faith as they did as religious leaders, black educators began to change their approach to white municipal and state officials. When educators like Ferdinand Fenderson stood up to improve the physical conditions of the Court Street School, he carried with him the moral authority of the church and the social innovation of the school. Efforts like his throughout the rural communities met with obstruction frequently enough that the need for civil rights organizations and collective public protest became impossible to deny. After more than fifty years of church work and public education, the institutions of racial equality began to emerge throughout the rural corridor.

Black communities across the state continued to develop within a context of stringent racial segregation, despite the existence of an 1881 state law prohibiting discrimination.[27] That same year, African Americans in Asbury Park requested a segregated school at Bangs Avenue for their children to avoid mistreatment at the hands of white school administrators. Black historians from northern New Jersey reported that the desire for black teachers and concern about white resistance to integration motivated the request.[28] Asbury Park's black business owners pursued school and political integration as ideals under the New Jersey Civil Rights Act of 1884. Yet segregation and racial exclusion in Asbury Park's beaches, hotels, restaurants, and schools survived into the 1940s.[29] The Bangs Avenue Elementary School kept white and black students in different wings of the same building with separate times for lunch and recess.[30] White investors in Asbury Park even attempted to establish an African American university in 1891. The anonymous group of investors supported a two-hundred-thousand-dollar proposal to open an institution modeled after Fisk University for five hundred African Americans.[31] The project was slated for completion in the fall of 1892, but the funding drive failed and the plans were abandoned.

When African Americans like Ermon Jones sued New Jersey's municipalities for equal conditions and resources, the transformation of the school system unfolded swiftly. Challenges to these inequalities resulted in the revision of the state constitution in 1948. However, as with the 1884 state law, nothing changed in the school districts without intervention by civil rights groups. Ermon Jones became president of the Asbury Park–Neptune branch of the NAACP in 1961. Leading a coalition of churches, businesses, and home owners, Jones desegregated housing developments, workplaces, and schools along the Jersey shore over the next three decades. His belief in college education for African American youth and his career as a military technician gave him credibility with local leaders, both black and white. The NAACP successfully created the first Head Start program for black children in Monmouth County in 1964 and desegregated the Neptune school system in 1969.[32] Without the earlier work of the teachers and ministers within the segregated systems in New Jersey, these efforts to reshape the municipal and state institutions would have floundered.

The legacy of racial separation at all levels of education persisted into the twenty-first century in Cape May. Franklin Street School formally closed its doors in 1948, but the structure stood as a testimony to the era through the first decade of the twenty-first century. Franklin Street served a larger community than the Court Street School from 1928 to 1948.[33] However, the two buildings housed adults committed to imparting a first-class education to all of the African American children who walked through their doors. Neither school enjoyed electricity or running water until their final decade of operation. Each site enjoyed an unprecedented surge in public appreciation at the end of the twentieth century, when they were registered as historic sites by the State of New Jersey.[34] Franklin Street and Court Street schools serve as potent reminders of the transition from the central authority of the black church to the decentralized organizations for racial equality that emerged after 1960.

CONCLUSION

Churches established the foundation of black communities in the late nineteenth century. New Jersey's rural corridor would change politically, culturally, and economically as a result of their presence. The challenge to racial segregation in the state's school system rose from these small towns as reason and faith intersected in the activism of the black church. Heroes, including Ermon Jones, Lila Stevenson, Marion Russell, and William Bloodsaw, pursued the accomplishment of racial equality in the twentieth century with single-minded devotion. Civil rights organizations formed a system of public accountability that transformed the United States in the second half of the twentieth century. Against prevailing notions of black inferiority, New Jersey's black churches and schools taught pride and dignity in ways that redeemed the promise of America. A new standard of leadership and organization united religious and educational leaders in this project. Civil rights ceased to be the radical cry of abolitionists of the late nineteenth century and became the core principle of democracy at the start of the twenty-first century.

African Americans created the network of churches and schools in their rural communities from nothing but their determination and creativity. The discussions about the nature of black identity and the balance between religious and educational institutions were often difficult for the diverse migrants who came together for the first time in the early decades of the Great Migration. Their sense of shared sacrifice and painful memories of the oppression they faced provided a common commitment to surviving any adversity. Their love for the children and hope for a brighter future shaped the opportunities for higher education and better jobs that these communities enjoyed at the height of the civil rights movement. Groups like the NAACP and Urban League developed their agendas and support as a result of the connections forged by the churches and schools in the first half of the twentieth century. Their organizational success created the greatest transformation of American democracy in the nation's history by 1970.

NOTES

1. Wendell A. White, *Small Towns, Black Lives: African American Communities in Southern New Jersey* (Oceanville, NJ: Noyes Museum of Art, 2003), 69.

2. James D. Anderson, *The Education of Blacks in the South, 1860–1935* (Chapel Hill: University of North Carolina Press, 1988), 232, 273.

3. Gary Hunter, *Neighborhoods of Color: African American Communities in Southern New Jersey, 1660–1998* (n.p., 2002), 31.

4. Ibid., 32.

5. Ibid., 34.

6. Ibid., 64.

7. Ibid., 63.

8. C. Eric Lincoln and Lawrence Mamiya, *The Black Church in the African American Experience* (Durham, NC: Duke University Press, 1990), 115–62.

9. Bill Myers, interview by Andrea Alcott, Rowan University Color Line Projects, April 2, 2001, 3.

10. C. P. Williams, ed., *Second Baptist Church 100th Anniversary Booklet* (privately published, 1987), not paginated.

11. Ronald Tucker, interview by Jane O'Donnell, Rowan University Color Line Projects, April 17, 2002, 8.

12. Barbara Ransby, *Ella Baker and the Black Freedom Movement: A Radical Democratic Vision* (Chapel Hill: University of North Carolina Press, 2005), 90–91.

13. Ibid., 139, 309–10.

14. New Jersey Bureau of the Census (NJBC), *New Jersey State Census—1915* (ms.), schedule 1.

15. Richard Walling and Middlesex County Vocational-Technical High School Students, *The African American Experience in Western Monmouth County, New Jersey: Two Historic Black Communities in Manalapan/Millstone and Freehold Townships* (Manalapan: Friends of Monmouth Battlefield, Inc., 1996), 25, 27; Griffith, *Freehold*, 38.

16. Joseph Ham, "Freehold," *New Jersey Afro-American*, 29 March 1941, 15; Joseph Ham, "Freehold," *New Jersey Afro-American*, 12 April 1941, 15; Joseph Ham, "Freehold," *New Jersey Afro-American*, 12 April 1941, 15.

17. McKay, *The Blacks of Monmouth County*, 45–47.

18. Jane McCosker, *Historical Perspectives of Social Welfare* (Freehold: Monmouth County Board of Social Services Publication, 1986), 31–33.

19. YMCA Committee, "Colored YMCA," *Monmouth Democrat*, 30 November 1916, 4.

20. "Colored YMCA," *Monmouth Democrat*, 26 July 1917, 4; "Colored YMCA," *Monmouth Democrat*, date unknown.

21. "Review of YMCA," *Monmouth Democrat*, 4 October 1917.

22. "Blacks Remain a Small Fraction of Fulbright Scholars," *Journal of Blacks in Higher Education* 48 (Summer 2005), 32–33.

23. James S. Brown, *Manalapan in Three Centuries* (Manalapan: Township of Manalapan Publication, 1991), 53.

24. Richard J. Dalik, *Images of America: Manalapan and Englishtown* (Dover, NH: Arcadia Publishing, 1998), 110. Brown, *Manalapan in Three Centuries*, 65–66.

25. Walling and Students, *The African American Experience in Western Monmouth County, New Jersey*, 16–19.

26. Ibid.

27. Though Asbury Park was ostensibly Republican in the late nineteenth century, in opposition to Democratic Long Branch, the two local parties' views on the separation of the races were quite similar. The front page of the local paper often ran articles about the alleged "deviance" and violent nature of African Americans (*Shore Press*, 14 May 1885, 4).

28. L. A. Greene, "A History of Afro-Americans in New Jersey," *Journal of Rutgers University Libraries* 56, no. 1 (1994): 36–37.

29. Ibid., 37–38.

30. Correspondence of the National Association for the Advancement of Colored People (NAACP), "Asbury Park Negroes Demand that Board of Commissioners End Discrimination," 26 July 1928, Manuscript Division, Library of Congress.

31. "A Colored University," *Red Bank Register*, 7 January 1891, 1.

32. June West, "Interview with Ermon Jones," in *Remembering the Twentieth Century: An Oral History of Monmouth County, New Jersey*, ed. Flora T. Higgins, accessed 6 June 2002, http://www.visitmonmouth.com/oralhistory/bios/JonesErmon.htm.

33. White, *Small Towns, Black Lives*, 70–77.

34. "Community History Program," Center for Community Arts—Cape May, New Jersey, accessed 6 April 2008, http://www.centerforcommunityarts.org/history.htm.

FIVE

Civil Rights Beginnings

African American children in rural New Jersey pursued excellence in both their personal and their academic lives. These efforts to proclaim their humanity against the public presumption of their inferiority shaped dozens of small communities during the first three decades of the twentieth century. Parents, teachers, ministers, and local authorities all struggled to manage outbursts of exuberance among the black youth by blunting the force of their self-esteem. The imposition of authority taught them their "rightful place" in a society that preferred whiteness as the standard of excellence and acceptance. Where the church taught them to survive and the school taught them to succeed, the generations of black New Jerseyans who came of age after 1930 increasingly refused to accept second-best as a description of their lives.

Politics became the arena where the children of ministers and teachers could advance their dreams of equality. Where the schools and churches failed to challenge the boundaries of northern segregation, rural African Americans claimed the mantle of the "New Negro" and asserted their rights to justice and fair treatment. Negotiations with white elected officials rarely produced changes in the law or corporate policies restricting black access between 1900 and 1930. Lawsuits and protests held white authorities accountable for the violation of civil rights in the small towns across the state between 1930 and 1990. Sixty years of steady challenges to discrimination and segregation tested the mettle of both the activists and the conservatives who opposed them. Between 1930 and 1950, the defeats outnumbered the victories for black advocates. However, as black electoral power forced white legislative leaders to acquiesce at the state level after 1945, the tide began to turn. A full generation after African Americans in New Jersey organized chapters of the NAACP throughout the state, legislative breakthroughs became more common, and business owners abandoned the informal enforcement of racial restrictions in their restaurants, hotels, and stores.

The growth of church congregations in small, black towns led to the formation of several civil rights groups in the first half of the twentieth century. Several of the most politically and socially active black organizations operated out of the rural corridor. These included numerous Afro-Republican Leagues and the New Jersey Association of Colored Voters.[1] The Walters Literary Society discussed black art and contemporary politics.[2] The Knights of Pythias Lodge hosted a number of dinner parties and provided an informal version of unemployment insurance.[3] These dinner parties likely offered secular social interaction for multiple generations of single adults seeking prospective mates. The informal unemployment insurance gave lodge members support during the seasonal layoffs of the tourism-based economy. By paying into the lodge during periods of prosperity, members created a safety net for themselves when hard times inevitably arrived. In these instances, segregation strengthened African American migrants' desires to build community through their secular[4] and religious institutions.[5]

African American activism in Red Bank targeted the community's political and economic concerns. Lewis O. Summersett and William E. Rock published local black newspapers like the *Mail and Express* and the *Echo*, while holding leadership positions in many organizations.[6] In 1902, the Monmouth County Afro-Republican League was founded to question the levels of patronage blacks received from the Republican Party in return for their support. Since the 1870s, the Republican Party had abandoned its black supporters across the country by letting racism and Jim Crow segregation expand throughout the South without opposition. In one of the first meetings of the Afro-Republican League in September, Midas Washington, a member of the AME Zion church on Shrewsbury Avenue, denounced the local white Republicans as traitors to the cause of racial equality. He said, "The time had come when the Negroes in Monmouth County had to act and think for themselves; that they had been stabbed long enough in the house of their supposed political friends; and that these Negro haters must be given a rebuke."[7]

Washington used the rhetoric of self-determination to incite his audience to immediate action, directed against those who supported racism at the start of the twentieth century. The key reference to "supposed political friends" questioned the integrity of the Republican Party and asserted the betrayal African Americans had suffered in this relationship. The previous week the county's ministers had met with Summersett to discuss how the black community would vote.[8] New York's Reverend Charles S. Morris also visited Red Bank that month, addressing the continuing problems of racism in both the North and the South.[9] These discussions show the weakening of African American support for the Republican Party three decades prior to the national shift in black voting

patterns. Local blacks recognized that the Republican Party had no interest in either protecting southern blacks from lynching or addressing the
plight of northern blacks and was also resistant to the enforcement of
equal rights for all citizens.

Summersett and Rock benefited from the presence of a famous advocate for black equality in their midst. T. Thomas Fortune was a leading
voice among the affluent and educated members of Red Bank's black
community after 1900. Fortune, a colleague of Booker T. Washington,
founder of the National Afro-American League (NAAL, became the National Afro-American Council, NAAC, in 1898), and editor of the *New
York Age* from 1884 to 1907, spent the years between 1901 and 1910 in a
twelve-room house on a one-acre plot called Maple Hill.[10] His words
regarding the struggle for black equality in the United States also foretold
the obstacles facing the African American community in central New
Jersey. He wrote in 1890, "We expect that before the rights conferred
upon us by the war amendments are fully conceded, a full century will
have passed away. We have undertaken no child's play. We have undertaken a serious work which will tax and exhaust the best intelligence and
energy of the race for the next century."[11] Fortune served as master of
ceremonies for Reverend Morris's appearance and spoke at the initial
meeting of the local Negro Business League.[12] Fortune's role at the meeting gave the organization immediate legitimacy and made the meeting a
major event for the local black communities. Fortune's wife, Carrie, often
worked with Saint Thomas Episcopal Church, and his son, Frederick,
graduated from Red Bank High School in 1910—the only African
American in the graduating class.[13] T. Thomas Fortune also entertained
prominent African Americans like the noted political activists Judge Robert Terrell and Mary Church Terrell at Maple Hill.[14] Fortune's presence in
Red Bank stimulated the political atmosphere created by leaders like
Summersett and Rock by emphasizing politics as a means to uplift
African Americans, especially through racially integrated education.[15] As
a national figure involved in supporting and sanctioning local organizations, Fortune inspired other black citizens to participate in existing organizations and to start new organizations as well.

The Long Branch NAACP protested against the Ku Klux Klan and
filed complaints against segregation between 1920 and 1950, based on the
1875 New Jersey Constitution and the 1884 New Jersey Supreme Court
Pierce decision that had mandated desegregation of all public facilities.[16]
Much of the organization's work after 1920 laid the foundation for desegregation of the Long Branch school system during the 1930s and 1940s. It
also sponsored programs that reflected strategies used by the national
organizations. The 1944 Baby Contest, for instance, encouraged local
African Americans to submit their children's pictures for judging as the
"best baby" or "prettiest baby," with area residents donating money to

the NAACP in their nominee's name. This event brought in 664 new local members and 112 new subscriptions to the *Crisis*.[17]

Political education programs of the Long Branch NAACP were also popular, and youth involvement was important to the cause. The chapter hosted "Jim Crowism: How It Is to Be Defeated" in 1944. This event showcased the education and talent of its youth members, both black and white, who discussed several topics, including "Jim Crowism and the Law," "Racial Superiority as the Cause for Jim Crowism," "How Jim Crowism Affects the Home," and "Jim Crowism and Juvenile Delinquency."[18] NAACP activities in Long Branch relied on youth involvement to undo the inculcation of racist assumptions taught by everyday life in the North. Long Branch resident Vyeta Walker, a young adult at the time, described the political and economic conditions that motivated community support for the NAACP. "My grade school was all black—teachers and students—at Liberty Street. There were two theaters here—Strand and Paramount. They both kept black people in the balcony. There were never any signs for 'colored' or 'white'—I didn't see those until I went to Florida."[19]

The local NAACP stood to profit from the economic advances African Americans made in Long Branch by pushing to end racial segregation in all its forms and, thus, provide future opportunities for greater political access and opportunities. Although the NAACP focused on the issue of legal segregation, in Long Branch specifically and the United States generally, issues of employment discrimination and social segregation could not be separated from each other. They were two tentacles of the same beast. This was especially the case in the small towns on the Jersey shore. While the NAACP and other black organizations relied on the black middle class in larger cities, local civil rights groups like the Asbury Park and Long Branch NAACP chapters could not survive without broader support from the black poor and working class.[20]

African Americans in rural New Jersey created a new standard of civic engagement throughout the state. Often overlooked by the urban leadership in the state, leaders like J. C. McKelvie and Paul Prayer reformed municipal government and private business practices to expand opportunities for some of the most vulnerable black communities. Small protest organizations in New Jersey towns combined the lessons of family, history, and leadership in ways that churches and schools could not before 1930. The effects of home and public education gradually transformed the spheres of adult cultural expression into civil rights organizations through the third and fourth decades of the twentieth century. Rural black communities in New Jersey founded chapters of the NAACP, the Urban League, and the Universal Negro Improvement Association as well as local newspapers and Young Men's and Women's Christian Associations. These new organizations were the foundation for local and state civil rights reform efforts that utilized informal conversations, quiet negotiations, public demonstrations, and lawsuits to advance the cause of human equality.

Reverend J. C. McKelvie and other early civil rights activists in rural New Jersey acted out of frustration when confronting racism, but they were determined to maintain an air of dignity and integrity with their protests. This sensibility reflected the lessons taught at home and in schools about the fundamental self-worth that all African Americans possessed. In fact, the suffering of degradation at the hands of white authority only buttressed black confidence. Every time a business owner denied service to a black family or a local mayor dismissed complaints about unequal treatment, African Americans in these small communities became more determined to correct the fundamental wrongs in their world. Lawsuits forced white leaders to respect the words and deeds of black civil rights leaders in ways that the daily scholastic and religious endeavors never did.

Black activism in Asbury Park consistently challenged white racism between 1910 and 1940. In 1910 and again in 1911, white mobs nearly lynched two black men along the Jersey shore, showing that the North continued to resemble the white supremacist South.[21] The National Association for the Advancement of Colored People's magazine *Crisis* noted that police barely restrained a white mob from attacking one black man as he was transported to trial in the first incident. In 1911, another African American—who had faced false accusations of murdering a white woman in Lakewood—escaped a lynch mob in Asbury Park. In the words of historian Clement Price, "The color line was to be preserved, and extralegal police practices and violence against blacks were a potential means to that end."[22] These events, in addition to the presence and popularity of the Ku Klux Klan in the resort city, made the growth and relative prosperity of the area's black community even more remarkable.

Asbury Park's black community protested segregation of beaches, playgrounds, restaurants, and hotels throughout the first half of the twentieth century. African Americans were expected to use beaches in nearby Belmar or Seaside instead of the town beaches. The one nonsegregated local beach was near a sewage outlet—hardly an enticement to bathers. The local branch of the NAACP noted in 1928 that "colored people on benches along the Asbury Park beachfront had been requested by city police officers to 'move down where the colored people belong.'"[23] Yet segregated institutions persisted, in part, because African Americans businesses served the black community well. Racial segregation in New Jersey fueled the need for black business ownership, often overlooked in recent times.[24] Black consumers, like others, generally preferred to spend their money at businesses owned by members of their community. While Paul Prayer, president of the local NAACP between 1931 and 1934, challenged racial segregation in schools and on beaches, more conservative civil rights organizations (like the Monmouth County

Urban League) defended and promoted local black ownership aggressively. Scholars have noted civil rights organizations pursued a long-term strategy of racial equality alongside a short-term tactic of using segregated institutions for economic survival throughout the country in the first half of the twentieth century.[25] On Springwood Avenue alone, there were five black-owned social establishments during the 1920s.[26] NAACP meetings met in F. Leon Harris's Asbury Park funeral home—a product of prevailing racial segregation.[27]

African Americans in Asbury Park used the limited economic self-reliance prompted by segregation to promote an agenda of racial integration. Regardless of intraracial divisions about strategies and tactics to combat informal systems of segregation, the majority of local African Americans remained committed to ending racial segregation in education and discrimination in employment. Against the rising tide of racism between 1910 and 1930, African Americans created organizations to meet specific political and economic needs, such as the Universal Negro Improvement Association, NAACP, and Urban League. Many people were members of all three organizations, making the differences among them less clear. However, in general terms, the UNIA focused primarily on basic literacy programs and cultural-pride events, the NAACP battled segregation in public accommodations and schools, while the Urban League promoted an agenda for economic improvement within the west side community. Together, these groups fostered a more aggressive pursuit of racial equality in Asbury Park from the 1920s through 1940s. The local NAACP demonstrated its awareness of the national scope of unjust race relations when it protested lynchings in the South with editorials in the local newspaper. Paul Prayer, Asbury Park NAACP president, wrote: "Since 1892, 5,050 people have been lynched in the United States. Not a very fine record when we think of our boasted civilization. When [blacks] think of the many evidences of race prejudice, the utter lack of opportunity for those who are capable and the low economic status of the group generally due to these conditions, it is only the unfair or ignorant who would say that we have not made good."[28]

These civil rights organizations also brought attention to racially motivated crimes along the shore. The first major victory for racial equality in Asbury Park was the desegregation of the Bangs Avenue School in 1941 and the immediate promotion of the black assistant principal to principal with authority over both black and white students.[29] The UNIA relied on the local church institutions for hosting events, fund-raising, and membership drives. The Urban League had a strong relationship with the segregated school system in the form of various vocational education and work-training programs. These activities reflected the organization's commitment to work within the legal constraints and racial assumptions of the era.[30] The tactics employed by all three organizations demonstrate the ingenuity of each in finding new local residents. Asbury Park's black community became considerably more politically aware, economically developed, and culturally active during these decades because the individuals and families took their liberation into their own hands.

One sign of the rising tide of civil rights activism in the black community in Asbury Park was a boycott of international movie star and famous tap dancer Bill "Bojangles" Robinson's appearance in May 1941. Democrat Walter Reade owned and operated the State Theatre, which practiced racial discrimination by restricting African Americans to the balcony seats. Reade campaigned against incumbent Republican mayor Clarence E. F. Hetrick. African Americans formed a crucial constituency for both candidates. Reade paid Robinson to appear in an effort to draw black votes. Several dozen African Americans organized the boycott, and several black Reade supporters appeared to counter the demonstration, arguing the Democrat's history of philanthropy toward African Americans. Robinson allegedly turned down a one-thousand-dollar bribe to cancel the performance. A scuffle broke out involving participants on both sides as well as the police. Reade cancelled the performance and subsequently lost the election.[31] These political divisions among African Americans reflected the general shift from the Republican to the Democratic party among the national black community between 1936 and 1968.[32] The use of boycotting and political organizing was part of a larger national trend among civil rights groups during the same era.

The activities of McKelvie and Prayer illustrated the extent of segregation in rural New Jersey throughout much of the twentieth century. Each of these civil rights leaders made inroads against the prevailing system of racial oppression by reducing the ideological boundaries that existed between the national civil rights and racial uplift organizations. Small black communities could not afford the subversion and infighting that characterized some of the larger black communities in the state. White authorities held too much power over their jobs, homes, and lives. Instead, in the smaller communities, civil rights leaders incorporated groups with the same membership and elected leaders under different organizational names to avail themselves of the maximum amount of financial and political capital in order to overcome northern Jim Crow segregation. The results were inconsistent before 1950, but thereafter the improvement in African Americans' access to public facilities and better jobs indicated that gradual change was unfolding. The reputation of resort towns in New Jersey grew enough to attract internationally renowned entertainers to segregated venues after 1940. Celebrity events became new opportunities to unite local African Americans in both celebration of their achievements and organized protest against persistent discrimination.

The 1941 incident surrounding Bill Robinson's appearance illustrated the political importance of cultural events. Reade and Hetrick would have ignored the black electorate a generation earlier because their franchise was more effectively limited by municipal authorities. Only after the expansion of black voting rights in the North between 1933 and 1941 were African Americans influential voters in rural New Jersey. The Robinson incident shows that these debates were contentious, even among African Americans. Republican supporters viewed open legal challenges against white politicians as too provocative to effect lasting reform. Democratic voters rejected the gradualism of their parents and grandparents as unacceptable, given the evidence of black leadership in the federal legislative and executive bureaucracies. Celebrities like Robinson, Bill Basie, Billie Holiday, and Eartha Kitt became symbols of the importance of personal accountability on civil rights issues from the municipal through the federal levels of government.[33]

Nationally, the *Pittsburgh Courier's* "Double V" campaign inspired the next generation of African Americans to continue the movement for equality by linking "victory abroad" to a "victory (over racism) at home." It catalyzed the nascent energy for racial equality within the black community between 1941 and 1945.[34] Victories against Nazism abroad and racism at home provided a public framework for African Americans to challenge the social assumptions about their status and heritage. Newspapers like the *Afro-American* publicized the campaign for black patriotism and civil rights to dozens of small communities throughout New Jersey, reporting on activities of churches, schools, and civil rights organizations to hold the United States accountable to its rhetoric of human equality. Militant expressions of black pride and accomplishment became common for the first time in the state's history. New Jersey's Fair Employment Practice Law of 1945 and Civil Rights Act of 1949, and the creation of the Division against Discrimination in the Department of Education, opened the door for aggressive African American leadership within the state government. Over the next decade, a surge of black political involvement transformed urban areas like Newark, Trenton, Camden, and Atlantic City.[35] The rural corridor, however, remained a bastion of resistance against the movement towards greater black political influence for the remainder of the twentieth century. White leaders in small communities held fast to the traditional beliefs that white supremacy was divinely sanctioned, requiring the subordination of African Americans for a functional society.

CONCLUSION

Black families and communities in rural New Jersey met the challenges of northern segregation with the creation of civil rights organizations in the first half of the twentieth century. Local newspapers, the YMCA and YWCA, the UNIA, the Urban League, and the NAACP functioned as a single organization in many of these small towns, often with less than a dozen people maintaining the voice of thousands of farmers, cooks, and waiters in the public arena. Beginning with conversations and moving to negotiations, demonstrations, and lawsuits, civil rights groups made equality a political reality that no one imagined possible in 1900. Summersett, McKelvie, and Prayer all understood the sacrifices that previous generations of ministers and teachers made for them. These civil rights leaders had an opportunity to speak the truth to power in ways that would liberate their children. They showed the world African Americans with dignity and joy. Their message demonstrated how wrong it was to allow white supremacy to inform philosophy, science, and history. Their successes in redefining the laws of the Garden State made it possible for countless African Americans to become officers of the public trust, exercising decision-making power for the entire society. It was a great victory.

NOTES

1. "Monmouth County Afro-Republican League," *Red Bank Register*, 3 September 1902, 10; "National Negro Business League," *Red Bank Register*, 20 March 1907, 1.
2. "A Literary Society," *Red Bank Register*, 17 July 1900.
3. "Colored Lodge at Red Bank," *Red Bank Register*, 1 April 1903, 9; "Visited by a Lodge," *Red Bank Register*, 30 August 1905, 1.
4. Jane McCosker, *Historical Perspectives of Social Welfare* (Freehold, NJ: Monmouth County Board of Social Services Publication, 1986), 14.
5. August Meier, *Negro Thought in America, 1880–1915* (Ann Arbor: University of Michigan Press, 1966), 168–70.
6. Randall Gabrielan, *Images of America: Red Bank, Volume 2* (Dover, NH: Arcadia Publishing, 1996), 116; "Colored Men Organize," *Red Bank Register*, 20 March 1907, 1; Lenora W. McKay, *The Blacks of Monmouth County* (privately published, 1976), 47.
7. "Colored Voters Organize," *Red Bank Register*, 3 September 1902, 10; "Colored Voters Organize," *Red Bank Register*, 22 October 1902, 1.
8. "Ministers in Politics," *Red Bank Register*, 15 October 1902, 3.
9. "A Concert and Lecture," *Red Bank Register*, 8 October 1902, 10.
10. Emma Lou Thornbrough, *T. Thomas Fortune: Militant Journalist* (Chicago: University of Chicago Press, 1972), 289; Columbus Salley, *The Black 100: A Ranking of the Most Influential African-Americans, Past and Present* (New York: Citadel Press, 1994), 216.
11. Salley, *The Black 100*, 216.
12. "A Concert and Lecture," *Red Bank Register*, 8 October 1902, 10; "Colored Men Organize," *Red Bank Register*, 20 March 1907, 1.
13. Thornbrough, *T. Thomas Fortune*, 290, 348; Randall Gabrielan, *Images of America: Red Bank, Volume 3* (Charleston, SC: Arcadia Publishing, 1998), 117.
14. Ibid., 291.
15. Kevin K. Gaines, *Uplifting the Race*, 41, 58.
16. Clement A. Price, *Freedom Not Far Distant: A Documentary History of Afro-Americans in New Jersey* (Newark: New Jersey Historical Society, 1980), 226; L. A. Greene, "A History of Afro-Americans in New Jersey," *Journal of the Rutgers University Libraries* 56, no. 1 (1994): 34–36.
17. McKelvie to Baker, 19 August 1944, box C: 108, file "Long Branch, 1940–44," group II, NAACP, LOC.
18. Reeves to Hurley, 19 February 1944, box C: 108, file "Long Branch, 1940–44," group II, NAACP, LOC.
19. Vyeta Walker, interview transcript, 5 December 2000.

20. Kenneth L. Kusmer, *A Ghetto Takes Shape: Black Cleveland, 1870–1930* (Chicago: University of Illinois Press, 1976), 260–63; Gaines, *Uplifting the Race*, 247.

21. Untitled article, *Crisis*, June 1911, 60; Price, *Freedom Not Far Distant*, 191.

22. Price, *Freedom Not Far Distant*, 191–92; Greene, "A History of Afro-Americans," 42.

23. Correspondence of the NAACP, Manuscript Division, Library of Congress. "Asbury Park NAACP Wins against Beach Segregation," 24 August 1928. Although the title claims victory, the battles over the beach and playground persisted through the 1930s.

24. Greene, "A History of Afro-Americans in New Jersey," 36.

25. Ike Williams, "Asbury Park," *New Jersey Afro-American*, 12 April 1941, 15; Robert Weems, *Desegregating the Dollar: African American Consumerism in the Twentieth Century* (New York: New York University Press, 1998), 7–31; August Meier, *Negro Thought in America, 1880–1915* (Ann Arbor: University of Michigan Press, 1966), 168–70; Manning Marable, *How Capitalism Underdeveloped Black America* (Cambridge, MA: South End Press, [1983] 2000), 143–47.

26. McKay, *Mama and Papa*, 78, 81.

27. McKay, *The Blacks of Monmouth County*, 115.

28. "Lynching a Federal Offense," *Asbury Park Evening Press*, 4 January 1934, 8.

29. Marion Thompson Wright, "Extending Civil Rights in New Jersey through the Division against Discrimination," *Journal of Negro History* 38, no. 1 (January 1953): 96.

30. McKay, *Mama and Papa*, 52; Ike Williams, "Asbury Park," *New Jersey Afro-American*, 12 April 1941, 15; "Asbury Park," *New Jersey Afro-American*, 5 July 1941, 15; Ike Williams, "Asbury Park Residents Vacationing in Fla., Calif.," *New Jersey Afro-American*, 5 February 1944, 2; "New Jersey Afro Honor Roll," *New Jersey Afro-American*, 12 February 1944, 2.

31. "Crowd Spurns Free Show in Asbury Park," *New Jersey Afro-American*, 10 May 1941, 1–2.

32. American Social History Project, *Who Built America? Working People and the Nation's Economy, Politics, Culture, and Society*, vol. 2, *1877 to the Present* (New York: American Social History Productions, Inc., 2000), 436–39. African Americans began to vote for the Democratic Party after a generation of white northern Democrats built relationships with their communities and organizations (in addition to the neglect of their issues and aspirations by the Republican Party) between 1910 and 1930. Many African Americans, especially in the South, remained Republicans through the late 1950s, but the Kennedy and Johnson administrations' support for civil rights legislation created a political loyalty for the Democratic Party that resulted in the election of thousands of black elected officials between 1972 and 2008.

33. Mel Watkins, *On the Real Side: A History of African American Comedy from Slavery to Chris Rock* (Chicago: Lawrence Hill Books, 1999), 500. Watkins's discussion of Dick Gregory illustrates the ways many African American entertainers became public advocates for racial equality between 1955 and 1972.

34. Kevin K. Gaines, *Uplifting the Race: Black Leadership, Politics, and Culture in the Twentieth Century* (Chapel Hill, NC: University of North Carolina Press, 1996), 234–60.

35. Lizabeth Cohen, *A Consumer's Republic: The Politics of Mass Consumption in Postwar America* (New York: Alfred A. Knopf, 2003), 181–84.

SIX

Civil Rights Endings

Two decades of lawsuits and educational programs opened the door to civil rights reform in New Jersey. At the start of the twentieth century, white families in rural and resort communities remained staunchly committed to Jim Crow segregation and white supremacy. The local prominence of the Ku Klux Klan embodied the core concept that the United States was a republic for the descendants of Anglo-Saxons and no one else. African American families who moved into these towns faced this ideological obstacle with no illusions of transforming white perceptions in their lifetimes. Their best hopes were for their children. If the next generation could access secondary and postsecondary education by 1950, then the sacrifices that the early-twentieth-century migrants made might bear the greater fruit of substantive political reform.

As historian and legal scholar John Mulligan noted in 1956, there were no legal challenges to racial discrimination at the New Jersey Supreme Court between 1912 and 1926. In northern counties, individual African Americans sometimes gained relief from segregation and discrimination, but there was little evidence of this success south of New Brunswick.[1] Marion Thompson Wright, the dean of African American historians in New Jersey, wrote, "In 1881, a situation developed in Monmouth County which provoked the legislature to pass a law prohibiting the exclusion of any child from any school in the state because of nationality, religion, or color. This measure resulted in the elimination of the remaining separate schools in the northern counties, but it failed to affect any change in the practices of school officials in the southern counties."[2] Little changed in terms of civil rights until a 1936 statute passed by the legislature expanded the protections of the 1889 state constitution.[3] Three years later, the *Bullock v. Wooding* case granted a writ of mandamus to an African American plaintiff who demanded equal access to the beach in Long

Branch. By 1944, the *Hedgepeth* decision ordered the desegregation of the Trenton public school system.[4] The rising tide of change towards justice and equal opportunity peaked in 1947 with the revision of the state constitution. Article 1, section 5 stated that all citizens of the state enjoyed equal access to service in the state militia and public schools.[5] By the end of the decade, the Supreme Court issued multiple decisions consistent with the new constitution like *Seawell v. Macwithey* and *State v. Stewart*, which applied the principles of racial inclusion to housing and jury selection.[6]

The state law against discrimination in 1945 and the subsequent revision of the state constitution in 1947 cannot be overemphasized as monumental accomplishments in American history.[7] New Jersey had been one of the most conservative states in the Union at the start of the Civil War. It is the only northern state that voted against Abraham Lincoln in both 1860 and 1864. The state's commitment to white supremacy persevered through the nineteenth century and culminated in the ascendance of Woodrow Wilson to the presidency of the United States. Wilson embodied the elite intellectualism that defended white supremacy as both religiously and scientifically unquestionable. These attitudes towards racial equality made the Garden State fertile soil for the second Ku Klux Klan precisely during the period that Mulligan identified for its lack of civil rights cases. Noted historian of the African American experience Giles Wright noted that the passage of the 1947 New Jersey state constitution was a key factor in President Harry Truman's decision to desegregate the armed forces in 1948.[8] In one generation, New Jersey had changed from a national leader in the maintenance of racial segregation to the vanguard of equal protection for all people.

As immigrant families surged into rural and resort communities in New Jersey between 1935 and 1955, the moral imperative to maintain the color line wavered. Italian children knew the segregation of African American youth from firsthand exclusion from white classrooms themselves. Jewish children understood the ridicule and disdain their families encountered from Methodist and Baptist churches in their communities. As the children of immigrants became young leaders in adult civil society, they could not claim white identity in the ways their children would after 1960, but the foundation for that transformation came in the form of the legislative and judicial reforms that recognized the legitimacy of African American claims to full equality. These claims took the form of the *Pittsburgh Courier*'s Double V campaign during World War II. After the conflict, civil rights leaders like Mercer Burrell and Fred Martin seized the opportunity of constitutional revision. Martin said, "We ask that New Jersey lead the way in [the] democratic process."[9] The state responded affirmatively as a legislature and judiciary for the next thirty years, but local resistance to African American equality took deep root in the fast-growing real estate markets of the growing suburbs.

THE FAILURE OF NEW JERSEY'S CIVIL RIGHTS REFORMS

Legendary civil rights attorney Robert Carter's confrontation with the East Orange School Board over the segregation of the high school's swimming pool after 1930 represented the journey that many black activists experienced in twentieth-century New Jersey. His commitment to justice revealed a calling to correct the evils of white supremacy in American law for the next seventy years.[10] Yet, as the victories mounted and the laws changed, white authorities found new ways to maintain racial divisions in the United States. The economics of the housing market became a barrier against equal rights for African Americans after 1970. Employment and education within the larger American society became possible as New Jersey's previously segregated workplaces, schools, and colleges opened their doors to significant numbers of African Americans for the first time. Antidiscrimination law in the Garden State, especially, made it possible for the black middle class to reach heights of earning power that their parents never imagined. However, income turned into assets and wealth slowly because of the barriers against home ownership and business lending in black communities.[11] The reality of racial segregation replicated the problem Carter faced when he won his legal access to the swimming pool. He had gained entry, but he was the only one.[12] Legal integration fell short of the African American vision of racial uplift.

Civil rights organizations in the rural North did not anticipate the consequences of their legislative victories. The states with smaller cities and expansive farming counties (Connecticut, Delaware, and New Jersey) witnessed a sharp shift in the distribution of their populations between 1950 and 2000. Farms became residential suburbs. Black towns in the midst of rolling hills and acres of vegetable fields were surrounded by hundreds of thousands of single-family homes and new highway developments. In southern New Jersey, the exodus from Philadelphia and Camden to Burlington, Camden, and Gloucester counties was especially large.[13] Rural African American communities in the Garden State won the greatest victories leading up to 1950, and the accomplishments nearly eradicated these enclaves over the ensuing two generations. The political emphasis of the civil rights generations ignored the shifting economic terrain of the emerging service economy following World War II. Black advocates for racial equality did not prepare for a macroeconomic transformation that erased the nineteenth-century foundations for their homes, churches, schools, and jobs.[14] In the midst of massive residential resegregation as the rural corridor became part of the megapolitan stretching from Boston to Washington,[15] the fundamental strategy for organizations' pursuit of racial equality had no answers for the first generation of African Americans raised in an era of legal integration. (See Figures 6.1 and 6.2.)

The failure of civil rights groups in rural New Jersey to address the racial disparities in wealth after 1970 left the young people who formed the core of their programs vulnerable to changes in law enforcement and prison policy. Two institutions represent the significance of the late-twentieth-century trend towards criminalizing civil rights activism and incarcerating black youth in the New Jersey Training School for Boys in Jamesburg and the East Jersey State Prison near Rahway. As black communities integrated into predominantly white school districts and African American workers shifted into more demanding service-industry jobs, the core of the rural black working class shrank dramatically in New Jersey. In communities ranging from Hamilton to Neptune to New Brunswick, young African Americans faced increasing rates of impoverishment and unemployment without the stable foundations of church and school to help them avoid the pitfalls of drugs and violent crime.[16] Successful national and state campaigns to incarcerate offenders for longer periods of time, even for nonviolent offenses, led to dramatic surges in prison populations.[17] The youthful exuberance that produced the climate that transformed black communities in the middle of the twentieth century gave way to a profound cynicism as the paths to education, employment, and homeownership narrowed among African Americans in these small towns.

The reform school in Jamesburg housed the state's youth offenders stretching back into the nineteenth century. It was a place where boys with troubled family backgrounds could begin to find purpose and reclaim a productive adult life in the first half of the twentieth century.[18] Jamesburg's purpose changed towards a disciplinary model as larger numbers of African American and Latino children came there towards the end of the century. The state legislature and municipal governments expressed little support for the rehabilitation of troubled youth. East Jersey State Prison also reflected the changing priorities of law enforcement in the Garden State. Tensions between guards and prisoners steadily rose

Figure 6.1. Public Housing (Walter David Greason, 2001) These federally funded units often became homes for displaced farm workers in Freehold after 1970.

Figure 6.2.   Abandoned House (Walter David Greason, 2001) In Asbury Park, many of the African American residents of the west side lost their homes to foreclosure, and the collapse of the local economy left numerous homes abandoned, despite their proximity to the beaches.

in Rahway after 1950 with a number of escapes making the regional news.[19] Discrimination against African Americans became so prevalent at East Jersey that black guards filed lawsuits challenging the abuse they suffered at the hands of colleagues and supervisors.[20] The demographic shift in the prison population and the problems in the internal administration of the institutions occurred within a context where incarceration became a profitable industry by 2000. Opponents of racial equality had not merely succeeded in undermining the source of the civil rights reforms between 1930 and 1970. They had also established a financial return for the subversion of black activism.[21]

Nearly 80 percent of all prisoners in the state of New Jersey at the start of the twenty-first century were black or Latino. Among that number, almost half were arrested, tried, and sentenced in the rural corridor of the state.[22] The shift to the suburbs as the heart of business and residency in the northeastern United States transformed farming villages into exurban sprawl. It has also made these suburbs the main area of emphasis for law enforcement, especially in terms of controlling the presence and activities of racial minorities. The availability and profitability of prison labor only encourages state and local authorities to find new ways to incarcerate more of the young, poor, undereducated, and unskilled in the metropolitan region.[23]

These trends eradicated hundreds of rural African American homes, schools, churches, and civil rights organizations. As Michael Parenti wrote, the "real service of prison labor is ideological. Working convicts make prison look efficient, moral, and useful . . . we can pretend that prison labor rehabilitates. Thus convict labor becomes the ultimate conservative revenge fantasy."[24] Incarceration in the last decades of the twentieth century attacked the strategies and tactics of the Black Freedom Movement by sabotaging the participation of black children in the institutions that provided for their parents and grandparents. Locked away for decades, often from adolescence, African American boys and girls realized they had insufficient education or professional skills necessary to compete in the global economy that constructed and maintained the suburbs that enveloped them.[25] Their ancestors had overcome slavery and gradual emancipation. Their grandparents had built institutions to survive Jim Crow. Their parents had transformed the legal infrastructure of the nation. All of these strategies and sacrifices became either ineffectual or illegal in a new society rhetorically committed to equality, but functionally carrying out policies of benign neglect.[26] Civil rights organizations in rural New Jersey achieved their greatest victories between 1930 and 1970. The global economic rationale that obscured new forms of white supremacy required another wave of African American activism to promote democracy.

CONCLUSION

White legislators and residents in New Jersey did not simply surrender and take up the banner of black equality after 1970. For the next three decades, legal battles continued to define the limits of human equality within the law. One of the most profound changes was the criminalization of civil rights protest. Law enforcement officials developed strategies to marginalize and silence civil rights activists without using mass arrests or state violence to suppress demonstrators. Media outlets that provided sympathetic coverage to ministers and their congregations before 1970 increasingly ignored their actions or relied on police accounts of their activities in the last decades of the century. After the election of Ronald Reagan, conformity became a measure of patriotism. African American images on television, in movies, and in music rarely echoed the sounds and images that shaped the civil rights era. White Americans denied the substance of black cries of protest. Youth activism remained stifled behind prison walls.

One of the hallmarks of this rejection of civil rights groups was the assertion that color blindness was the standard Martin Luther King Jr. championed in his speech at the Lincoln Memorial in August 1963. King's opponents willfully mistook a literal reading of his "I Have a Dream" speech to negate civil rights advocates' calls for new laws and support for affirmative action. They misled the public to believe that any discussion of race and white supremacy shamed its perpetrators to the point of perpetuating racial inequality. Even as the racial disparities in wealth and business ownership widened between 1980 and 2000, many Americans believed that African Americans no longer faced any form of racism in their neighborhoods, homes, schools, jobs, or banks. New standards for white identity silently crept into American institutions ranging from the media to the church. Where supremacy stumbled, privilege arose.

NOTES

1. John P. Mulligan, "Perspective on: Civil Rights in New Jersey," *NJEA Review*, March 1956, 295.
2. Marion Thompson Wright, *Education of Negroes in New Jersey* (New York: Arno Press, 1971), 5.
3. Mulligan, "Civil Rights in New Jersey," 294.
4. Ibid., 295.
5. Richard Connor, *The Process of Constitutional Revision in New Jersey: 1940–1947* (New York: National Municipal League, 1970), 195.
6. Mulligan, "Civil Rights in New Jersey," 295–96.
7. Price, *Freedom Not Far Distant*, 258–69.
8. Giles Wright, *Afro-Americans in New Jersey: A Short History* (Trenton, NJ: New Jersey Historical Commission, 1989), 70.
9. Clement Alexander Price, "The Struggle to Desegregate Newark: Black Middle Class Militancy in New Jersey, 1932–1947," in *New Jersey History* 99, no. 3–4:224–25.
10. Gilbert Jonas, *Freedom's Sword: The NAACP and the Struggle against Racism in America, 1909–1969* (New York: Routledge, 2005), 77.
11. Lizabeth Cohen, *A Consumer's Republic: The Politics of Mass Consumption in Postwar America* (New York: Alfred A. Knopf, 2003), 219–21.
12. Stephen Bertman, *Vital Speeches of the Day* (Mount Pleasant, SC: City News Publishing, 2000), 290.
13. Matthew J. Countryman, *Up South: Civil Rights and Black Power in Philadelphia* (Philadelphia: University of Pennsylvania Press, 2006), 56; Howard Gillette, *Camden after the Fall: Decline and Renewal in a Post-Industrial City* (Philadelphia: University of Pennsylvania Press, 2005), 95–120.
14. Thomas J. Sugrue, *Sweet Land of Liberty: The Forgotten Struggle for Civil Rights in the North* (New York: Random House, 2008), 177–78.
15. Cohen, *A Consumer's Republic*, 212–22.
16. Manning Marable, *How Capitalism Underdeveloped Black America* (Cambridge, MA: South End Press, [1983] 2000), 210–20.
17. Jeff Sinden, "The Problem of Prison Privatization: The United States Experience," in *Capitalist Punishment: Prison Privatization and Human Rights*, ed. Andrew Coyle, Allison Campbell, and Rodney Neufeld (Atlanta: Clarity Press, 2003), 39–47.
18. Seth Mandel, "Training School Memories on Display at Lakeview," *Sentinel*, 26 January 2006, accessed 9 April 2008, http://ebs.gmnews.com/news/2006/0126/Front_Page/003.html.

19. M. Reilly, "Locked in Time: East Jersey State Prison Marks 100 Years of Changing Penal Roles," *Star-Ledger*, March 26, 1996.

20. Southern Poverty Law Center, "Guarding against Hate," *Intelligence Report* (Fall 2000), accessed 8 April 2008, http://www.splcenter.org/intel/intelreport/article.jsp?aid=227.

21. Angela Y. Davis, "Masked Racism: Reflections on the Prison Industrial Complex," *Colorlines*, Fall 1998, accessed 10 April 2008, http://www.colorlines.com/article.php?ID=309&p=1.

22. Larkin S. McReynolds and Gail A. Wasserman, "Risk for Disciplinary Infractions among Incarcerated Male Youth," *Criminal Justice and Behavior* 35, no. 9 (September 2008): 1177; "East Jersey State Prison," 8 April 2008, http://prisonplace.com/forums/p/664/675.aspx.

23. Ken Silverstein. "America's Private Gulag," in *The Celling of America: An Inside Look at the United States Prison Industry*, ed. Daniel Burton-Rose, Dan Pens, and Paul Wright (Monroe, ME: Common Courage Press, 1998), 158; Dan Pens. "Microsoft 'Outcells' Competition," in *The Celling of America: An Inside Look at the United States Prison Industry*, ed. Daniel Burton-Rose, Dan Pens, and Paul Wright (Monroe, ME: Common Courage Press, 1998), 116.

24. Christian Parenti, *Lockdown America: Police and Prisons in the Age of Crisis* (New York: Verso, 1999), 237.

25. Paul Wright. "Making Slave Labor Fly," in *Prison Nation: The Warehousing of America's Poor*, ed. Tara Herivel and Paul Wright (New York: Routledge, 2003), 116; Gordon Lafer, "The Politics of Prison Labor," in *Prison Nation: The Warehousing of America's Poor*, ed. Tara Herivel and Paul Wright (New York: Routledge, 2003), 125.

26. Charles M. Lamb, *Housing Segregation in Suburban America since 1960* (New York: Cambridge University Press, 2005), 139–40.

SEVEN

Resistance and Denial

What does it mean to be "normal" in terms of race in the United States? The emphasis within the history of race often focuses on the racial other. Native Americans, African Americans, and immigrants from Mexico, China, Japan, Italy, and eastern Europe have all encountered the classification of being different from white Americans through the twentieth century. Over the last two decades more scholarly attention has been directed at the question of what is a "normal" American identity. A foundation in English identity provides a starting point, but the ethnic and geographic components of the idea are not sufficient to understand the expansion of a white racial identity. Whiteness can be measured in terms of occupational access, uninhibited residential selection, opportunities for political authority, and chances for asset accumulation. These characteristics are not the exclusive domain of white Americans, but the intersection of all of them suggests an acceptance. One of the most powerful symbolic meanings of whiteness was its "purity." The presumed fragility of whiteness required its protection from corruption. No contact with other racial groups on equal terms could be allowed from the standpoint of public policy because such interactions would destroy the purity—intellectual, cultural, sexual—of the white race. Such racialist thought was the core assumption that drove the institutional mandate to maintain spatial separation of white from black throughout American history.

Residential segregation shaped the urban development of the United States between 1850 and 2000.[1] Distinct neighborhoods for African Americans existed in Philadelphia and New York City as early as 1800.[2] As gradual emancipation unfolded through the North between 1790 and 1860, free blacks lived in growing enclaves because of both white resistance to black neighbors and black preferences to live in comfort and safety. White discomfort with black presence and mobility contributed to

numerous race riots in northern cities throughout the nineteenth century.[3] Overt racial terrorism against African Americans was rare in rural
New Jersey after 1870.[4] There were a few lynchings, but never a massacre
like the events in Tulsa, Oklahoma, or Rosewood, Florida, where hundreds of African Americans died, were injured, or permanently lost their
homes.[5] As the politics of accommodation enabled African Americans to
build community organizations within the system of northern Jim Crow
during this period, these compliant behaviors also reinforced white assumptions about white racial superiority. Racist assumptions formed the
foundation of the laws, policies, and daily decisions that white
Americans enacted to maintain social and spatial separation from African
Americans.[6]

The nuances of an ideology designed to maintain second-class citizenship for millions of human beings based on their physical appearance
deserves as much study as the strategies the victims of oppression used
to overcome their suffering. Changes in legislation and private policies
fall short of transforming the thinking that supported the expansion of
those abuses. An infrapolitics of oppression nurtured the development of
formal political, economic, and cultural authority in the United States.
Too often, white supremacy is understood historically as a manifestation
of state authority. This conception of the phenomenon dramatically
underestimates the flexibility and multiplicity of its power. White supremacy, and its late-twentieth-century derivative, white privilege, simultaneously functioned as federal, state, and local law as well as individual,
family, and organizational behaviors. The infrapolitics of whiteness in
rural New Jersey reflected strategic decisions to transform small farming
communities into expansive exurban regions to the detriment of assertive
and organized working-class and middle-class African Americans.

WHITENESS AS AN IDEA

The difficulty of identifying whiteness only amplifies the frustration of
trying to explain it. David Roediger took this task to document and to
explore white racial experiences that shaped the last five centuries. *Working toward Whiteness* focuses on the influx of European immigrants into
the United States between 1880 and 1930. Phrenology, Egyptology, crani-
ology, and eugenic theory all flourished during this time period in various intellectual attempts to explain the material disparities among civil-
izations, while ignoring or justifying colonialism and the global exploitation of nonwhite human beings. In the second half of the twentieth century, Italians, Jews, Greeks, Irish, and Poles were unquestionably part of the
"white American community." Roediger maps the racial transformation
of these ethnic immigrants across generations through labor experiences,
religious adaptations, and marital liaisons. The year 1924 receives Roedi-

ger's attention as a turning point in the cultural history of white identity. The political push supporting the immigration restrictions of that year reflected several countervailing influences. The largest constituency wanted to protect against the assimilation of social values ranging from Communism to Catholicism into the white, Anglo-Saxon, Protestant culture developed from the eighteenth and nineteenth century. When the first Red Scare abated in 1923, it was clear that radical labor organizations were not acceptable within the American political society. The establishment of Prohibition demonstrated the strength of the Protestant church nationwide, minimizing the public voices of other faiths. However, the Supreme Court distinguished between Mexican, Asian, and European immigrants in its decisions during this time period.[7] The legal distinctions of race taught ethnic European individuals and communities the value of whiteness. Over the next two decades, children of these "new immigrants" carefully expanded the veil of white identity to include all of Europe, while blatantly "othering" people of Asian, Chicano, and African descent—most notably during public defenses of Japanese internment between 1943 and 1946. Senator Theodore Bilbo of Mississippi increasingly abandoned his attacks on ethnic Europeans as separate races during this stage of his career. "He assured all that he acted out of 'the respect and love I have for the Caucasian blood that flows not only in my veins but in the veins of Jews, Italians, Poles, and other nationalities of the White race [whom] I would not want to see contaminated with Negro blood."[8] Franklin Roosevelt accelerated the naturalization of Italian immigrants and rescinded their enemy alien status, while maintaining the restrictions on Japanese American naturalization. Prominent Italian Americans asserted their familiarity with discrimination in order to assert some antiracist ideas, but these opinions waned sharply as racial integration of schools and neighborhoods advanced in the North. The collapse of white ethnic antiracism during the era of *Brown v. Board of Education* created the conditions that obscured white supremacy for the next generation. Adaptive racism pressured and accelerated the assimilation of the new immigrants' grandchildren. As a result of this new inclusion, the alliances between new immigrants and African Americans, Asian immigrants, and Mexican Americans were all wiped away like burnt cork from the face.

Richard Delgado and Jean Stefancic's collection of essays, *Critical White Studies*, shows the ways that whiteness and suburbanization have worked together to shape suburban communities in America.[9] The Federal Housing Administration (FHA), the Home Owners' Loan Corporation (HOLC), and the Veterans Administration (VA) encouraged the migration of white families to suburbs after 1940, guaranteeing them access to low-interest mortgages and student loans for white families. The ability of white men to gain an education allowed many to move from blue-collar jobs to technical and professional occupations. Education, together with home ownership, enabled the white middle class in America to expand. Racially exclusive education and property ownership enabled the children of European immigrants to participate in suburbanization after 1940 in the form of housing developments surrounded by malls, stores, restaurants, and theaters. All of this growth relied on federal agencies to subsidize its creation. White identity became a requirement for inclusion in suburban America.[10] However, the dynamic interplay between white families' desire for suburban living and the federal government's policies to encourage residential and commercial spending created a complex and evolving relationship that enabled white supremacy to transform into white privilege by the end of the twentieth century.

FOUNDATIONS OF WHITENESS IN THE RURAL CORRIDOR

Small towns were the vanguard of the maintenance of white identity in New Jersey. In the early twentieth century, this was particularly true of the Jersey shore. Long Branch was a solidly Democratic enclave in local and state politics during the second half of the nineteenth century. Conservatism in both economic and social affairs characterized elected office holders in this area.[11] Prominent entrepreneurs such as George W. Childs, owner of the *Philadelphia Public Ledger*, and Louis P. Brown, a leading local financier, promoted several gambling houses and racetracks in Long Branch.[12] In racial matters, local white leaders steadfastly rebuked efforts to ratify the Fourteenth and Fifteenth Amendments (which defined individual citizenship and restricted government limitations on voting rights, respectively) and actively encouraged noncompliance with civil rights laws pertaining to education and public accommodations.[13] Racist attitudes, and an economic agenda promoting small business and limiting railroad subsidies, characterized the local Democratic Party into the early twentieth century.[14] Many Long Branch business owners rallied to the Democratic call for small business and used African American laborers to suppress wages for white workers. Local whites also committed themselves to the residential, educational, and social segregation of African Americans, in defiance of New Jersey's 1884 civil rights law banning racial segregation in public places.[15]

Few whites rejoiced at the steadily increasing numbers of African Americans in Long Branch in the early twentieth century. The city's leaders and prominent businesspeople actively supported the South's right to secede before the Civil War, white political supremacy during Reconstruction, and Jim Crow segregation in the early twentieth century. As the economy shifted from tourism toward light manufacturing, local white citizens felt increasingly threatened by the growth of the local African American population. A 1911 fictional story in the *Long Branch Daily Record* titled "The 'Nigger Teacher'" by Walter Hendricks was indicative of these trends. Hendricks plotted a story of Cyrus Vanderveer, a black abolitionist teacher in Alabama in 1861 whose school was burned down by Confederate officials. The fire at the school inadvertently spread to one of the Confederates' homes and endangered the life of his daughter. Vanderveer heroically ignores the destruction of the school and rescues the child, earning the respect of her father before leaving the area to fight for the Union army. The story concludes in 1868 with the child (now a woman) turning away white suitors, waiting for her black savior. The narrator then reveals himself to be Vanderveer, returned from the North to claim his white bride.[16] Hendricks constructed this grossly ahistorical tale to appeal to the paternalistic sympathies in rural northern readers by making Vanderveer an educated abolitionist and Union supporter in the Deep South. However, he then uses the psychological demon of interracial love and marriage to scandalize his subject and offer a cautionary tale for those who might sympathize with African Americans. Vanderveer's role in public discourse reflected what historian George Frederickson calls "romantic racialist" ideas.[17] African Americans were either humorous idiots, savages enlightened into voluntary service, or educated threats to the purity of Anglo-Saxon America. These images served to justify the economic subjugation of and discrimination against the black community in Long Branch, much as they did throughout the nation.

Long Branch's citizens concentrated on issues of temperance and Protestant piety between 1900 and 1930 in an effort to appeal to local native-born whites.[18] These "New Idea" Democrats grappled for local political power with the reform-minded Republican Party official strongholds in Asbury Park and Red Bank. The candidates advocating the strongest reforms of corporate influence on state and local politics lost their primaries in both the Republican and Democratic parties during the first decade of the twentieth century. However, their supporters demonstrated that they could be a key voting bloc. Each party raced to adopt New Idea reforms such as equal taxation of railroads and franchise limitations (especially on municipal utility franchises) as part of their platforms. Public debate around these issues culminated in Woodrow Wilson's election as governor of New Jersey in 1910.[19] As Wilson rose to national (and then international) prominence, he maintained close ties with New Jersey. He launched his reelection campaign in the summer of 1916 from the Shadow Lawn mansion in West Long Branch.[20] The mansion was a symbol of American industrial wealth previously owned by John A. McCall, president of the New York Life Insurance Company, and loaned to Wilson by Joseph B. Greenhut, the principal owner of Siegel, Cooper, and Company department store. The location assured Wilson that he rested among friends and allies who shared his economic pragmatism, nationalist idealism, and racial conservatism. By 1920, Long Branch embodied the heart of whiteness in New Jersey, much to the frustration of local African Americans.

THE PINNACLE OF WHITE SUPREMACY

The second Ku Klux Klan (KKK) rose to prominence in rural New Jersey after 1920.[21] Indeed, across many parts of the nation, native-born white unease found a voice through the secret organization.[22] New Jersey was the third-strongest Klan state in the Northeast (behind Pennsylvania and New York), with sixty thousand registered members.[23] Long Branch's chapter of the Ku Klux Klan epitomized native-born white anxieties, especially fear of the growing African American community. "By 1923," historian David Chalmers notes, "the Klan had found its real home amid the bluffs, dunes, and beaches of Monmouth County."[24] Within the state, Long Branch was a major center of Klan activity. Attracted by the opportunity to protest growing Italian and Jewish, as well as African American, populations in the area, Klan leader Arthur Bell organized for temperance and against shoreline tourism in conjunction with local Methodist churches.[25] Bell's ascent through the ranks of the KKK began as a local Kleagle (recruiter) and culminated in his election as New Jersey's grand dragon (state president) in 1925. With Bell in charge, the Ku Klux Klan played a significant role in Long Branch's political transformation. Incensed at the rising white ethnic and African American populations at the shore, Bell opened a new headquarters in the Elkwood Park section of Long Branch. Campaigning around temperance issues as they did throughout the country in this period, the KKK constituted a large portion of the local New Idea voting bloc after 1915.[26] Local politicians could not risk alienating Klan voters between 1918 and 1925 without jeopardizing their own political ambitions. This political reality prevented any substantive discussion of racial segregation or inclusion of African American political perspectives in public policy.

The Klan reached its peak strength between 1923 and 1926 along the central Jersey shore. A May 1923 Klan parade illustrated the growing membership and resultant social power of the Long Branch KKK. A local Irish laborer, Dennis O'Connor, attacked the marchers, punching Klansmen randomly and snatching the hoods from their heads. Spectators then surrounded and pummeled O'Connor until several police pulled him from the melee with the threat of pistol fire. The march proceeded to Asbury Methodist Church in North Long Branch, where Reverend De Witt Clinton Cobb delivered a sermon. With over five thousand onlookers in attendance, the town's fascination with the Klan was clear.

In April of the next year another Protestant minister, Reverend F. A. DeMaris, pastor of the First Episcopal Church, accused Mayor E. F. Hetrick of hosting a "wet" party with nude prostitutes at the Deal Inn. A grand jury dismissed the charges, largely because the Klan was suspected of having bribed the primary witness—Walter Tyndall, a publisher from Asbury Park.[27] With a growing popular base, the KKK continued to push their agenda of maintaining white supremacy, exclusion of Catholics and

Jews from public life, and the condemnation of alcohol, gambling, and burlesque entertainment.

Three major events galvanized the Klan presence in Long Branch during the mid-1920s: a Tristate KlonKlave, the Imperial Klaliff's Day, and a Fourth of July celebration. Each attracted thousands of attendees. These events drew national Klan leaders like Walter Bossert and Norris Freeman, while incorporating minstrel shows, fireworks displays, and beauty pageants. Following just weeks after DeMaris's accusations about Hetrick, the Tristate KlonKlave celebrated Independence Day with a four-hour parade to Elkwood Park, a 175-acre beachfront resort with a campground, restaurant, swimming pools, tennis courts, and a golf course. Local church services and summer concerts dominated the advertisements at the event, serving to link the Klan's supremacist message with vacation fun in the sun. Arthur H. Bell served as president of the Elkwood Park Association and stood to profit mightily from its emergence as a resort center. His wife, Leah E. Bell, organized the statewide Women of the Ku Klux Klan from this location, making it the leading Christian family entertainment location for native-born white Protestants in the mid-1920s.[28] Thousands of Klan families from all over New Jersey, eastern Pennsylvania, and Delaware responded to the Bells' siren song—making the Long Branch KKK a major economic force at the resort. The number of local advertisers who paid to support their events grew from nine in 1924 to fifty-five in 1926.[29] As access to local services increased, the crowds who came to support the Klan grew larger. Linking the native-born working class's desire for a relaxing day at the beach to the economic success of local business through the prisms of Protestant and white supremacy fueled the rapid expansion of Klan activities in Long Branch over the next two years.

The impact on the local white ethnic and African American communities was equally dramatic. In the wake of the 1924 KlonKlave, many Jewish and Catholic residents left Long Branch permanently within the next year. African Americans, who often could not afford to leave, stayed at home for several days.[30] In some parts of the state and the country, white ethnic communities organized legislative, social, and even violent resistance to the Klan.[31] These patterns of resistance did not emerge in Long Branch during the first half of the 1920s. In May 1925, two large Klan events signaled the peak of the organization's success at the shore. On May 10, eight thousand Klansmen gathered at the Ocean Grove Auditorium to honor American mothers. Arthur Bell told the assemblage that loyalty to one's mother guaranteed loyalty to the nation. Such vague appeals to universal inclusion implicitly applied to only the native-born white Protestant Americans, however. Imperial Klaliff (National Sergeant-at-Arms) Walter Bossert attended at evening program in his honor on May 23, granting the Long Branch KKK considerable legitimacy as a leading chapter in the state. The day's events ran nearly ten hours in length, ranging from the ubiquitous opening public procession through vaudeville and minstrel shows in the evening, continuing naturalization ceremonies for new members, and fireworks near midnight. Twenty thousand people from throughout the Northeast attended these events.[32]

Bell had established Long Branch as the heart of the New Jersey Klan and himself as the leader of the movement. He emphasized the organization's cultural conservatism in regard to Anglo-Saxon American identity, virtuous womanhood, and Protestant piety. Appeals tailored to Long Branch's resort history were used to enlist new members. In so doing, Bell followed the national Klan outreach strategies.[33] The sudden, explosive success of Bell's organization attracted business advertisers from all over Monmouth County for the three-day Fourth of July celebration in 1926. Imperial Wizard (National President) Hiram Evans agreed to appear at one of the church services on Sunday, July 4, to speak about the national Klan agenda. The previous evening New Jersey's "Miss 100 Percent America" was crowned at a ball in her honor. Monday, July 6, was the signature day for this celebration. The programs began at 6:30 a.m. with the raising of the American flag and closed at 11 p.m. with a burning cross. Bell and several local ministers spoke in the morning, and then all in attendance read the Declaration of Independence aloud. The 1926 parade took place that afternoon with a reminder for participants to keep their visors down to avoid recognition. The last formal event was the pageant and coronation of Miss 100 Percent America in a program written by Leah Bell, followed by fireworks.[34] Klan chapters from all parts of New Jersey participated that day, but it was the last major celebration of the Klan that Long Branch would see. The Klan's antitourism rhetoric began to cost them valuable local support as larger numbers of working-class white immigrant tourists avoided the area they considered a haven for intolerance.[35] Rigid commitment to temperance severed their connections with the local Democratic Party.[36] This forced an awkward alliance with the Republicans, who had often relied on white ethnic and African American support. By the end of the decade, the Klan held little political power or economic influence. The increasing assimilation of European immigrants into shore society marginalized the most extreme supports of white supremacy.

Understanding 1924 as the turning point for the idea of white identity in the United States offers a useful lens for the examination of Klan nationalism. In the years following World War I, the public desire for cultural festivals claiming the society's greatness was strong. Klan rallies allowed Americans to celebrate the accomplishment of the nation's industrial might and world standing, while also fueling a xenophobic pride in the unique nature of American identity. The National Origins Act of 1924 was the legislative manifestation of a cultural movement to preserve white American purity against allegedly inferior races. Minstrel shows, vaudeville acts, and quilting bees taught everyone who desired recognition as a true American what was funny, intelligent, and trustworthy. Summer gatherings at the beach with fireworks and beauty pageants established a national ethos sense of normality that explicitly defined certain thoughts, words, and behaviors as racially white.

After 1925, European immigrants in the United States possessed a clear framework for their assimilation into white America. The Red Scare was testament to the hostility white Americans held for radical labor politics. Public discussion of socialist ideas like communal land ownership or federal unemployment insurance would result in arrest and potential deportation from the United States. The rhetoric of white racial superiority was openly celebrated across much of the country. As European immigrants internalized these lessons and adopted public postures to affirm white supremacy and reject radical politics, they took their first steps towards American assimilation. More importantly, white Americans became less anxious about the threat of European immigrants in response to the new legislation and the national campaign against radical activists. White identity expanded because more immigrants learned how to perform its rituals and native-born Americans accepted their actions as respectful and admiring.[37]

The last stage of the transition from European immigrant to true American was the movement to exclude people of African, Asian, and Mexican descent. The history of racial intermixture functioned among white Americans to marginalize Chicano and Latino migrants to the United States as "idle," "thriftless," and "worthless."[38] Asian immigrants spoke languages and held beliefs that the descendants of Europeans found unintelligible. Meanwhile, African American urban social behaviors in churches and nightclubs insulted the sensibilities of many home owners in segregated white communities. For Irish and Italian Catholics (not to mention eastern European Jews) to ever successfully assimilate into white Americans, they had to distance themselves socially and physically from Latinos, Asians, and African Americans.[39] As the resort communities in New Jersey grappled with changes in civil rights law at the state and federal level, the children of "new immigrants" made choices about how race relations would unfold in these small towns. Their own credibility as white Americans lay in the balance as they chose the shape and form of racial integration in a developing metropolitan context.

MIDDLE-CLASS WHITE IDENTITY

Asbury Park's prosperity grew as whiteness became synonymous with middle-class recreation, and the city became a major tourist attraction in rural New Jersey.[40] Making his purchase in 1870, James A. Bradley (a devout Methodist and land speculator) incorporated the municipality in 1879. Property valuation reached over 1.5 million dollars by 1880.[41] Located fifty-four miles from New York City and eighty-nine miles from Philadelphia, Asbury Park was an ideal location for a family weekend at the shore.[42] With a large boardwalk and casino at cheaper costs, this resort town offered a summer retreat to the middle class. Bradley's enthusiasm and entrepreneurial vision combined to create a haven, which was named after Methodist circuit rider Francis Asbury. Bradley's devout Christianity and commitment to temperance attracted middle-class families who wanted to avoid the risqué gambling houses and horse racing of Long Branch. With strong religious and moral convictions, Bradley imagined a shore resort free from the twin sins of liquor and gambling.[43] All commercial deeds in Asbury Park included a clause prohibiting the sale and distribution of alcohol.[44] As a result, this small city became an attractive summer weekend stop for a growing white middle class between 1880 and 1940.

Asbury Park was not a playground for the wealthy, and the local political progressivism reflected this. Progressivism in the northern United States served as the Republican Party's response to rural populism at the end of the nineteenth century. Blending support for big business with a commitment to Protestant conservative values, the progressive movement rebuked the racial egalitarianism of Thaddeus Stevens and Charles Sumner in favor of xenophobia and corporate privileges between 1870 and 1900. Bradley, a Civil War veteran and staunch Republican, won election to the state senate over Long Branch's Democratic candidate, Henry S. Terhune.[45] Yet, like most Republicans, his progressivism on social matters ended at his pocketbook. In the 1880s, Bradley closed Asbury Park's public beaches to African Americans.[46]

Seacoast National Bank, John Steinbach's department store, and Clayton and Clayton Real Estate all did millions of dollars in local business between 1880 and 1930.[47] By 1889, there were two hundred hotels and eight hundred private homes in the city.[48] Ed Mitchell opened the Asbury Park Bathing Company to provide lifeguards, attendants, and special police for summer visitors to the shore. He paid the city between 18,500 dollars and 105,000 dollars a year for the privilege.[49] These conservative interests considered Asbury Park their playground. They differed little from Long Branch's Democrats, with whom they shared the notions of white supremacy.[50] Both groups agreed that the resorts on the Jersey shore were best used in service to white visitors. All politicians viewed the area's African Americans as a necessary evil in providing a quality vacation experience. Not only were these tourist-related businesses expanding, but the number of year-round residents also increased. Asbury Park's immediate future looked prosperous, indeed.

"Swell and near-swell and folks 'just comfortable' go to places like Asbury Park," one local newspaper reported at the turn of the century.[51] This statement reflected the city's new prominence and popularity among the middle and upper-middle classes of the Mid-Atlantic states.

While the town's year-round population barely topped four thousand in 1902, the summer population that year was some sixty-five thousand.[52] The number of bathhouses, pavilions, and piers multiplied in the first decade of the twentieth century. A local reporter recalled these early developments: "The fishing pier featured a pavilion including oriental carpeting, live palms, rocking chairs, and writing desks. On summer days, pavilions would be literally packed to the rafters."[53]

By 1904, there were eight hundred hotels, 4,500 oceanfront bath-houses, and one thousand rental lockers in Asbury Park.[54] Industrial and manufacturing development suffered as a result of the growth of tourism. In 1890, the Betsy Ross Farm opened, specializing in jellies, jams, and relishes, and employed the majority of industrial and agricultural workers in Asbury Park through the 1920s.[55]

Local entrepreneurs filled their pockets with visitors' coins between 1880 and 1910. They then looked for ways to fortify their political strength along the shore. On the heels of the 1892 state antigambling legislation, Bradley seized the shore's state senate seat in 1894. One of his first votes helped reaffirm this ban, cementing Asbury Park's status as Monmouth County's preeminent resort.[56] The resort city had already established policies to ensure the comfort of its white, middle-class summer patrons. Mr. and Mrs. Harry Thompson, an interracial couple, fled to Massachusetts after undisclosed conflicts relating to race. The local newspaper commented, "The trouble had its foundation in the difference of race, and . . . the ill-mated couple started for Worchester yesterday morning."[57] Such feelings continued as the white residents of the West Sewall section protested an African American, Samuel Marrow, purchasing a home in that neighborhood in 1900.[58] Discrimination also affected Jewish and Italian migrants to the area, who were often forced to live among African Americans. In 1912, the Bergen Place School in nearby Red Bank opened with the intended purpose of serving the Italian and African American elementary students who lived on the west side.[59] The creation of a separate elementary school for the children of Italian immigrants and African Americans spoke to those groups' increasing numbers through the early 1900s. Ostensibly meant to accommodate young people who did not live close to the existing elementary school, the "west side" elementary served the xenophobic and racist local native-born whites. Still, this particular form of discrimination also reflected the prevailing notions of race in this era. The idea of "white" racial identity attracted much social debate as waves of southern and eastern European immigrants came into the United States. Italians, Greeks, and eastern European Jews had not yet assimilated American cultural practices by this point.[60] This was the underlying reason for their inclusion with African Americans as "nonwhites" within Red Bank's social and educational structures. These rigid forms of residential separation between white and nonwhite people did not encourage southern and eastern Europeans to join the black community's pursuit of racial equality. On the contrary, these new immigrant families sought to distance themselves from their black neighbors and climb the racial hierarchy to assimilation into the white American community. As in the rest of the nation, Asbury Park's leaders established white identity as the racial and cultural ideal, causing divisions among white ethnics and racial minorities who competed for the political and economic opportunities they were denied on the basis of race and ethnicity. Jewish and Italian immigrants migrated to the area looking for opportunities after 1910. While ethnic whites blended into the native white population in suburban areas, the different religious and cultural practices of ethnic whites in New Jersey's rural corridor made them targets for white resentment throughout much of the period of northern Jim Crow segregation.

German Jews constituted the first wave of new migrants to the Howell area after World War I. They founded the Central Jersey Farmers Cooperative Association (CJFCA) almost immediately upon arrival.[61] By the mid-1920s, the CJFCA had evolved into the Jewish Agricultural Society, which developed settlement loan programs for prospective Jewish farmers. Many Jews took advantage of these programs to make new homes in rural central New Jersey. Older Jewish residents opened a cultural center where courses in literature, language, and history were taught to newer Jewish immigrants. By the 1940s, the younger, more liberal, and professionally educated Jews rejected many of the "old" ways, but still faced rejection from the native-born white community in Howell.[62] Anti-Semitism rose in this region. The Peskin family experienced cross burnings on their property and violent threats against their children from Klan sympathizers in the 1920s.[63] Jewish resident Rose Staples offered another perspective on the differences between local native-born whites and Jewish families before World War II. She said, "My father was civic minded and very broad-minded. When I was young, I recall, when African Americans came into your house, other people looked at you very strangely. But my father thought nothing of it. Or of going to their houses. Or going to their churches for their church dinners. I didn't think of it as racial tension."[64]

Although the Jewish community did not identify itself with the black population during this period, their sensitivity to discrimination and persecution fostered resistance to traditional, racist attitudes. In patterns seen throughout the rural corridor, local whites saw their community in Howell changing from a farming village to a commuter suburb. They responded to those changes with uneasiness, resistance, and flight through the first half of the twentieth century. White privilege emerged in these communities as the overt rejection of white supremacy developed. Instead, many white Americans began to favor the maintenance of informal, material advantages in comparison to African Americans and Mexican immigrants.

FROM WHITE SUPREMACY TO WHITE PRIVILEGE

White American Tim Wise's book, *White Like Me*, reveals the ways institutional racism and white advantages shaped American life after 1950. "Belonging" is the core privilege unique to white identity.[65] The acceptance in the public eye presents a fluid and dynamic power. Moving from place to place and situation to situation without scrutiny affords individuals freedoms and expectations that stunt an individual's ability to sympathize with those considered "different" or "other." Describing his own collaboration with white supremacy *in the midst* of his activism to confront and overturn apartheid in South Africa, Wise reveals honesty and a humility that should have been the bedrock of post–civil rights white identity starting in the 1950s. He confesses that the raw inequalities within the New Orleans community he called home never drew his attention while he protested the subordination of black South Africans.[66] Exposed and humiliated publicly for overlooking local systems of injustice, he does not convert his embarrassment into rage against the African Americans who did not recognize his well-intended efforts to combat racism. Wise used introspection to expand his commitment to include an aggressive redefinition of himself. Wise captures the horror of his growth as an antiracist thinker confronting the embedded racial narcissism in the heart of his color-blind role model, his mother. While drunk and, later, suffering from Alzheimer's disease, his mother lapses into the use of the word "nigger" to describe African Americans.[67] Angry and hurt at the fundamental betrayal of the values she inculcated, Wise comes to dread the power of white supremacy to corrupt even the most spirited defender of racial equality. He comprehends the scope and range of the problem that took four centuries to create. Until government authorities take action to undo white privilege, no legislative or political reform will affect any amelioration of racial segregation or wealth disparities.

In 1968, the Kerner Commission on Civil Disorders asserted that whites did not primarily migrate to suburbs to avoid blacks and other minorities. Instead, they moved because of the "rising mobility and affluence of middle-class families."[68] The commission's analysis did not account for the explicit bias in the federal programs that encouraged suburbanization. Growing suburbs transformed white identity, and white identity fueled municipal expansion on the urban fringe. Prospective white home owners and private lenders used federal policies that pushed for suburbanization. White identity changed from a simple matter of physical appearance to a social construction of educational and economic status. White Americans saw "new immigrants" as an "in-between" racial group before 1940. These new immigrants generally held more social status than African and Asian Americans, but white Americans (typically of western European descent) viewed them as inferior. The transitional status of the new immigrants, between the extremes of racial identities, allowed varying degrees of assimilation to occur in those communities between 1940 and 1980. The acceptance of the new immigrants became clear as they enjoyed access to New Deal programs and federal housing incentives between 1935 and 1970.[69]

CONCLUSION

Accepting the new immigrants before African Americans offered the newcomers the advantage of suburban access—a chance to assimilate into white America. Once white Americans accepted a more inclusive view of white identity, the process of transforming race from a biological concept to an adaptive, social idea was complete.[70] A range of suburban communities in New Jersey demonstrate the spatial consequences of expanding white racial identity in the second half of the twentieth century. These townships are often near segregated communities, whether predominantly white or predominantly black. Federal policies caused the formation of majority white communities in New Jersey's suburbs. East Brunswick and Pennsville both attracted large numbers of white migrants by 2000—77 percent and 97 percent of the residents, respectively. In East Brunswick, most African Americans lived in an "apartment district." Zoning in East Brunswick pushed to keep multifamily housing units away from single-family units.[71] The attempt to isolate nonwhite families in apartment buildings away from white residential developments continued the spatial maintenance of white privilege in New Jersey. White suburbanites allowed some suburban access to racial "others," but clear boundaries reinforced historical patterns of white authority in those neighborhoods. In Pennsville, 97 percent of the population is white, while neighboring Salem City has a population that is 57 percent black. Pennsville was able to deny most black prospective home owners, but a few African Americans gained access to the majority white neighborhood using lawsuits alleging violations of civil rights.[72] White elected officials and home owners maintained segregation in some suburban communities by fostering racial divisions at the neighborhood level within the townships. The governmental and private practices of defining "good" neighborhoods as "white" solidified the relationship between racial categories and economic opportunities.[73] Although minorities eventually gained access to certain communities, white home owners, lenders, and real estate agents preserved racial segregation within the region by informal strategies such as "steering."[74] Black persistence in asserting equal opportunity did not encourage white acceptance of the principles of racial inclusion in the second half of the twentieth century. White residents in rural New Jersey became more committed to informal strategies to undermine the use of federal and state authority to include African Americans in the promise of democracy.

Roediger's *Colored White* offers a prescription for the lack of awareness about the functions of race in American society and provides an opportunity to consider different possibilities for a racially just society. The starting point is the power of white ridicule. By studying the racial disdain propagated by Rush Limbaugh, the power of white perception in mocking black leadership, intelligence, and expertise becomes apparent. Limbaugh's tactics convey a visual message about the prevalence of African American ineptitude and the dominance of white authority, even when his face only appears in a corner of the television screen.[75] The popularity of Limbaugh's images and indictments reveals the power of white racial bonding and the continuing commercialization of black images as property.[76] Conservative speakers can reassert and relive the privileges of ownership and control through visual fantasies about the stupidity and iniquity of black racial uplift. Rush Limbaugh embodies the ways that white supremacy adapted to programs, policies, and images of human equality. These patterns emerged in the eighteenth century and continued to inform public perceptions through the start of the twenty-first century.[77]

The possibilities of white, masculine, heterosexual Christian identity grounded in the praxis of human equality unfold in this examination of white privilege. Instead of the mass production of media-driven "angry white males," how can we understand the racial transformations of young white men who embrace hip-hop, martial arts, and salsa dancing?[78] How can white men engage the diversity of human culture in ways that do not reproduce the evils of white supremacy? White men did not understand the diverse and unique ways white supremacy damaged them as individuals in the twentieth century. Redefining the cultural aspects of white identity is the crucial project of self-reflection for white men who might participate in the creation of a new global society.

White Americans demonstrated considerable flexibility in the process of transforming the ideology of white supremacy into the practice of white privilege between 1920 and 1990 in New Jersey's rural corridor. The effect of this transformation was the isolation of working- and middle-class African Americans in these small towns, using the imperatives of racial segregation before 1950 and the loopholes in the enforcement of racial integration after 1950. In the absence of state and federal authorities to maintain the Ku Klux Klan's agenda in the region, private and individual decisions preserved the social order that entrenched white expectations of residential separation. The resilience of white determination to deny racial equality stems from the difficulty in articulating its existence. Silence and denial conspire to perpetuate racial segregation and white privilege. Grappling with the informal authority of racist discourse in homes, clubs, and businesses in the ways Tim Wise and David Roediger propose is essential. An infrapolitics of oppression keeps the informal power of whiteness alive in the United States. Honesty and integrity among white Americans in private spaces like their homes, businesses, and social clubs may enable some future generation to escape the responsibility of understanding white supremacy. Rejecting the advantages white Americans enjoy in neighborhoods, schools, churches, and businesses in the coming decades constitutes a path to the realization of the beloved community envisioned by the civil rights movement.

White racist violence did not vanish from American society over the last fifty years. The sharp decline in lynchings and race riots forcefully demonstrates the movement away from white supremacy that the society has experienced. Benign neglect became the prevalent form of racial intolerance after 1970.[79] White Americans denied accountability for the emergence of white privilege and the material advantages they continued to enjoy in the process of creating metropolitan suburbs and destroying black rural communities. The frequent emphasis on the color-blind nature of the global economy only served to further obscure the persistence of the benefits of whiteness. The insulation of white communities against the gun violence in many black neighborhoods numbed white Americans to the need for constructive engagement across the twenty-first-century color line.[80] The politics of black protest fell on deaf, if not hostile, ears. Neglecting black suffering and ignoring white privilege allowed the principles of the Klan's true Americanism to shape the processes of metropolitan growth and the global service economy over the last three decades of the twentieth century.

NOTES

1. Douglas Massey and Nancy Denton, *American Apartheid: Segregation and the Making of the Underclass* (Cambridge, MA: Harvard University Press, 1993), 17–59.

2. Winthrop Jordan, *White Man's Burden: Historical Origins of Racism in the United States* (New York: Oxford University Press, 1974), 155–64.

3. Paul Gilje, *Rioting in America* (Indianapolis: University of Indiana Press, 1999), 87–115.

4. Gary D. Saretzky, ed., "The Murder of Mingo Jack," *Olde Monmouth Times*, February 1999.

5. James S. Hirsch, *Riot and Remembrance: The Tulsa Race War and Its Legacy* (New York: Houghton Mifflin Harcourt, 2002), 77–116; Stewart E. Tolnay and E. M. Beck, *Festival of Violence: An Analysis of Southern Lynchings, 1882–1930* (Chicago: University of Illinois Press, 1995), 211.

6. David M. P. Freund, *Colored Property: State Policy and White Racial Politics in Suburban America* (Chicago: University of Chicago Press, 2007), 9–10.

7. David R. Roediger, *Working toward Whiteness: How America's Immigrants Became White—The Strange Journey from Ellis Island to the Suburbs* (New York: Basic Books, 2005), 153–56.

8. Ibid., 241.

9. Martha R. Mahoney, "Residential Segregation and White Privilege," in *Critical White Studies: Looking behind the Mirror*, ed. Richard Delgado and Jean Stefancic (Philadelphia: Temple University Press, 1997), 273–74; James R. Barrett and David Roediger, "How White People Became White," in *Critical White Studies: Looking behind the Mirror*,

ed. Delgado and Stefancic, 402–5; Kenneth Jackson, *Crabgrass Frontier: The Suburbanization of United States* (New York: Oxford University Press, 1985), 199.

10. Freund, *Colored Property*, 18; Ira Katznelson, *When Affirmative Action Was White: An Untold History of Racial Inequality in Twentieth-Century America* (New York: W. W. Norton, 2006), 116.

11. William E. Sackett, *Modern Battles of Trenton: History of New Jersey's Politics and Legislation from the Year 1868 to the Year 1894* (Trenton, NJ: John L. Murphy, printer, 1895), 148, 171, 259.

12. Thomas Fleming, *New Jersey: A Bicentennial History* (New York: W. W. Norton and Company, Inc., 1977), 139, 141; Sackett, *Modern Battles of Trenton*, 443–45; New Jersey Writers Project (NJWP), *Entertaining a Nation: The Career of Long Branch* (Bayonne, NJ: Jersey Printing Company, 1940), 45.

13. John P. Milligan, "Perspective on Civil Rights in New Jersey," *New Jersey Education Association Review*, March 1956, 294.

14. Ransome E. Noble, *New Jersey Progressivism before Wilson* (Princeton, NJ: Princeton University Press, 1946), 1–4.

15. Marion Thompson Wright, "Extending Civil Rights in New Jersey through the Division against Discrimination," *Journal of Negro History*, January 1953, 94; John P. Milligan, "Perspective on Civil Rights in New Jersey," *New Jersey Education Association Review*, March 1956, 294.

16. Walter B. Hendricks, "The 'Nigger Teacher,'" *Long Branch Daily Record*, 1 July 1911. 2. Hendricks's plot is improbable on several points, but, most notably, the idea of an abolitionist teacher (white or black) in Alabama in 1861 is ridiculous.

17. George Frederickson, *The Black Image in the White Mind: The Debate on Afro-American Character and Destiny, 1817–1914* (Hanover, NH: Wesleyan University Press, 1971), 103–6.

18. Alan Rosenthal and John Blydenburg, eds., *Politics in New Jersey* (New Brunswick, NJ: Rutgers University, 1975), 44–45; Edgar I. Vanderveer, *County, City, Town, Township, and Borough Officials of Monmouth County, 1917* (Keyport, NJ: The Weekly Print, 1917), 5.

19. Ransome E. Noble, *New Jersey Progressivism before Wilson* (Princeton, NJ: Princeton University Press, 1946, 66, 78–79, 153.

20. August Heckschner, *Woodrow Wilson* (New York: Charles Scribner's Sons, 1991), 401–15.

21. L. A. Greene, "A History of Afro-Americans in New Jersey," *Journal of the Rutgers University Libraries* 56, no. 1 (1994): 47; Randall Gabrielan, *Images of America: Long Branch, People and Places* (Charleston, SC: Arcadia Publishing, 1998), 31.

22. David Chalmers, *Hooded Americanism: The History of the Ku Klux Klan* (Durham, NC: Duke University Press, 1987), 11; David R. Contosta, *Lancaster, Ohio, 1800–2000: Frontier Town to Edge City* (Columbus: Ohio State University Press, 1999), 171–72.

23. Kenneth T. Jackson, *The Ku Klux Klan in the City: 1915–1930* (New York: Oxford University Press, 1967), 237. Pennsylvania listed 150,000 registered Klan members, while New York listed 80,000.

24. Chalmers, *Hooded Americanism*, 245; Jackson, *The Ku Klux Klan in the City*, 179.

25. Ibid., 246, 249.

26. Ibid., 245.

27. James F. Durnell, "The Ku Klux Klan of Monmouth County: A Brief History," *Long Branch Daily Record*, 26 May 1971, special insert.

28. Ku Klux Klan (KKK), *Tri-State KlonKlave Souvenir Program*, 4 July 1924, George Moss Collection, Long Branch, NJ, not paginated; NJWP, *Entertaining a Nation*, 136–37.

29. KKK, *Tri-State KlonKlave Souvenir Program*, 4 July 1924, not paginated; KKK, *Imperial Klaliff's Day Program*, 23 May 1925, George Moss Collection, Long Branch, NJ, not paginated; KKK, *Fourth Annual Fourth of July Celebration*, 3–5 July 1926, George Moss Collection, Long Branch, NJ, not paginated.

30. NJWP, *Entertaining a Nation*, 136–37. In keeping with the promotional spirit of this work, the authors argue that the local Klan collapsed as result of the ethnic popu-

lations' flight from the area. This seems counterintuitive. The Klan would have gained strength from this success, not fallen apart.

31. David Goldberg, "Unmasking the Ku Klux Klan: The Northern Movement against the KKK, 1920–1925," *Journal of American Ethnic History*, Summer 1996, 32–36.

32. Durnell, "The Ku Klux Klan in Monmouth County," *Long Branch Daily Record*, 26 May 1971, special insert; KKK, *Imperial Klaliff's Day Program*, 23 May 1925, not paginated.

33. Goldberg, "Unmasking the Ku Klux Klan," 32–33.

34. KKK, *Annual New Jersey Klan July Fourth Celebration Program*, 3–5 July 1926, not paginated; Kathleen M. Blee, *Women of the Klan: Racism and Gender in the 1920s* (Berkeley: University of California Press, 1991), 160.

35. Chalmers, *Hooded Americanism*, 250.

36. Ibid., 249.

37. Matthew Frye Jacobson, *Whiteness of a Different Color: European Immigrants and the Alchemy of Race* (Cambridge, MA: Harvard University Press, 1998), 82–85.

38. Ronald Takaki, *A Different Mirror: A History of Multicultural America* (New York: Back Bay Books, 2008), 161, 299.

39. Jennifer Guglielmo, *Are Italians White? How Race Is Made in America* (New York: Routledge, 2003), 29–59; Karen Brodkin, *How Jews Became White Folks and What That Says about Race in America* (New Brunswick, NJ: Rutgers University Press, 1999), 103–37.

40. Women's Club of Asbury Park (WCAP), *An Historical Review of Business and Other Organizations Operating in Asbury Park* (Asbury Park, NJ: City Publication, 1929), 2.

41. Ibid.

42. Mustin, Maurice, ed., *A Sketch of Monmouth County, New Jersey, 1683–1929* (Camden, NJ: M. Mustin Co., 1929), 37.

43. Helen-Chantal Pike, *Images of America: Asbury Park* (Charleston, SC: Arcadia Publishing, 1997), 7.

44. WCAP, *An Historical Review of Business*, 2.

45. Pike, *Images of America: Asbury Park*, 99.

46. Ibid., 100.

47. WCAP, *An Historical Review of Business*, 3, 8, 10, 16.

48. Pike, *Images of America: Asbury Park*, 119.

49. WCAP, *An Historical Review of Business*, 3.

50. W. Earle Andrews, *Asbury Park Beachfront Improvement* (New York: privately published, 1945), 12.

51. Fleming, *New Jersey*, 143.

52. Pike, *Images of America: Asbury Park*, 119.

53. Marie A. Sylvester, "Beating Heat at the Shore," *Asbury Park Press*, 12 April 1999, B2.

54. Pike, *Images of America: Asbury Park*, 113, 122.

55. Mary B. Sim, *Commercial Canning in New Jersey: History and Early Development* (Trenton: New Jersey Agricultural Society, 1951), 427.

56. Sackett, *Modern Battles of Trenton*, 456. Pike, *Images of America: Asbury Park*, 99.

57. "White Married Black," *Shore Press*, 20 June 1890, 1.

58. "Asbury Park Folk Object to a Negro as a Neighbor," *Monmouth Press*, 21 April 1900.

59. Randall Gabrielan, *Images of America: Red Bank, Volume 3* (Charleston, SC: Arcadia Publishing, 1998), 77. No records concerning the reasons and methods preceding the school's establishment survived.

60. Jacobson, *Whiteness of a Different Color*, 52–68.

61. Alan S. Pine, Jean C. Hershenov, and Aaron H. Lefkowitz, *Peddler to Suburbanite: The History of the Jews of Monmouth County, New Jersey* (Deal Park, NJ: Monmouth Jewish Community Council, 1981), 109.

62. Ibid., 118–20.

63. Ibid., 182–83.

64. Flora Higgins, "Interview with Rose Staples," 12 July 2000, in *Remembering the Twentieth Century: An Oral History of Monmouth County*, ed. Flora T. Higgins, http://www.visitmonmouth.com/oralhistory/bios/StaplesRose.htm.

65. Tim Wise, *White Like Me* (New York: Soft Skull Press, 2005), 8, 25.

66. Ibid., 114.

67. Ibid., 124–25.

68. Mahoney, "Residential Segregation and White Privilege," in *Critical White Studies: Looking Behind the Mirror*, 273–74.

69. Barrett and Roediger, "How White People Became White," in *Critical White Studies: Looking Behind the Mirror*, 402–5.

70. Ibid.

71. James Lamond, "Development of East Brunswick, NJ," online archive for Race and the Suburbs discussion group, accessed 10 July 2006, http://groups.yahoo.com/group/Race_Suburbs,

72. Holly Bittle, "Pennsville Township in Salem County, NJ: History, Present Time, and an Optimistic Future," online archive for Race and the Suburbs discussion group, accessed 7 July 2006, http://groups.yahoo.com/ group/Race_Suburbs; Ermon Jones, "Housing and Head Start Issues," Court Street School Education Community Center file, Freehold, NJ, 2009.

73. Mahoney, "Residential Segregation," in *Critical White Studies*, 273–74.

74. Charles M. Lamb, *Housing Segregation in Suburban America since 1960: Presidential and Judicial Politics* (New York: Cambridge University Press, 2005), 192.

75. David R. Roediger, *Colored White: Transcending the Racial Past* (Los Angeles: University of California Press, 2002), 51.

76. Ibid., 52.

77. Robert M. Entman and Andrew Rojecki, *The Black Image in the White Mind: Media and Race in America* (Chicago: University of Chicago Press, 2001), 57; George M. Fredrickson, *The Black Image in the White Mind: The Debate on Afro-American Character and Destiny, 1817–1914* (Hanover, NH: Wesleyan University Press, 1971), 3–5.

78. Roediger, *Colored White*, 237.

79. Lamb, *Housing Segregation*, 139, 141.

80. Entman and Rojecki, *The Black Image in the White Mind*, 78–93.

EIGHT

Suburban Regions

An investigation into the transformation of New Jersey from the Garden State of the nineteenth century to the Suburban State of the twenty-first century might yield numerous answers (and even more rewarding questions) in an effort to create a new narrative chronology. The rural corridor, stretching from Somerset County to Gloucester County, provides an ideal starting point to examine the possibilities of societies outside of the urban centers in the twentieth-century United States. On first glance, this region appears to have undergone an industrial leap. This metropolitan region had evolved from a collection of rural villages to a set of suburban communities without any widespread industrial development. Furthermore, African Americans composed between 7 and 10 percent of the total population in the rural corridor throughout the century. Race relations were not exclusive to northern urban spaces and southern rural spaces — the rural North revealed additional dimensions of the socioeconomic composition and evolution of the United States.

Between 1940 and 1970, in particular, the children of European immigrants became white Americans as they continued the de facto practices of segregation and discrimination against African Americans during the processes of transforming rural New Jersey's resort communities and farming villages into a suburban exopolis. The relationship between deindustrialization and globalization shaped the economic processes that defined the last three decades of the twentieth century. Suburbanization and regionalization are equally important facets to understanding the emergence of color-blind conservatism after 1970, because the spatial organization of these areas created a limited sense of social inclusion.[1] The suburban home owner drove the consumption economy of the entire world with increasing force due to federal and state largess in the form of tax credits and incentives by 2000.[2] The citizen consumer created an un-

sustainable political drive for conglomerate political authority that supplanted local and state restrictions across the country.[3] The millions of
new residents in the "Suburban State" from both New York City and
Philadelphia often accepted an idea of exclusionary American communities based on the mythology of cultural assimilation inherited from
their parents and grandparents.[4] In a complete inversion of Ben Franklin's colonial metaphor, New Jersey became a vacuum inhaling from both
ends, transforming communities in Morristown, Red Bank, Randolph,
and Franklin. These towns reveal the range of outcomes that unfolded in
New Jersey as rural areas became suburbs.

Isolated rural towns in the northern portion of New Jersey's rural
corridor did not experience waves of industrialization before 1950 because their residents relocated there to escape the culture and lifestyle of
the larger cities. Commuting by railroad and automobile (as well as the
lack of private financing for homes) prevented thousands of families
from moving to these areas. However, the lack of access also intensified
the desirability of rural enclaves among the urban working classes. With
the passage of New Deal legislation, improved wages through federal
labor laws, and new federal bureaucracies to stimulate consumer credit
for home ownership, hundreds of thousands of New Yorkers moved to
the suburban plots of their parents' dreams. Morristown and Randolph
grudgingly accepted the well-heeled newcomers who found their way
there. Red Bank experienced its peak of prosperity during the middle
decades of the twentieth century because residents flocked to the banks
of the Navesink River. Franklin, Howell, and Freehold all became service-industry hubs, especially for retirees, by 1990.

MORRISTOWN

Morristown developed as a result of railroad expansion in northern New
Jersey. In 1916, the *New York Times* described early evidence of Morristown's growth when it offered the opinion that the town possessed
"many advantages for the suburban resident." Picturing the homes of
several Morristown residents including Mr. and Mrs. P. T. Francis of the
Normandie Park neighborhood, the article explained, "Its local and
neighboring clubs and accessibility to the popular social centers of Ber-
nardsville and Madison, with excellent transit facilities to New York"
create an ideal suburban escape from urban living.[5] Given that the Delaware, Lackawanna, and Western Railroad Company ran straight through
the town, it was an ideal residence for wealthy families throughout the
northeastern United States.[6] Historian Kenneth Jackson described an elit-
ist retreat when he said, "In some communities, like Morristown, New
Jersey, membership in 'the club' was a prerequisite for residence in the
suburb."[7] The development of the automobile changed the face of subur-

ban development as the dominance of steam power decreased between 1920 and 1960. Jackson also said, "In the nineteenth century the image of suburbia as an affluent community of railroad commuters was set, and the image remained until the interstate suburbs developed in the 1960s."[8] As highways dictated the value of real estate, Morristown did not grow as quickly as smaller rural communities in southern New Jersey because of higher property values. In 1951, the Morristown planning board put together a master plan for the area in order to evaluate the importance of economic and social elements to bringing people into the area. According to the plan, Morristown's share of the total population of Morris County declined from 13.7 percent in 1930 to 10.4 percent in 1950. Local retail sales also dipped throughout the county, dropping from 34.8 percent in 1929 to 26 percent in 1948.[9] This first effort to link demographic and economic trends in useful ways for politicians and business owners laid the foundation for a series of studies through the rest of the twentieth century.

In its report, the planning board also examined the importance of bringing new industry into the area in order to stimulate job growth. In the decade of World War II, Morristown's industrial employment doubled. Planners believed new industrial growth was necessary to stimulate the regional economy. They believed that their success would attract new residents and boost retail businesses with increasing automobile traffic through the area. Corporate firms started to follow suburbanites out of older cities such as New York, Newark, and Paterson in search of lower overheads and a wealthier customer base.[10] Though Morristown attempted to entice new business and residents to the area, other places prepared more effectively for expanding suburban development. Morristown's early growth crippled the area's ability to take part in the later regional expansion of suburbia that took place in New Jersey after 1950. Places like Franklin and Freehold offered developers and businesses vast tracts of undeveloped land for the taking, while earlier suburbs like Morristown had little available land to offer.

The industrial economy powered a sense of nationalism among Americans between 1870 and 1950. As the nation recovered from the wounds of civil war, the growth of the international steel economy and the United States's role as a world power reinvigorated the domestic sense of purpose and identity. Americans created rural towns as rewards for their hard work during this period. Morristown offered a place for rest and renewal in preparation for the new demands of the industrial world. However, the industrial world still did not include much of Asia, Africa, and Latin America. Rural retreats appealed to residents seeking the provincialism of patriarchy, white supremacy, and Protestant Christianity. The hunger of industrial capital for innovation and new markets provided an opportunity to challenge these core assumptions of early American identity. As seen in chapter 7, conflicts over the meaning of

American culture shaped the forces of metropolitan growth and the emergence of conglomerate capital in the second half of the twentieth century in New Jersey's rural corridor.

RED BANK

Between 1920 and 1950, Red Bank transformed from a tiny village into a small city. Both retail and industrial bases in the area grew rapidly through the 1920s, suffered setbacks during the 1930s, and made modest gains in the 1940s. Red Bank's total population nearly doubled during this period from 7,400 to 12,700.[11] Yet, after World War II, many of the most prosperous white business owners in Red Bank began to seek residence in neighboring municipalities like Shrewsbury, Rumson, and Tinton Falls. Lower taxes and the opportunity for greater political influence contributed to this migration. Meanwhile, the local African American population in Red Bank grew steadily during these three decades as migrant families established permanent residences. This period marked both the pinnacle of Red Bank's economic strength and the beginning of its decline.

The 1920s witnessed dramatic growth in Red Bank's retail and service economies. As local horse-and-carriage shops and hotels closed, auto dealerships and department stores opened. Numerous local hotels closed due to the Depression, but the Molly Pitcher and the Globe survived.[12] Van Syckle Dodge dealership opened on Front Street in 1924, and Prown's National Five and Ten Cents Store followed in the next year. Riverview Medical Center began its operations in 1929.[13] Red Bank opened an airport in 1926, and a group of local white women opened a business institute to teach business skills for female entrepreneurs.[14] The Great Depression significantly curtailed Red Bank's retail success, but, more importantly, it ended the city's centrality to the county economy. Through the 1930s, this trend slowed, though the Electrical Industry Manufacturing Company started and Eisner's uniform company grew considerably.[15] The 1940s brought a major shift in Red Bank's economy as the United States Army established a signal lab, and insurance companies replaced many of the retail stores.[16] Baird-Davison was the town's only remaining farm-machinery shop after World War II.[17]

After 1920, Red Bank attracted white entrepreneurs who saw the declining prospects in tourism-based Long Branch and Asbury Park. Business owners like C. E. Conover, Sigmund Eisner, and Fred D. Wickoff opened factories and stores in Red Bank, while also building their homes nearby to live close to their workplaces. The Elkins and D'Onofrio families moved to the area with hopes of new beginnings. The D'Onofrios came from Italy in 1920, and their son, Joseph, would found the Red Bank Electric Company in the late 1940s. New York Court of Appeals judge

Abram Elkus moved to Red Bank in the mid-1920s. His daughter won election as the town's first woman mayor in 1951.[18] These families' experiences establish a pattern of native and ethnic whites finding success in the town during the decade. However, by 1940, many white families no longer saw Red Bank as a middle-class retreat.

Red Bank's loss of social status after 1940 illustrated the counterpart to Morristown's narrative of economic stagnation. The former community never retained the wealthy year-round residents who constituted the population of the latter. As a result, more working-class African Americans purchased and rented homes in Red Bank than in Morristown through the middle decades of the twentieth century. Increasing black residency, even as legislative integration began to unfold, meant fewer new businesses, lower household incomes, and higher unemployment rates in New Jersey's rural corridor. (See Figure 8.1.) In nearly all of these communities studied in this chapter, the de facto barriers against African American success and inclusion such as housing discrimination, educational segregation, and job discrimination remained effective until the start of the twenty-first century. Morristown never integrated racially, so it did not experience the worst effects of uneven development. Red Bank's African American community grew dramatically after 1950, so state and local authorities isolated it using public law-enforcement tactics and private strategies of disinvestment as seen in chapters 6 and 7. Randolph offered some of the most pronounced examples of this social division and its economic consequences over the last sixty years.

RANDOLPH

Randolph Township was a rural area until 1940. That year, Randolph's population was 2,160 people. The racial makeup of the town remained almost entirely white. Only 2.3 percent of the total population was black in 2000. In 1931, the state built Route 10, running through Randolph and increasing access to surrounding communities and cities. Randolph's vacation-resort businesses had operated since the end of the nineteenth century. With the construction of Route 10, it quickly became a popular vacation spot for the tristate region (New York, New Jersey, and Connecticut). Vacation spots like Ackerman's mountain resort offered customers the facilities for swimming, fine dining, and skiing in the appropriate seasons. The advent of air travel and the expansion of superhighways after 1960, however, gave tourists access to more exotic destinations. The end of the resort era in Randolph was swift.[19]

In 1960, only 20 percent of Randolph's municipal land was developed. Of the total 13,939 acres that comprised the municipality, residential space comprised the highest percentage (9.4) of land usage.[20] The 1960 census showed that from 1950 to 1960 Randolph's population more than doubled as tourists became permanent residents.[21] According to the Randolph Township comprehensive plan, many of the new people in the area still commuted to other areas throughout the greater New York–Philadelphia metropolitan region. Randolph emerged as a suburb at the very beginning of its economic development. The township dedicated only 0.3 percent of its land to commercial space and 1.7 percent to industrial space, choosing to maintain its resort infrastructure. Areas like Mount Freedom offered tourists a rural getaway from the cities. Hotels made up 3.5 percent of the total land mass in Randolph.[22] Retail space was mostly concentrated in Mount Freedom, by the Sussex Turnpike to the southwest, and also near Route 10, which divided the north and south parts of town. The township planners recognized the future importance of "an orderly concentration of residential development" in 1960.[23] They recognized that this would require the installation of new infrastructure to ensure the orderly development of neighborhoods. Randolph designed a general "neighborhood concept" for future developments. This plan proposed residential zones in a grid with a school, church, park, fire station, and neighborhood shopping center.[24] Secondly, Randolph planners envisaged the growth of commercial space on two levels—regional and neighborhood. In this way the township believed it could both serve the current population and attract new residents to the area. Finally, the plan emphasized the importance of attracting industrial development to the community. In order to accomplish this goal, the 1960 plan conveys the importance of installing sewer/water facilities and fire stations in close proximity to the new residential zones. In its plan for future ratables, Randolph targeted industries like metal fabrication, scientific/professional instrument manufacturing, and furniture manufacturing.[25]

The population of Randolph rose steadily in response to the implementation of the zoning plan. The town's predominantly white population persisted into the twenty-first century and was the focus of local planning efforts. The banking and real estate interests in Randolph maintained the racial and economic standards that ensured the exclusivity of the community. This made it quite difficult for African Americans to move into these suburban neighborhoods.[26] The barriers of racial and economic segregation created and maintained by private lenders using federal guidelines persisted in New Jersey and across the United States until the end of the twentieth century.[27] Local advertising for the rural resort communities in New Jersey reinforced this discrimination. On the front of its advertising brochure, Ackerman's featured a photo of its white-only patrons. Countless examples of this symbolic exclusion accompanied by the overt racial requirements of government lending for housing effectively perpetuated the legacy of northern Jim Crow segregation for decades.[28] Even as towns in New Jersey's rural corridor adapted to the global economy of the late twentieth century, the assumptions of black inferiority shaped neighborhoods, jobs, and wealth creation under the emerging, new system. (See Figure 8.2.)

FRANKLIN

Some of the most dramatic transformations of the rural corridor into a metropolitan space occurred in northern New Jersey's Somerset County in Franklin Township. Suburban sprawl changed Franklin after 1950. By the end of the decade, it was not a rural community with a reliance on agriculture, but a suburban community. The township's population grew from 5,912 to 19,601 between 1940 and 1950.[29] This explosion occurred because many New Brunswick residents preferred the lower-density residential areas in Franklin. Large subdivisions forced the community to extend their road, electrical, and water systems in order to accommodate the new population after 1960. Many farmers sold their properties to incoming developers who constructed acre after acre of single-family homes.

Most of the residential zone in Franklin lay in the northeastern portion, closest to New Brunswick. Sociologist Robert W. Lake noted that Franklin's residents at this time were, "mid-level, white-collar relocates."

Figure 8.1. Frederick Douglas Apartments (Walter David Greason, 2001) Douglass did vacation in the area during the peak of its popularity in the late nineteenth century, but using his name to market vacancies to low-income families betrayed the legacy of racial equality he envisioned. *Note*: The housing developer made a common error in misspelling Frederick Douglass' name with a single "s" on their sign. His error is replicated in labeling this figure for the sake of accuracy in representing the name of the apartments.

**Figure 8.2.   Rug Mill Towers (Walter David Greason, 2001) One example of de-
velopment that included options for low-income and multiple-family structures
came in the form of Freehold's Rug Mill Towers. However, it was located adjacent
to one of the poorest neighborhoods in the region and did not attract middle- or
high-income residents.**

Between 1970 and 1982, the area grew rapidly as Interstate 287 brought
an influx of new businesses to the area.[30] Despite the commercial expansion, according to Franklin's 1982 comprehensive plan, 80 percent of the
municipal land remained undeveloped.[31] Efficiency supplanted innovation in Franklin after 1970 as residential developers produced standard-
ized housing to maximize profits. Inattentive planners in search of quick
methods of attracting new residents and businesses failed to think about
the long-term effects of their decisions, prompting general disdain for the
suburban culture of mass consumption. Historian Dolores Hayden
shows, "Excessive private consumption was not inevitable. It was the
result of sustained pressure from real estate interests and their allies in
government to marginalize the alternatives to unlimited private subur-

ban growth."[32] While assumptions about infinite residential space prevailed, the loss of a sense of community throughout the rural corridor created feelings of tremendous isolation, even within families, by 2000. Franklin illustrated the dramatic social costs of this isolation in the second half of the twentieth century.

Lake examined the changes in the African American community in Franklin after 1950. Pine Grove Manor, a large apartment complex that was redeveloped and marketed to New York residents who looked to move to the suburbs, reveals layers of racial tension that emerged as the town grew. It became a cooperative apartment building and opened all sections in 1959. The down payment for two- and three-bedroom apartments was five hundred dollars. White buyers swarmed the location within the first year. Seeking to avoid African American residents, complex managers actively prevented black applicants purchasing apartment units. However, a few did manage to acquire units. In 1959, black residents constituted approximately 6 percent of Pine Grove Manor's population. When residents discovered that building management had discriminated against prospective black applicants, indictments followed. The apartment complex's board signed a nondiscrimination agreement, and the proportion of nonwhite residents expanded as a result. But, as the percentage of African Americans in Pine Grove grew, white residents departed.[33]

In 1963, with African Americans forming 12 percent of Pine Grove's population, there was also a 10 percent vacancy rate. White flight changed from an urban phenomenon to a metropolitan process. Levitt and Sons opened a new development of single-family homes less than two miles away from the apartment complex.[34] Home ownership certainly attracted some Pine Grove residents, but there were also racial concerns. In 1964, the *New York Times* documented more activity by the Levitts, who announced the opening of Strathmore at Franklin, a four-hundred-acre project that would house more than eight hundred single-family structures ranging in price from twenty thousand dollars to thirty thousand dollars. The homes would boast all the amenities of a luxurious single-family residence, including central air-conditioning and a two-car garage.[35] As many white families looked for single-family housing, they found many desirable options in Franklin.

Interracial tensions in Franklin only increased after this announcement. The confrontations about real estate surrounding Pine Grove Manor foreshadowed the tensions among the youths of the area. Between 1940 and 1960, the black population in Franklin grew over 500 percent. From 1960 to 1980, it more than doubled again in response to availability of housing units in the suburbs.[36] The sharp increase in the African American community combined with massive growth in the general population to foster youth violence across the town. Racial eruptions of violence became commonplace throughout New Jersey's rural corridor. In

1969, the Afro-American Youth Council staged a nonviolent sit-in demanding "more Afro-American history courses, the teaching of Swahili, the hiring of more Negro faculty members and counselors, and a greater say in school disciplinary studies."[37] Reactions to racial inequality by youths continued over the next decade. On April 7, 1973, the Newark *Star-Ledger* reported a major interracial brawl at Franklin Township High School. Police suppressed the violence and monitored school activities in plain clothes. The incident began when a white student attacked a black student. According to the School Superintendent Dr. Robert E. Maxwell, "high school [had] been closed three or four times within the last four years because of fights usually between black and white students."[38] The emergence of black suburban communities in formerly all-white enclaves stimulated conflict over the traditions of unchallenged white superiority. Racial fragmentation in Franklin illustrated the difficulties of managing social change as a region changes in response to metropolitan development.

The reformulation of white identity in the burgeoning American suburbs following World War II unified a new generation of young workers in pursuit of a global service economy based on technological innovation. The inclusion of rural black workers in the plans to build centerless cities was never an option for the political elites in the Garden State's farms and resorts. African Americans were crucial participants in the maintenance and expansion of rural New Jersey's communities through the first half of the twentieth century. After 1970, white authorities maintained the legacy of racial segregation by isolating black communities in small boroughs near social services. Blocked from the opportunities for economic and educational development that accompanied the emergence of the global service economy, thousands of African American families attempted to maintain middle-class standards of living (over nine thousand dollars a year in 1979) in areas without any working-class opportunities (employers who provided indoor, salaried work). The promise of a color-blind, merit-driven society that would lead the world into a brighter tomorrow at the start of the twenty-first century never materialized. The traditions of racial inequality adapted and thrived, just as they had over the previous three centuries.

NOTES

1. David M. P. Freund, *Colored Property: State Policy and White Racial Politics in Suburban America* (Chicago: University of Chicago Press, 2007), 396–99.

2. Myron Orfield, *American Metropolitics: The New Suburban Reality* (Washington, DC: The Brookings Institution, 2002), 70–73, 95–96.

3. Kevin M. Kruse, *White Flight: Atlanta and the Making of Modern Conservatism* (Princeton, NJ: Princeton University Press, 2005), 251–58.

4. Freund, *Colored Property*, 375–79.

5. "Building New Homes at Morristown, NJ," *New York Times*, XX4.

6. The primarily rail line came into town parallel to Madison Avenue in the southeast, before crossing town just south of Morris Avenue, then turning north along Speedwell Avenue.

7. Kenneth Jackson, *Crabgrass Frontier: The Suburbanization of the United States* (New York: Oxford University Press), 98.

8. Ibid., 102.

9. McHugh and McCrosky Consultants, Town of Morristown, New Jersey (n.p., 1951), 10.

10. Ibid., 18.

11. Walter D. Greason, "From Village to Suburb: Race, Politics, and Economics in Monmouth County, New Jersey, 1890–1990," PhD diss. Temple University, 2004, table 11.

12. Gabrielan, *Red Bank*, 41, 76.

13. Randall Gabrielan, *Red Bank in the Twentieth Century* (Dover, NH: Arcadia Publishing, 1997), 28, 58.

14. Randall Gabrielan, *Images of America: Red Bank* (Dover, NH: Arcadia Publishing, 1995), 81, 99.

15. Maurice Mustin, ed., *A Sketch of Monmouth County, New Jersey, 1683–1929* (Camden, NJ: M. Mustin Co., 1929), 43; Gabrielan, *Red Bank in the Twentieth Century*, 72, 74.

16. McKay, *The Blacks of Monmouth County*, 34; Gabrielan, *Red Bank in the Twentieth Century*, 23, 46, 73.

17. Randall Gabrielan, *Red Bank, Volume 2* (Dover, NH: Arcadia Publishing, 1996), 46.

18. Gabrielan, *Red Bank, Volume 2*, 88, 91; Gabrielan, *Red Bank*, 114–15.

19. Township of Randolph, "Getting to Know Us: History, Our Grand Hotels," Randolph Township Online, 13 July 2006, http://www.randolphnj.org/get_to_know_us/grand_hotels.

20. Community Planning Associates, *Randolph Township Comprehensive Development Plan—Report and Recommendations*, 1960, 3.

21. Ibid., 4.

22. Ibid., 3.

23. Ibid., 15.

24. Ibid., 17.

25. Ibid., 24.

26. Freund, *Colored Property*, 221. Restrictive zoning measures relied on the racial assumptions about land use and value that dominated the market between 1910 and 1940.

27. Jackson, *Crabgrass Frontier*, 196–218.

28. Ibid.

29. United States Bureau of the Census (USBC), *1960 Census of Population, Volume II* (Washington, DC: United States Government Printing Office), 36. Table 15; idem., *1970 Census of Population, Volume II* (Washington: United States Government Printing Office), 55. Table 17; idem., *1980 Census of Population, Volume II* (Washington, DC: United States Government Printing Office), 35. Table 17; Inter-University Consortium for Political and Social Research (IUCPSR), "Study 00003: Historical Demographic, Economic and Social Data: United States, 1790–1970" (Ann Arbor: ICPSR), http://fisher.lib.virginia.edu (25 December 2002); "Population Estimates, New Jersey" http://www.wnjpin.net/OneStopCareerCenter/LaborMarketInformation/lmi02/ncinj.htm (5 April 2006).

30. Robert W. Lake, *The New Suburbanites* (New Brunswick, NJ: Center for Urban Policy Research, 1981), 90.

31. Township of Franklin, *Comprehensive Plan Township of Franklin Somerset County, New Jersey*, 1982, 8.

32. Dolores Hayden, *Building Suburbia: Green Fields and Urban Growth, 1820–2000* (New York: Random House, 2003), 18.

33. Lake, *Suburbanites*, 93.

34. Ibid.

35. "Levitt Acquires Tract in Jersey," *New York Times*, 9 February 1964, R4.

36. United States Bureau of the Census (USBC), *1960 Census of Population, volume II* (Washington, DC: United States Government Printing Office), 36, table 15; USBC, *1970 Census of Population, volume II* (Washington, DC: United States Government Printing Office), 55, table 17; USBC, *1980 Census of Population, volume II* (Washington, DC: United States Government Printing Office), 35. Table 17; Inter-University Consortium for Political and Social Research (IUCPSR), "Study 00003: Historical Demographic, Economic and Social Data: United States, 1790–1970" (Ann Arbor: ICPSR), 25 December 2002, http://fisher.lib.virginia.edu; "Population Estimates, New Jersey," 5 April 2006, http://www.wnjpin.net/OneStopCareerCenter/LaborMarketInformation /lmi02/ncinj.htm.

37. "Franklin Township in School Sit-In," *Newark News*, 13 March 1969.

38. Robert Misseck, "Student Boycott Shuts High School," *Newark Star-Ledger*, 7 April 1973.

NINE

Race and Consumption

The expansion of the black middle class in the United States in the second half of the twentieth century transformed the educational and economic aspirations of African Americans. Between 1790 and 1860, few free blacks could expect equal compensation for the same work that a white person completed. The very idea of black education was highly debatable, even among white Americans who favored the abolition of slavery. One hundred and fifty years later, the institutions of government in New Jersey began the task of redefining the meaning of democracy with the inclusion of the descendants of former slaves. Racial categories had limited African American socioeconomic achievement. African Americans made great economic progress for the first time in American history after 1950. These opportunities changed their interpretation of social equality. Where income, occupation, and education were the keys to African American perceptions of social status between 1800 and 1950, net worth (especially home ownership) and conspicuous consumption emerged as the keystones to black respectability in rural New Jersey by 2000.

Civil rights laws provided the foundation for legal challenges against overt segregation and discrimination between 1965 and 2000. However, widespread poverty, unemployment, and crime often increased in African American neighborhoods in both the Garden State.[1] Rates of black home ownership and new business creation fell in the two decades following the Civil Rights Act of 1965.[2] Black leaders made varying attempts to define a continuing strategy for racial uplift in economic terms after 1970. At the opposite ends of this spectrum were advocates for black capitalism and supporters of black socialism. Conservative commentary emphasized the need for African Americans to participate in the market economy, regardless of whatever disadvantages they encountered in the competition.[3] Liberal analysts asserted that racially motivated disinvestment continued to frustrate economic development in predominantly black cities and towns, fueling a need for cooperative investment strategies with public ownership and profit-sharing agreements.[4] As civil rights laws dramatically increased African American purchasing power, opportunities for industrial- and service-business ownership in black communities of rural New Jersey declined sharply in the second half of the twentieth century.

African Americans became some of the most aggressively acquisitive households in the United States after 1950. In earlier generations, community investment guided much of the spending of the black professional class. From the story of Dr. James Still in the early nineteenth century through the activism of Ermon Jones during the civil rights era, African Americans used their dollars to support projects to transform the life opportunities of their neighbors and children. A different pattern took shape after political integration. Individual spending, driven by sophisticated marketing techniques, dissipated the resources families and communities had relied on twenty years earlier. These fragmented spending patterns simultaneously cloaked the layers of socioeconomic divisions among all Americans and reified the rhetoric of the rugged individual among African Americans in New Jersey's suburbs. Conglomerate consumerism was the system of mergers and acquisitions after World War II that produced the largest private corporations in world history in response to American middle-class consumer habits. In the late twentieth century, this system produced broad but shallow encounters with transient global communities of interest through radio, film, television, and the Internet. This transformation made New Jersey's exurbs the center of several urban networks. These networks formed the Boston–Washington transportation and communication corridor as a single, regional culture and economy after 1970. This regional corridor allowed families, organizations, and businesses access to various forms of human capital around the world. African Americans who participated in the construction and maintenance of these networks became increasingly isolated from both family and neighbors by the start of the twenty-first century.

EARLY HISTORY OF THE BLACK ELITE

Springtown was one of the most significant centers of black professional settlement in the nineteenth century. Founded by free blacks during the period of gradual emancipation in New Jersey, the village became a center for the Underground Railroad and northern abolitionism. Levin Still and his sons, William and James, epitomized the lives of educated African Americans in rural New Jersey before 1900. William lived in Philadelphia and became one of the most important conductors of escaped slaves to the North. James became a medical doctor who was famous throughout New Jersey. His advice to free blacks foreshadowed the accommodations many later African American leaders would endorse in the worst years of Jim Crow segregation: "Merit alone will promote you to respect." His approach to race relations was both dignified and deferential, framing the limits of racial uplift in New Jersey for almost a century.[5]

Several other all-black towns formed in rural areas as a result of African Americans' escapes from slavery before 1870 and their search for work until 1920. Places like Gouldtown, Guineatown, Saddlertown, and Timbuctoo offered chances for a peaceful life, if not total relief from racial segregation.[6] The majority of the residents were working-class or impoverished workers, employed on a daily basis as manual labor or domestic servants.[7] Their lives centered on the sense of discipline and integrity that James Still emphasized in his autobiography. Still wrote, "Should you conduct yourselves on true moral principles, not gaudy in manners nor boisterous in talk, your ways calm and decisive, your word so sacred that 'tis never violated, your promises fulfilled, your debts paid, modest in all things and meddlesome in none, you shall find the monster Prejudice only a thing to be talked about."[8] Without the ability to gather the meager resources available in these small towns, the black residents' dreams of improved lives for their children would remain unrealized.

The few African Americans who achieved professional status in their careers possessed a crucial responsibility in the confrontations with slavery and segregation. Their existence in a nation where nearly every white citizen believed that black excellence was a laughable myth opened the door for social change. Their ability to seize the opportunity to transform the discourse about racial capacities—moral, intellectual, physical, social—laid the foundation for the possibility to imagine a multiracial democracy. In New Jersey, the physical manifestation of black professionals' work was the all-black town. These places functioned to undermine the institution of slavery both covertly through the Underground Railroad and overtly through the promotion of abolitionists' rhetoric and policies. With a base of operations and a cohort of organized families, the impetus for racial equality in the Garden State grew from the fertile soil of black achievement.

The values of black family, history, and leadership required the financial support and collaborative effort of African American professionals in the late nineteenth and early twentieth century. Without the efforts of individuals like William and James Still, there would have been no Underground Railroad, no Tuskegee Institute, no National Association for Colored Women, and no National Association for the Advancement of Colored People in later generations. Educated African Americans reached across socioeconomic divides to work for racial uplift that improved the jobs, schools, and homes of thousands of working-class African Americans in these small towns, as seen in chapters 3 and 4. The steady investment of financial and cultural capital invented the idea of a black race as defined by African Americans. The black image in the black mind offered portraits of decency and dignity in addition to the creation of organizations and institutions for political and economic opportunities. As Anna Julia Cooper wrote, "A sound manhood, a true womanhood is a fruit which the lowliest can grow. And it is a commodity for which the supply never exceeds the demand. There is no danger of the market being glutted. The world will always want *men*. The worth of one is infinite. To this value all other values are merely relative. Our money, our schools, our governments, our free institutions, our systems of religion and forms of creeds are all first and last to be judged by this standard: what sort of men and women do they grow?"[9] Rural resort communities offered places within northern segregation to foster new growth based on the aspirations of the professional classes in the all-black towns.

LONG BRANCH

Imagine life as an emancipated African American after 1870. The struggle to reunite family, to find gainful employment, and to understand the extent of a newly acquired freedom might overwhelm any individual. Now add to this the effort to find a new home, far from the painful reminders of slavery. This was the challenge facing African American migrants to New Jersey. Coming predominantly from Maryland, Virginia, and North Carolina, the new black citizens of the rural corridor settled in places like Long Branch that contained as few as 140 African American residents in 1860 and only 223 by 1880.[10] These few came seeking employment opportunities as waiters, cooks, and janitors at shore hotels like the Arcade, the Ocean, and the Continental.[11] When the railroad lines opened in 1881, they provided additional work for black men as porters.[12] The African American presence in these small towns developed in step with their recreational economy. As affluent whites enjoyed life in the late nineteenth century, they expected black waiters, porters, cooks, and janitors to attend their needs. In 1880, African Americans composed approximately 5 percent of Long Branch's total population.[13] This number grew to over 10 percent just before the First World War.[14] For African American migrants used to smaller, rural settings, Long Branch between 1870 and 1890 combined some of the economic opportunities of a larger city with the comfort of a small community.

Industrial cities attracted the largest numbers of black migrants to the Garden State in the late nineteenth century, obscuring the impact African Americans had on resort towns.[15] Newark and Atlantic City's black enclaves approached ten thousand each by 1910, and over six thousand African Americans lived in Camden during the same period.[16] These larger neighborhoods grew and coalesced around hopes for greater social mobility, creation of religious and social institutions, and a sense of safety in numbers, just as they did on a smaller scale in villages like Long Branch.[17] Even Frederick Douglass had chosen a summer home among the black community in 1892 in Long Branch.[18] The African American population of Long Branch increased tenfold between 1870 and 1900. The new arrivals founded two churches (Second Baptist and Trinity AME) and developed lifestyles that fused elements of both urban and rural living, as Lenora Walker McKay's life showed in chapter 1.[19] Unlike the black migrants from the South who sought employment at the beach every summer, the year-round black residents of the Jersey shore laid the foundation of their new lives with brick and mortar in the form of their homes and churches.

Segregation dominated everyday life along the Jersey shore during the last decades of the nineteenth century. As they did throughout much of the country, African Americans attended separate schools like Brook Street Elementary and churches like Second Baptist because they were treated as second-class citizens in white churches and barred from white classrooms.[20] They could not shop at the Reid Ice Cream Company or Alps Kandy Shoppe or stay in hotels where they worked, such as the Ocean or the Continental.[21] This exclusion allowed local whites to effectively ignore the growing black population on a day-to-day basis. Even in late-nineteenth-century local elections (when black votes might have made a difference), few whites showed any public interest in the lives of local African Americans. Many white voices from that era proclaimed the lack of lynchings and riots in these small towns as an indicator of the area's exemplary race relations. As long as African Americans endured daily comic strips like *Poor Ol' Robinson Crusoe* depicting them involved romantically with apes or *Sambo and His Funny Noises* revealing the stupidity of black social dignity, white leaders and families accepted the presence of a racial minority.[22] Still, the practice of consistent, political repression of African Americans also allowed Long Branch's white population to continue assumptions about their racial superiority. Comments like "Our Negro friends are in their glory. The watermelons are ripe" appeared frequently in the weekly newspapers.[23] These same assumptions cemented white resistance to the social mobility that African Americans sought when settling in Long Branch. Nonetheless, lured by jobs that offered steady pay, over one thousand African Americans lived in Long Branch by 1900.[24]

Despite the organizational success of the black church in the late nineteenth century (see chapter 4), the effects of white supremacy stood out in the Long Branch economy. Prior to 1910, two-thirds of New Jersey's African American population worked in agriculture or domestic service.[25] Between 1870 and 1900, local white employers consistently relegated African American workers to the lower-status, lowest-paying occupations. Many of the black men in Long Branch in the late nineteenth century found employment as waiters or laborers. Black women were most often housekeepers, laundresses, or cooks.[26] This pattern reflects the national trends in black employment, with women and men outside of agricultural work occupied most often as servants or unskilled laborers, respectively.[27]

Given local whites' antipathy toward black residents in Long Branch, why did more African Americans migrate to the area during World War I? Why did Long Branch's black population skyrocket during the fifteen years following the war?[28] Several factors encouraged African American migration, but the major inducement was employment opportunity. Between 1910 and 1930, the number of African Americans working in manufacturing in New Jersey increased from 8,345 to 31,871—a growth rate of over 280 percent. This numerical increase reflected a twofold increase (from 2.1 percent to 4.8 percent) in the percentage of industrial workers who were African American between 1910 and 1930.[29] As elsewhere, the job opportunities provided by the absence of white men because of service during World War I allowed African American migrants to gain industrial jobs for the first time.[30] Opportunities for work at sauce factories in Long Branch like Tomaini and Tomaini and McDowell, Noah, and Company caused the local African American population to grow 120 percent during this period.[31] Between 1900 and 1930, just over 10 percent of Long Branch's garment and canning workers were African American.[32]

With the opening of Fort Monmouth after 1925, economic opportunities for African Americans matched their peaks from the resort's heyday in 1880, as seen in chapter 8. Long Branch's black population reached about 9 percent of the total, mostly because of migrants choosing the town as a second or third stop after arriving in the North.[33] This surge in the African American population occurred even as Long Branch declined as a tourist attraction. Although the overall labor demand in the locality dropped, African American migrants still found work as domestic servants, laundresses, and garment and farm laborers (with very few light industrial workers) until the mid-twentieth century.[34] Women typically gained employment in these fields in larger numbers than men. As a result, adult women in Long Branch outnumbered adult men by a nearly two to one ratio between 1900 and 1930. Women continued to outnumber men—872 to 376.[35] By 1921, African American women worked mostly as domestic servants and semiskilled workers. Black men were mostly unskilled laborers. By 1930, both groups were experiencing higher rates of unemployment due to the Great Depression. Some black men, however, found work as domestic servants or semiskilled workers. The tightening job market may have forced black women into more domestic work from 1930 to 1950, while men moved into the semiskilled positions during the same time period.

Despite the continuing decline of tourism-related employment in Long Branch during the first three decades of the twentieth century (see chapter 8), African Americans were able to find jobs, support families, and form communities because local manufacturers (and, later, a military installation) needed their labor. Local, native-born whites had lost their legendary seaside resort. Black migrants developed a rapidly growing community characterized by its political activism and religious commitment. At the same time, racial tensions grew. Just as the hotels and casinos closed through the first three decades of the twentieth century, Long Branch's small factories were stymied between 1930 and 1941. The Great Depression eliminated jobs for everyone in the town, but African Americans experienced the "last hired, first fired" phenomenon as well. Without jobs, the economic base that empowered black churches and organizations shrank. African American life along the rural corridor's eastern shore lost much of its luster after 1930. This tarnish was especially ugly, given Long Branch's status in the late nineteenth century as the gem of the Jersey coast line.

Vyeta Walker spoke of the despair many felt in 1930 when she said, "At Christmas time one year, we went down to the bank to get our money and everybody was there crying because Citizen National [Bank] was closed, out of business." [36] This dissatisfaction led to a call for political change in Long Branch, as it did across the country. In the 1932 presidential election, Franklin Roosevelt defeated Herbert Hoover in Long Branch 4,699 votes to 3,709 votes, despite split votes for the Democratic and Republican parties in the state and local races. [37] Long Branch textile producers fired nearly a third of their workforce during the early Depression years, but these losses were far smaller than those experienced nationally. In 1934, American Silk Mills employed 295 people and 179 people worked for Long Branch Fur Dressing and Dyeing—a significant reduction in total workers for both businesses. Still, Long Branch continued to house forty-one industrial businesses in 1934. [38] Some recovery occurred over the next four years. Kay-Dunhill, Inc. (a dressmaking company) became Long Branch's leading employer with 360 workers, and A. Hollander and Son, Inc. (formerly Long Branch Fur Dressing and Dyeing) expanded its number of laborers to 281 people. Forty-five industrial businesses operated in the "Branch" in 1938, but hard times continued for many African Americans in New Jersey's small towns. [39]

The presence of African American workers was essential to the image of a prosperous resort town. Long Branch catered to the sensibilities of the white American elites by providing black servants as the final touch of a luxurious vacation. African Americans seized these chances to escape the realities of sharecropping and unsteady maid service. White Americans' desires for comfort shaped the possibilities of better wages for black American workers. In the years following the Civil War, black resort workers in rural New Jersey claimed the legacy of the nineteenth-century black professionals. Long Branch was not only the state's crown jewel of entertainment and vice after 1870. The town was also a portal for black workers seeking better pay, homes, and schools within the restrictions of a segregated society.

Asbury Park and Atlantic City supplanted Long Branch as a tourist destination after 1920. Yet African American migrants continued to arrive in pursuit of futures beyond urban congestion and southern sharecropping. The establishment of military bases like Earle Naval Ammunition Depot and Fort Monmouth failed to employ black workers in the same numbers as the hotels and restaurants had done for the previous generation. National defense and military communication employers denied the intellectual ability of African Americans to successfully execute the required duties until the Second World War.[40] Black service workers reinforced the ideas of racial inferiority, while African American soldiers and technicians challenged those notions. The socioeconomic structure of black communities in rural New Jersey became more complicated after 1940. Early signs of a black middle class between the professionals and the unskilled workers formed around the waiters, chefs, porters, and entertainers by 1950.

RED BANK

Many African Americans also moved to nearby Red Bank between 1890 and 1950 seeking jobs and homes. By 1920, there were several black-owned businesses in the town, most notably a newspaper titled the *Echo*.[41] This setting attracted perhaps the region's most notable African American professional and served as the launching pad for a representative of the emerging black middle class. T. Thomas Fortune and William "Count" Basie symbolized the socioeconomic diversity within the local black community, as seen in chapter 5.[42] Without detailed accounts of black family life for the majority of African Americans in Red Bank, these two men's lives represent an important transition within the rural corridor. Fortune was a member of the national African American elite who chose Red Bank as a quiet retreat near the end of his life. Basie grew up in Red Bank's working-class black community, directly experiencing both educational and occupational discrimination. This created his preference for urban living in New York City during his adult life.

Despite the dignified accommodation that both men embodied in their lives in the region, many Red Bank businesses refused to employ African Americans between 1870 and 1950. Retail shops (and auto dealerships in the early twentieth century) relied on comfort, knowledge, and trust between their customers and salesmen. Local white businessmen did not consider any of the nearly one thousand local African Americans qualified for these jobs. African Americans still found work as personal servants, coachmen at horse and carriage shops, and janitors at the few local hotels.[43] Some blacks like Joseph White, a domestic servant in Justice Henry J. Childs's office, and William Reid, a sexton at the Second National Bank, held domestic and personal-service jobs.[44] These occupations generally paid little, so black families in Red Bank often took in boarders to help with expenses. Reid, a single man, was an exception to this rule and acquired ownership of three houses on the west side of town.[45] Work was also available at timber mills along the river and with the Eisner Company making uniforms.[46] Overall, the small towns along the Jersey shore presented opportunities for black migrants, but often the cost was the acceptance of prevailing systems of racial oppression.[47]

Survival was the primary concern among the recent migrants and unskilled workers of the late nineteenth century in the rural corridor. With few friends and family available, African Americans tried to secure steady work first, and then sent word to their families to follow. Black professionals like the Still family in Burlington County and George White's investment group in Cape May County encouraged church attendance and good work habits between 1870 and 1910. The emphasis on Christian stability in the small towns proved successful in places like Long Branch by 1920. Living simple lives of work, faith, and thrift enabled African Americans to acquire homes, to build schools, and to send a child to high school or college (as seen in the first half of this study). Historian Robert Weems notes that efforts like those in rural New Jersey led to surges in black literacy, employment, and income nationwide.[48] Self-help and racial accommodation helped rural black communities grow throughout the state. The larger racial ideologies regarding white supremacy and black inferiority buttressed white Americans' general resistance to the recognition of the achievements in the black community as seen in chapters 3, 4, and 5.

ASBURY PARK

Consumer power provided one method to challenge prevailing ideas about racial differences and their social importance. In the decade following the First World War, condescension and ridicule characterized the little attention whites paid to black workers as consumers. Despite the increasing income of African American households as they migrated to new regions like rural New Jersey, white business owners routinely excluded them from their shops. This discrimination against a growing segment of the market stimulated the growth of black-owned businesses between 1920 and 1950. All-black towns created branches of the National Negro Business League to encourage African American consumers to purchase from black-owned businesses.[49] In places like Long Branch, African American consumers filed lawsuits to gain access to beaches, restaurants, and stores as early as 1921 (as shown in chapters 3 and 5).[50] Previous generations of black professionals built a framework for survival within the northern Jim Crow system. The emerging consumer power of the black working class developed into a chance to challenge the entire structure of racial oppression. When Eugene K. Jones asserted that African Americans held nearly two billion dollars in purchasing power in 1935, he framed an argument for black equality in financial terms that national corporations and the federal government could understand.[51]

Ada Bryan's life in a resort town illustrates the transformation of black consumption between 1920 and 1950. Her family moved from the Newark area to Asbury Park in 1922. They encountered discrimination and segregation immediately, as they were denied access to the home they had purchased before the realtor realized that they were African American. Both she and her parents experienced discrimination on the job and as consumers through 1970. Despite the racial restrictions they faced, the Bryan family enjoyed their life at the shore. Bryan only possessed an eighth-grade education, and she maintained a life full of career achievements, church leadership, and political involvement. Her childhood shows several facets of social life for black families in rural New Jersey. "I played hide and seek, hopscotch, jacks. I liked ice skating in the winter, and I could play some tennis. In Asbury Park, it was sleigh riding. There was a place called Sand Hill, and all the kids would go up on the hill and come down on their sleighs."[52] The community-oriented games reflected the widespread interactions among the town's children outside of the formal settings of work, school, or church, even though informal types of racial segregation remained prevalent. While travel formed a part of the family's recreation, many of the ways Ada enjoyed herself as a child did not cost much money. Money was a resource reserved for more serious endeavors among rural African Americans before 1940.

One of the few indulgences that Bryan's father allowed was the purchase of a radio for the family. She recalled hearing Kate Smith singing "America, the Beautiful" and listening with rapt attention to the nightly news broadcasts. The Hindenburg disaster also made a strong impression on Bryan. "I can still hear the reporter's voice in my ear. He was so, so upset. Everybody in my house was crying."[53] Her first experience of television was at the 1939 World's Fair, where she also saw an exhibit illustrating the growth of highways filled with thousands of cars. Bryan came to Asbury Park to enjoy a slower, less urban lifestyle than her family had in Newark. Yet the radio kept them connected to the larger world in ways that foreshadowed the role of television and computers in the late twentieth century. The Bryan family did well enough to vacation around the region on an annual basis. Ada kept a fascination with the innovations of the future, even if she preferred a quieter life in a simpler place.

One of the recurring keys to the quality of life the Bryan family enjoyed in Asbury Park was the ability to own a home. Beyond the initial access to a steady job that earlier migrants had needed to settle in the rural corridor, home ownership transformed the long-term possibilities for socioeconomic improvement. Black consumers who could secure a property in a small town became part of the vanguard of the civil rights movement during the middle decades of the twentieth century. Educated African Americans believed that systems of local, state, and federal government could be reformed through organizations like the NAACP and the National Urban League between 1920 and 1970. These groups provided security and agency in the pursuit of equal rights.[54] In Bryan's case, her home became the foundation for her career, church work, and political activism. Working-class and poor African Americans struggled to survive economically in their communities and potentially alienating a landlord with civil rights activism posed an unnecessary risk.[55] Even in the absence of a high-school education, Bryan enjoyed a life that most black domestic servants and manual laborers could barely imagine two generations earlier. In the larger urban areas of New Jersey, home ownership before 1950 was extremely rare.[56] As black residents overcame discrimination in purchasing a home, their children's educational achievements improved. "When we cut through the disadvantages of class, African Americans actually demonstrate a greater level of commitment to education than their white counterparts, despite anecdotal or ethnographic evidence to the contrary. Within comparable economic strata African Americans behave in much the same way that many other ethnic, national, or religious minorities do: they put great stock in education as a route to upward mobility. Net worth is the second most important predictor of attaining the increasingly important college degree (after parental education level)."[57] The transformation of the black community in rural New Jersey between 1920 and 1950 indicated the power of African American consumers in terms of political reform and educational access. "The [consumer society] provided a wide range of black Americans with an available and legitimate recourse for challenging racial discrimination. Mass consumption begot a mass civil rights movement."[58]

Bryan's narrative also illustrates how the technological and commercial changes between 1940 and 1970 affected the lifestyle of the black middle class. Her childhood involved many of the same games and interactive experiences of larger cities.[59] She enjoyed a familiar world of frequent contacts with other children and adults that fulfilled the hopes of nineteenth-century black professionals like James Still. As Bryan grew older and the economic prospects in resort towns like Long Branch and Asbury Park declined after 1970, entertainment technologies like radio, television, and the movies became a larger part of her recreational experience. Her family's success in becoming part of a black middle class could be measured by the new technologies they brought into the home. The function of commercial media in the home coincided with the corporate realization of black consumer power. As a result, the expanding black middle class used its increased influence to abolish northern Jim Crow in the state legislature and to gain access to the public spaces (restaurants, hotels, and stores) that were denied their parents and grandparents. The most influential product of this activism was the Urban Colored Population Commission to the state legislature, which guided civil rights reforms at the state level for a decade. The commission's report declared, "Every resource must be utilized in an uncompromising campaign to make the virtues of democracy mean something more than empty, insincere words."[60] The sacrifices among New Jersey's black professionals at the start of the twentieth century opened the door for families in small black communities to pursue their individual dreams of consumer spending.[61]

Born in 1924, Ermon Jones lived in Neptune, New Jersey, his whole life. Jones's parents had moved to Neptune from Virginia in an effort to secure a better chance for their children's college education. Ermon graduated from Neptune High School in 1942 before serving in the United States Army from April 1943 to December 1944. Jones then completed his bachelor of science degree at Morgan State University in May 1951 and his master of science degree from Columbia University in December 1951. His career in signal technology engineering at Fort Monmouth stretched from 1952 to 1986. He retired from the army as the chief of the Equal Opportunity Office. Like Ada Bryan, Jones's life reflected the transformation of the black middle-class experience in rural New Jersey.

Jones's work as a civil rights leader in the region helped define racial equality throughout the state. In 1959, Jones filed suit against a suburban housing developer in Neptune who refused to sell homes to African Americans. The New Jersey State Supreme Court ordered the developer to open home sales to all potential buyers, regardless of race, in 1964. Jones also started one of the first federal Head Start programs in the region that year. Over the next four decades, thousands of children received early-childhood education that surpassed the resources many African American children received through the sixth grade before 1940. Jones's efforts with the local NAACP, Board of Education, Board of Chosen Freeholders, and county planning board expanded the chances for African Americans to work safer jobs, to earn higher pay, to own better homes, and to achieve higher degrees of education.[62] All of these achievements rested on Jones's successful completion of college and his employment with the United States Army's Electronics Command, especially as the Equal Employment Opportunity officer from 1969 to 1976.[63] Jones displayed his leadership and negotiation skills during the height of a confrontation between the state legislature and the Neptune school district between 1967 and 1972. From 1969 to 1972, a group of white parents worked under the name of the Consolidated Citizens Organization to prevent school integration. Superintendent Victor Christie asserted that he would exhaust all legal alternatives to prevent "some students" from returning to the schools "permanently."[64] Jones challenged the underlying assumptions behind Christie's reasoning. "Racism is a fact academic institutions must live with but constantly seek to root out. It is odd how expeditiously we attempt to eliminate or solve racial problems legally rather than attack these situations humanely."[65] Christie and Jones continued to negotiate the ways white teachers and black students had to adapt to each other. By 1976, the Consolidated Citizens Organization disbanded, and all students could attend Neptune High School without incident.[66]

When Jones demanded the end of residential segregation and educational discrimination, he championed a legacy of racial uplift that reached back into the nineteenth century. The 1964 formation of the Head Start program traced its roots back to the segregated schoolhouses in Franklin and in Freehold through its founders and staff who remembered the lessons of black agency these institutions offered. The 1959 housing lawsuit relied on the claim of black consumer power that had developed over the previous twenty years. Placing these changes in national context requires an acknowledgement of racial transition in suburbs across the country. African Americans who succeeded in challenging the racial restrictions on home ownership, education, and employment often found that white neighbors, educators, and employers would leave the area rather than tolerate civil rights reforms.[67] The activist, black middle class in rural New Jersey underestimated the strength of white resistance to racial integration. African Americans could participate in conglomerate capitalism at the local level by shopping at the nearest mall, but white Americans had little interest in greater social contact. As a result, suburban development in New Jersey's rural corridor displaced and uprooted many rural black communities like Timbuctoo and Gouldtown by forcing African American families into larger cities like Newark or suburban slums like Asbury Park after 1970.

Jones's life also illustrates the reliance of the black middle class in small metropolitan suburbs on governmental employment. His career with the United States Army kept him at the Jersey shore. Many other African American households in New Jersey gained civil-service jobs as the legislative reforms for racial equality swept through the state and federal legislatures.[68] This dependence on the public sector for stable employment made the black middle class vulnerable to political shifts at the end of the twentieth century and placed a lower ceiling on the potential lifetime earnings of their households, compared to similarly educated, white households in the same period with access to private-sector jobs.[69] This employment pattern expanded the consumer power among African Americans in the middle class. Yet black households became more aggressively acquisitive (and less organized as activists) after

1970.[70] While the northeastern megapolitan became the center of a global information economy, African Americans like Ada Bryan and Ermon Jones lost the access to participate in the political, economic, and cultural choices that shaped their towns. Jones said, "Public corruption continued to frustrate economic growth here in Asbury and Neptune, especially under Governor Christie Whitman."[71] Conglomerate strategies for mass marketing transformed the function of black consumerism from a vehicle of political agency into a symbol of integrationist acceptance by a color-blind society. Bombarded by commercial images daily, the black middle class lost its historic connection to the mission of racial equality in the United States after 1970. "The collective wisdom of the past generation has not been transmitted to the new one. The end result is symptomatic not only of the bankruptcy of corporate capitalism vis-à-vis its ability to meet the fundamental needs of masses of people, but also of the fundamental shortcomings of solutions and strategies proposed by both the Civil Rights and Black Power movements a generation ago."[72]

African Americans at the start of the twenty-first century reflected much of the social isolation that characterized the entire nation at the time.[73] Market segmentation divided the society by race, gender, religion, age, and geography. Even individuals within families found less common time to share and communicate with each other. The loss of a common sense of purpose made New Jersey's metropolitan communities disconnected culturally from the global economy their residents managed and organized during the workweek. Mass media in all its forms fostered oversimplified answers to prepackaged questions, undermining critical thought and public engagement. Falling into paradigms of a "classless" nation and individual meritocracy, middle-class African Americans in New Jersey's small towns stopped organizing groups for social change as they did before 1950 (see chapters 3 and 5). Buying the newest television,

Figure 9.1.   Battleground Ridge development, Manalapan (Walter David Greason, 2001) As black resort and farm workers struggled to keep their homes in the rural corridor, real estate developers made record profits by building large, expensive homes where African American families used to live.

computer, or cell phone became the focus of personal freedom. Sustained commitment to community organizations appeared old-fashioned and out of date. The abolition of legal segregation failed to achieve the dream of racial integration as the black middle class decided that style was preferable to substance. James Still, Vyeta Walker, and Ermon Jones all used the resources at their disposal to create systems of social justice that would dismantle white supremacy in theory and in practice. Without the same commitment to community engagement at the end of the twentieth century, black Americans became increasingly materialistic after 1950. (See Figure 9.1.) In this way, the trends toward greater social isolation had profound consequences for race relations.[74] While all Americans experienced fewer opportunities to develop social capital through leisure activities and private organizations, African Americans continued to carry an additional burden of spatial isolation based on their racial identity. The consumer culture that emerged after 1950 emphasized individual satisfaction in ways that disrupted the relationships that sustained churches, schools, and civil rights organizations between 1920 and 1970.[75] In that sense, consumerism as a force was color-blind, but its effects remained racially disparate because of continuing residential segregation based on race.

African Americans in New Jersey have the opportunity to revitalize their communities and the global struggle for human rights by engaging in the reformation of segregated institutions like corporations, universities, and churches. Martin Luther King Jr. said in 1967, "We as a nation must undergo a radical revolution of values."[76] He spoke directly to the crisis of global capitalism. Corporations did not adopt the principles and values of the civil rights movement and the Black Freedom struggle between 1955 and 1972. Chapters 10 and 11 will show that the global service economy developed in ways that reflected the continuing denial of African American agency that white migration from black towns represented over the last half century. As chapter 6 demonstrated, the preservation of white privilege maintained gross inequalities of personal and national wealth that stymied any movement toward international human rights by maintaining racial inequality in the United States.[77] Uneven development on a global scale relies on the isolation of individuals in their small towns. Black middle-class consumption fueled the continuing uneven development of metropolitan New Jersey, as seen in the collapse of resort towns like Long Branch, Red Bank, and Asbury Park in the next chapter.

NOTES

1. Myron Orfield, *American Metropolitics: The New Suburban Reality* (Washington, DC: Brookings Institution, 2002), 23, 49.

2. Robert E. Weems Jr., *Desegregating the Dollar: African American Consumerism in the Twentieth Century* (New York: New York University Press, 1998), 80–116; Manning Marable, *How Capitalism Underdeveloped Black America: Problems in Race, Political Economy, and Society* (Cambridge, MA: South End Press, 1983), 133–68.

3. Claud Anderson, *PowerNomics: The National Plan to Empower Black America* (Bethesda, MD: PowerNomics Corporation, 2001), 31–62; Thomas Sowell, *Basic Economics: A Common Sense Guide to the Economy* (New York: Basic Books, 2007), 495–17.

4. Marable, *How Capitalism*, 255–65.

5. Giles R. Wright, *Afro-Americans in New Jersey: A Short History* (Trenton: New Jersey Historical Commission, 1988), 39–41.

6. Ibid., 39.

7. Walter D. Greason, "From Village to Suburb: Race, Politics, and Economics in Monmouth County, New Jersey, 1890–1990," PhD diss., Temple University, 2004, tables 3 and 4.

8. Wright, *Afro-Americans in New Jersey*, 41.

9. Anna Julia Cooper, *A Voice from the South* (Xenia, OH: The Aldine Printing House, 1892), 281.

10. Wright, *Afro-Americans in New Jersey*, map 4. Estimate; Monmouth County Archives (MCA), *Enumeration 1880*, schedule 1. Few African Americans resided in resort towns throughout the year before 1890, so these figures mostly reflected migrant laborers.

11. Gabrielan, *Images of America: Long Branch*, 34, 77, 90.

12. Ibid., 56.

13. MCA, *Enumeration 1880*, schedule 1.

14. New Jersey Bureau of the Census (NJBC), *New Jersey State Census—1895* (ms.), schedule 1.

15. Barbara Cunningham, ed., *The New Jersey Ethnic Experience* (Union City, NJ: William H. Wise and Company, 1977), 77.

16. Wright, *Afro-Americans in New Jersey*, 45.

17. Ibid.

18. NJWP, *Entertaining a Nation*, 44; John W. Blassingame and John R. McKivigan, eds., *The Frederick Douglass Papers: Series One: Speeches, Debates, and Interviews*, vol. 15, *1881–1895* (New Haven, CT: Yale University Press, 1992), xxvii.

19. McKay, *The Blacks of Monmouth County*, 45; NJWP, *Entertaining a Nation*, 174, 181, 189; James Borchert, *Alley Life in Washington: Family, Community, Religion, and Folklife in the City, 1850–1970* (Chicago: University of Illinois Press, 1980), xii.

20. NJWP, *Entertaining a Nation*, 164; McKay, *The Blacks of Monmouth County*, 45.

21. Wright, *Afro-Americans in New Jersey*, 49–52; NJWP, *Entertaining a Nation*, 164; Ku Klux Klan, *KlonKlave Souvenir Program*, 4 July 1925, George Moss Collection, Long Branch, NJ.

22. Cartoons like these appeared in the *Asbury Park Evening Press* regularly between 1909 and 1911.

23. "Shore Briefs," *Shore Press*, 15 August 1879, 5.

24. NJBC, *New Jersey State Census—1895* (ms.), schedule 1.

25. Egerton E. Hall, *The Negro Wage Earner in New Jersey: A Study of Occupational Trends in New Jersey, of the Effect of Unequal Racial Distribution in the Occupations, and of the Implications for Education and Guidance* (New Brunswick, NJ: Rutgers University Press, 1935), 27.

26. MCA, *Enumeration 1880*, schedule 1; NJBC, *New Jersey State Census—1895* (ms.), schedule 1.

27. USBC, *Negro Population in the United States*, 508.

28. Cunningham, *The New Jersey Ethnic Experience*, 77. New Jersey's black population tripled from just fewer than 70,000 to approximately 210,000 between 1900 and 1930; Wright, *Afro-Americans in New Jersey*, 56–57. Maps 6 and 7 (for 1910 and 1930, respectively).

29. Hall, *The Negro Wage Earner in New Jersey*, 31, 48.

30. Ibid., 27, 47–48; August Meier, *Negro Thought in America, 1880–1915* (Ann Arbor: University of Michigan Press, 1966), 170.

31. Mary B. Sim, *Commercial Canning in New Jersey: History and Early Development* (Trenton: New Jersey Agricultural Society, 1951), 427.

32. USBC, *Fourteenth Census of the United States—New Jersey (1920)* (ms.), schedule 1.

33. NJWP, *Entertaining a Nation*, 133.

34. Sim, *Commercial Canning in New Jersey*, 217; Maurice Mustin, ed., *A Sketch of Monmouth County, New Jersey, 1683–1929* (Camden, NJ: M. Mustin Co., 1929), 37; Hall, *The Negro Wage Earner in New Jersey*, 37.

35. USBC, *Negro Population in the United States*, 771, table 1.

36. Vyeta Walker, interview, 5 December 2000.

37. "The Vote of Monmouth County," *Long Branch Daily Record*, 9 November 1932, 9.

38. Bureau of Statistics and Records, New Jersey State Department of Labor, *The Industrial Directory of New Jersey—1934* (Trenton: New Jersey Industrial Directory Publishing Company, 1934), 274.

39. Bureau of Statistics and Records, New Jersey State Department of Labor, *The Industrial Directory of New Jersey—1938* (Trenton: New Jersey Industrial Directory Publishing Company, 1938), 424–25.

40. Richard Thomas, "Blacks and the CIO," in *Civil Rights Since 1787*, ed. Jonathan Birnbaum and Clarence Taylor (New York: New York University Press, 2000), 292–97.

41. "A Monmouth County League," *Red Bank Register*, 24 October 1888; "Lived over 100 Years," *Red Bank Register*, 30 October 1912; McKay, *The Blacks of Monmouth County*, 73–81.

42. Emma Lou Thornbrough, *T. Thomas Fortune: Militant Journalist* (Chicago: University of Chicago Press, 1972), 289–91; Count Basie and Albert Murray, *Good Morning Blues: The Autobiography of Count Basie* (New York: Random House, 1985), 24.

43. NJBC, *New Jersey State Census— 1915* (ms.), schedule 1; Hall, *The Negro Wage Earner in New Jersey*, 39–40.

44. "Digs His Own Grave," *Red Bank Register*, 19 February 1913, 2; "Slave and Soldier," *New Jersey Standard*, 26 October 1901. Both men also fought in the Civil War.

45. Ibid.

46. Gabrielan, *Red Bank in the Twentieth Century*, 12, 18–19.

47. Greason, "From Village to Suburb," tables 12 and 13.

48. Weems, *Desegregating the Dollar*, 9–10.

49. Juliet E. K. Walker, *History of Black Business in America: Capitalism, Race, Entrepreneurship* (New York: Twayne Publishers, 1998), 182–224.

50. "Long Branch Unit NAACP," 30 August 1940, box C: 108, file "Long Branch, 1940–1944," group II, National Association for the Advancement of Colored People (NAACP), Library of Congress (LOC); "Long Branch NAACP Chartered," 8 December 1940, box C: 108, file "Long Branch, 1940–1944," group II, NAACP, LOC.

51. Weems, *Desegregating the Dollar*, 28–29.

52. June West, "Interview with Ada Bryan," 17 October 1999, in *Remembering the Twentieth Century: An Oral History of Monmouth County*, ed. Flora T. Higgins, http://www.visitmonmouth.com/oralhistory/.

53. Ibid.

54. Andrew Weise, *Places of Their Own: African American Suburbanization in the Twentieth Century* (Chicago: University of Chicago Press, 2004), 129–32.

55. Robin D. G. Kelley, *Race Rebels: Culture, Politics, and the Black Working Class* (New York: Free Press, 1994), 82–84.

56. Lizabeth Cohen, *A Consumer's Republic: The Politics of Mass Consumption in Postwar America* (New York: Alfred A. Knopf, 2003), 171.

57. Dalton Conley, *Being Black, Living in the Red: Race, Wealth, and Social Policy in America* (Los Angeles: University of California Press, 1999), 56, 75, 81.

58. Cohen, *A Consumer's Republic*, 190.

59. Caroline Goodfellow, *How We Played: A History of Childhood Games* (New York: The History Press, 2008), 3–5.

60. Cohen, *A Consumer's Republic,* 181.

61. Ibid., 406.

62. June West, "Interview with Ermon Jones," 5 September 1999, in *Remembering the Twentieth Century: An Oral History of Monmouth County,* ed. Flora T. Higgins, http:// www.visitmonmouth.com/oralhistory/.

63. "Equal Opportunity Fighter Administers Fort Agency," *Asbury Park Sunday Press,* 12 October 1969; "For Community Service," "Ermon Jones file" folder, Neptune, NJ, Segregation and Fire Services, 1970–1976, Court Street School Education Community Center archive.

64. "Neptune High Disorders Discussed," *Asbury Park Evening Press,* 24 February 1972, 1, 3.

65. Ermon K. Jones, "Response to Public Comments and Recommendation of the Superintendent of Schools Dr. V. J. W. Christie at the Board of Education Meeting, 23 February 1972," "Ermon Jones" file folder, Neptune, NJ, School Integration, 1972, Court Street School Education Community Center archive.

66. "Dismissed City School Board Attorney Defended," *Asbury Park Press,* 14 September 1976, D-1.

67. Andrew Wiese, *Places of Their Own,* 247–49.

68. Jaime J. Fader, Michael B. Katz, and Mark J. Stern, "The New African American Inequality," *Journal of American History* 92, no. 1 (June 2005): 90–92.

69. Ibid., 107; Conley, *Being Black,* 95–101.

70. 70. Wiese, *Places of Their Own,* 218; Weems, *Desegregating the Dollar,* 103–5; Conley, *Being Black,* 105–7.

71. Ermon K. Jones and Blanche Jones, interview transcript, 18 July 2008.

72. Ernest Allen Jr., "Making the Strong Survive: The Contours and Contradictions of Message Rap," in *Droppin' Science: Critical Essays on Rap Music and Hip Hop Culture,* ed. William Eric Perkins (Philadelphia: Temple University Press, 1996), 184.

73. Neil Postman, *Amusing Ourselves to Death: Public Discourse in the Age of Show Business* (New York: Penguin, 1986), 135–36.

74. Robert D. Putnam, "Bowling Alone: America's Declining Social Capital," *Journal of Democracy* 6, no. 1 (1995): 66–70.

75. Conley, *Being Black,* 15, 29–30; Weems, *Desegregating the Dollar,* 100–4, 116.

76. Martin Luther King Jr., "A Revolution of Values," *Spirituality and Practice,* accessed 14 May 2008, http://www.spiritualityandpractice.com/quotes/ quotes.php?id=18695.

77. Chuck Collins and Felice Yeskel, eds., *Economic Apartheid in America: A Primer on Economic Inequality and Insecurity* (New York: The New Press, 2005), 59.

TEN

Metropolitan Poverty

The suburb as a nineteenth- and twentieth-century phenomenon defies the conventional stereotype of the affluent, white enclave. Andrew Wiese and Becky Nicolaides have troubled this image by exploring the working-class suburbs and suburbs of color that existed in the United States over the last two centuries.[1] By proposing a framework for the study of metropolitan regions, Wiese and Nicolaides draw attention to the processes of suburbanization rather than the descriptive characterization of these spaces in both the past and the present. Metropolitan spaces include urban, suburban, and rural areas in both the nineteenth century and the twentieth century. However, the idea of metropolitan space still lacks specificity when applied to areas where people did not travel frequently or rapidly from urban center to rural enclave. The distant suburb in the late nineteenth century often resembles many farming or resort communities before 1920. This intellectual haze cannot withstand the historical scrutiny that accompanied the emerging centrality of the modern suburb as the building block of residential life in the twenty-first century. In the northeastern United States before 1920, there were rural, suburban, and urban areas, but the extent of social contact and interaction across those political boundaries remains unclear. Expansive Main Line mansions outside Philadelphia coexisted peacefully among hundreds of square miles of farms and orchards. The recreational escape from the city that the barons of industrial wealth sought required the presence of the countryside, or the farm and village. Few workers maintained the frequency of travel between the industrial center and rural fringe that characterized the social elites. Understanding the variations of the socioeconomic experience of the metropolitan region is crucial to an examination of the processes of urbanization, suburbanization, and rural contraction.

141

The suburb, the proximate retreat, emerged on the urban periphery—most commonly, the adjoining periphery. Reliance on street cars and carriages, along with the limited development of labyrinthine road systems, discouraged suburban development outside of the immediate environs of major cities. This limitation preserved the countryside as a distant escape from the pace of urban and emerging suburban culture. Only after 1940 did the exurb—the independent suburb—emerge. Automobiles facilitated a daily commute ranging over twenty miles and more as the century proceeded. More importantly for the suburban historian, the fast-paced lifestyle of the inner-ring suburb increasingly supplanted the seasonal rhythm of rural culture. The exurb began to consume the farm. This process was essential to the consolidation of the metropolitan region. Vast areas of isolated space frustrated economic growth and social exchange in the nineteenth and early twentieth century. However, the growing connections among metropolitan spaces reproduced many of the racial and socioeconomic boundaries that defined these earlier periods.[2] Working-class and African American suburbs are just two of the types of metropolitan spaces that illustrate this problem.

Andrew Wiese offers an initial framework for the discussion of black suburbs within a larger suggestion of working-class suburbs in American history. The four types of suburbs he describes are based on either occupational experiences or spatial design features—industrial suburbs, domestic-service suburbs, unplanned subdivisions, and bungalow suburbs. Industrial suburbs conformed to the model of ethnic European urban enclaves, characterized by dangerous labor and unsafe living conditions. Domestic-service suburbs grew in response to the demand for black labor by white elites and offered some greater flexibility for black owners. Unplanned subdivisions provided the greatest autonomy for African Americans, but also the least legal protections for their property rights. Bungalow suburbs were almost exclusively located in the South and counted black professionals (educators, ministers, etc.) as their residents. As useful as this framework is, there remains room for refinement. In particular, questions about the distinctions between rural and suburban in the case of the domestic-service and unplanned subdivision suburbs as well as the differences between urban and suburban space vis-à-vis industrial suburbs persist.[3] While urban, suburban, and rural land uses compose aspects of a broader metropolitan category, historians must be careful not to overlook these distinctions and their basis in historical experience. Cities, farms, and suburbs are intentional spaces. People have alternately pursued political power and public resources as both ends and means. When real estate developers and politicians collaborated in the writing of land-use legislation, their primary goal was the completion of a short-term residential commercial project. The passage of the legislation led to the repetition of the same process without careful oversight for decades. These efforts produce metropolitan spaces that simultaneously reinforced and undermined racial inequality. As a result, overt racial segregation became embedded in the economic justifications for metropolitan sprawl.

In the consideration of metropolitan areas, the patterns of uneven development deserve closer scrutiny. The processes of suburbanization focusing on fringe residential growth outside of major cities reflect similar transformations of rural areas into suburbs beyond the range of urban municipal borders. To consolidate the concept of metropolitan regions that include urban, suburban, and rural spaces, scholars must account for all facets of social and physical movement. The examination of resort towns like Red Bank, Long Branch, and Asbury Park, New Jersey, which blended rural and suburban characteristics at the start of the twentieth century, reveals the consistency of uneven development after 1960 with earlier patterns of racial segregation. The resilience of white supremacy in both residential and commercial spaces over this time period demonstrated the limitations of African American agency throughout the twentieth-century Black Freedom Movement. The framework of African American activism often initiated a transition from white segregationist municipal authorities to black integrationist elected leaders between 1965 and 1980. As white social and economic disinvestment in urban centers and older suburbs occurred, the economic foundations of the Black Freedom Movement collapsed.[4]

There are many potential starting points for a productive inquiry into the various kinds of suburban regions in New Jersey. Due to the fragmented nature of the surviving sources within the state's multiple municipal madness,[5] local and oral histories provide crucial hints. Careful scrutiny and analysis yield a narrative that addresses the following questions: How racially homogeneous were suburban and rural populations in the first half of the twentieth century? How did migration—local, regional, national, and international—shape these populations at different points? Did northern Jim Crow dictate the patterns that were later reinforced by socioeconomic forces in the private real estate market? The examination of Red Bank, Long Branch, and Asbury Park demonstrates the complexities of both prosperous and impoverished populations in metropolitan settings. Within the framework of global megapolitans in the United States, pockets of uneven development as represented by these towns emerged by 2000. In New Jersey's rural corridor, areas of suburban poverty and nonwhite population density resulted from the collision of planning policy, service economics, and conglomerate consumerism. The concentration of the black and Latino upper-working classes (predominantly employed in public governance) in county seats and smaller exurban boroughs only exacerbated the neglect of the suburban poor and the insulated affluence of the white and Asian immigrant elite households.

RED BANK

One of the smallest New Jersey resorts in the twentieth century; Red
Bank had a general population that grew slowly between 1890 and 1950.
The local retail economy rested on two department stores, the Globe
Hotel, and two manufacturing plants. The only trolley lines in Monmouth County between 1900 and 1920 ran in Red Bank. Major rail lines
and steamboat ports connected to all of central New Jersey through the
small town.[6] It experienced a significant increase of European immigrant
residents between 1895 and 1915.[7] Men like Basil Bruno—a child of Italian immigrants who sought their American dream in Red Bank—were
elected to public office and actively pursued their cultural assimilation
into an American cultural mainstream typified by the dominance of Anglo-Saxon and Protestant values. Life experiences like Bruno's preceded
the widespread transformation of late-nineteenth-century "new immigrants" into "average Americans" after the Second World War.[8] However, native-born whites remained the majority population, and local progressive Republicans demonstrated the same racism and nativism that
characterized the nation in the early twentieth century. Red Bank's Ku
Klux Klan demonstrated its popularity during the 1920s by holding numerous parades and newspaper polls.[9] Few of the largest enterprises
survived the Great Depression, and many local white entrepreneurs fled
to neighboring municipalities. During the 1940s and 1950s, Eisner's uniform factory continued to employ the largest numbers of workers, followed by several civil-engineering firms and electronics suppliers.[10]
While once it was the epitome of white middle-class life in Monmouth
County, Red Bank became a burned-out shell by the 1970. As local investors sought greater economic opportunity in commercial and residential
development in western Monmouth County, the retail economy in Red
Bank fell into disarray. The suburbanization of central New Jersey reflected the uneven development of metropolitan expansion that characterized the phenomenon across the country.[11] Suburbanization attracted
many more residents and businesses to small towns that competed with
each other for tax revenue and state grants to maintain and expand their
water, sewer, and electrical infrastructure. As a result, the fastest-grow-
ing communities received public financial support at the expense of their
neighbors.

Despite the prevalence of racial discrimination, many African
Americans moved to Red Bank between 1890 and 1950 seeking better jobs
and homes. By 1920, this town was a center for black economic achievement in the area.[12] Several of Monmouth County's most politically and
socially active black organizations operated out of Red Bank.[13] Leaders
like Arnold Rock and Dr. James Parker Sr. established benchmarks for
social achievement in Red Bank, as seen in chapters 3 and 4. Long-standing institutions such as Saint Thomas Episcopal Church, Calvary Baptist

Church, and the Knights of Pythias Lodge provided bases for community education and cooperative economic support for local African Americans.[14] Even during the economic downturn of the 1930s, these organizations helped keep people employed, fed, and housed. African American hopes for jobs, homes, and prosperity were frustrated as the declining retail economy buckled under the pressure of nonexistent private investment during the Cold War era. Churches and community institutions could no longer meet the overwhelming demand for economic support from a larger population.

By 1946, the national Young Men's Christian Association disallowed segregated branches, but the well-organized Westside Y persisted until 1958 because the local black middle class supported it. Several families created an enduring fund-raising and cultural pride event through the YMCA in 1950 when they developed a debutante cotillion. The event was a celebration of youth, beauty, parenting, and scholarship. Twenty-eight debutantes appeared at the first cotillion, and the number increased steadily through the next decade. Count Basie even agreed to come back to his hometown and play for the event in 1952 and 1956, adding prestige to the festivities.[15] Local black professionals sustained the tradition of black leadership in Red Bank that persisted past 1970. The existence of a rural black middle class during the middle decades of the twentieth century adds complexity to the analysis of metropolitan development. Not only did these African American families maintain networks of survival, solidarity, and success across geographic and socioeconomic boundaries, but their ability to effectively challenge white authority reshaped the spatial and racial relationships that defined political and social integration in their communities between 1940 and 1970.[16]

African Americans in Red Bank in the first half of the twentieth century built their homes and churches in the shadow of intransigent racial assumptions about their appropriate roles in the resort community. White tourists expected to be served by black service workers. They believed that African American servers provided a level of comfort and quality that no other ethnic group could provide.[17] If white employers and patrons did not value black workers during this period, African Americans would have likely experienced a greater degree of outright hostility in response to their growing numbers. Racial segregation in small towns like this one reconciled the white desire for social status and white revulsion at the presence of black people in general. The success of individuals like Fortune and Basie does not indicate a broad opportunity structure for African American success in the segregated environment. However, their achievements do show a determination on the part of black workers to improve their social and economic circumstances in these communities, where white assumptions about their role allowed the possibilities of home ownership and secondary or higher education. White Americans' paternalistic views of African Americans and their allegedly racial inferiority had its roots in the eighteenth century. In one breath, white racial philosophers of the early twentieth century described black people as children. In the next, they conjured the dangers of racial contact using images of Africans as beasts.[18] African Americans like Rock and Parker established churches, benevolent societies, and community organizations that contradicted this discourse. Within the black community, they taught the lessons of family, history, and race leadership through the first half of the twentieth century.

These segregated institutions within the black community had the ability to teach families how to adapt to the unique racial atmosphere in the rural North.[19] For southern migrants and new arrivals in northern cities, these groups provided invaluable messages and strategies about surviving the first months and years in New Jersey's rural corridor. White commitment to segregation did not wane in these years, and the frequent contact between white authorities and black workers required greater negotiation of the racial politics in small towns than the violence of the rural South or the blanket exclusion of the urban North. The difficulties arose when new leadership in these black communities tried to challenge the previously accepted limits on their freedom. By adapting so flexibly on a regular basis, the infrapolitics of resistance in the rural North developed more slowly than it did in other black communities, as chapter 4 showed.

When southern African Americans packed their bags or sabotaged their employers' farms before the Great Migrations to the North, their actions furthered a strong tradition of resistance against the abuses of slavery and sharecropping. Northern African Americans openly defied white mob rule and governmental suppression through increasingly effective use of the ballot during the first half of the twentieth century. In small-town New Jersey, neither of these paths of resistance could yield the same successes for racial equality. Any advancement in race relations relied on the maintenance of mutual respect between white authorities and black institutions.

LONG BRANCH

Located in the middle of Monmouth County's eastern shore, Long Branch emerged as a major tourist destination for the affluent after 1870. Illicit activities including gambling drove Ocean Township's (the original name of the incorporated municipality) rapid development from 1870 to 1900.[20] However, by 1920, Long Branch's resort status had declined precipitously. Political transformation did not accompany the economic changes of the early twentieth century. Long Branch remained a haven for the Democratic Party in Monmouth County. Political stability combined with economic changes to open the town to European immigrant and African American workers, but the native-born white citizenry only tolerated these groups as long as they did not challenge the social status quo. The Great Depression effectively ended significant economic opportunity in Long Branch, while new towns adjacent to the city sprang up. Oceanport, Monmouth Beach, and West Long Branch each had fewer than 1,000 people in 1920. Between 1930 and 1940, Long Branch's population declined slightly from 18,000 to under 17,500. Meanwhile, Oceanport, Monmouth Beach, and West Long Branch all experienced notable growth.[21] Many of the remaining citizens of Long Branch joined the public welfare rolls or struggled to find work on the farms in Colts Neck, Howell, and Freehold. Between 1940 and 1990, Long Branch's retail stores, textile and paint factories, and tourist attractions (most notably, its recreational pier and boardwalk) served as the basis of its weakened economy. Despite this resilience, Long Branch's population declined between 1970 and 1990, with white entrepreneurs leading the exodus. Only one of Monmouth County's top ten employers operated in Long Branch after 1990.[22] This dip in economic opportunity combined with the population decline to complete the resort's collapse.

The African American presence in Long Branch paralleled the development of its recreational economy. As the affluent enjoyed life there in the late nineteenth century, they expected black waiters, porters, cooks, and janitors to attend their needs. However, as Jewish and Italian immigrants took jobs in the growing garment industries, African American migrants replaced the immigrants as domestic servants, laundresses, and porters in the hotels, homes, and train cars.[23] Local African Americans formed four churches, a chapter of the NAACP, and a branch of the American Legion between 1870 and 1930.[24] African Americans constituted a larger percentage of Long Branch's population in the decades after World War II, reaching 20 percent by 1980.[25] As central New Jersey developed as a region through the remainder of the twentieth century, working-class and poor African American families faced greater social and spatial isolation.

Second Baptist Church served as an organizational center for many of the social and political activities the growing African American community in Long Branch demanded. Several pastors guided the church between 1910 and 1930, including Reverend Emmett Flowers, Reverend Albert S. Grayson, Reverend R. C. Williams, and Reverend L. K. Jackson. Flowers focused his energies on the development and expansion of the church building, helping to make it a source of pride for the black congregants.[26] His successor, Reverend Grayson, established a community-oriented atmosphere in the church that inspired greater ambition and achievement among the worshippers. Vyeta Walker, a young member of the church under Grayson, recalled: "We used to have morning and evening services. Back then, you had to testify to join church, and, then, when you went to school the next day, [the] teacher wanted to see a change in our lives. Christmas programs were the best with our oranges, candy, presents, and recitations. Church was the place to be on most days of the week."[27]

Church programs stimulated the sense of belonging among the migrants in their new home and gave opportunities to take pride in individual and collective accomplishments. Walker also underscores the interconnections between religious and secular life during this period. The importance of reinforcing moral lessons and social customs at home, in school, and at church stands out as a part of the foundation of this emerging culture. The most decisive victory for Long Branch's black community during this era was also a product of leadership based in Second Baptist Church. Ministers organized the campaign and civil suit that led to the legal demise of segregation at New Jersey beaches in 1939. The little surviving evidence shows that they pulled together financial and advisory support from local social clubs, the NAACP, and the other churches.

> On July 17, 1938, Mrs. Allie Bullock applied for a permit and was assigned to Beach No. 3, the segregated beach. She requested a permit for one of the other three beaches but was refused a permit to any save Beach No. 3. Attorneys Robert S. Hargrove, Walter J. Upperman, and Robert M. Yancey, representing the Long Branch, New Jersey, branch of the NAACP filed a petition for a writ of Certiorari on August 29, 1938. On September 11, 1939, the New Jersey Supreme Court denied certiorari but established the rights of Negroes to be protected from segregation.[28]

This victory proved fleeting as local resistance continued in spite of the order. McKelvie continued to protest the exclusion of African Americans at beaches 1 and 2 through October 1940 because their proprietors defied the court's order.[29] Continuing legal challenges stalled as miscommunications between the local and national NAACP offices multiplied. In at least one case, the national NAACP did not take the small black community seriously.[30] The spatial and social isolation of rural and suburban African American communities within the metropolitan milieu did not prevent civic engagement and political activism within these communities. Instead, black families referenced national organizations and state affiliates as symbolic leverage in their negotiations with white authorities about segregated public facilities and legal claims to uphold and recognize black property ownership.[31]

Most of the successes African American leaders secured affected the occasional access to public spaces in rural resorts like Long Branch. In many small resorts, legal challenges formed the next level of conversation to gain some foothold for the improvement of social conditions facing African Americans. However, these efforts encountered the reality that municipal, state, and federal courts all affirmed the property rights of white businessmen before any consideration of African American protection from discrimination.

New Jersey resembled much of the Mid-Atlantic region in its struggles for enfranchisement of African Americans, which did not begin to reshape state politics until 1945. Nearly a full generation of African American migrants to the major cities was needed before civil rights issues gained any momentum in the state legislature. Even with African Americans as a significant minority voting bloc, the concessions to African American community leaders' demands for social reforms did not occur until political pragmatism coincided with cultural embarrassment in the wake of global confrontation with Nazi propaganda about racial superiority. White supremacy could no longer be valid if it was the primary platform of the German government. Americans died to prevent the spread of that ideology. Elected officials used the vocabulary of social science to articulation the foundations of human equality as part of the superiority of the United States.[32] Yet this process of rhetorical transition only changed formal policies like the desegregation of industrial employment and the armed forces slowly.[33] African Americans in small towns like Long Branch continued to face public segregation and discrimination in the workplace after 1950. Worse, the adaptation of segregation and discrimination to a metropolitan environment in the second half of the twentieth century made legal challenges to continuing inequality much more difficult.[34] As the evidence in chapter 7 showed, color-blind racism continued to obstruct progress towards racial equality between 1970 and 2000.

Both the local and the national NAACP focused on the most obvious examples of racial inequality in their efforts to enforce equal protection of the law as guaranteed by the Fourteenth Amendment. The inadequacy of these tactics became apparent in New Jersey's rural corridor as the area transformed into a network of suburban communities. Wealth became the singular barrier to spatial integration across the historic race line. Black institutions continued to target public spaces, job discrimination, and educational access, but none of the reforms enabled African American families to secure more valuable homes, to open new business ventures, or to experience income from capital investments until the last decade of the twentieth century. Instead, the legislative accomplishment of racial integration caused black home and business ownership in small towns to plummet. Formerly middle-class families struggled to maintain the traditions of consistent employment, community investment, and personal thrift. Debt became the marker of black identity after 1970, and it was a burden that isolated African Americans in the rural North as effectively as Jim Crow ever had.

ASBURY PARK

As Long Branch's tourism declined early in the twentieth century, Asbury Park's prosperity grew. This resort town offered middle-class visitors a casino and larger boardwalk than Long Branch's and was less expensive. James Bradley, a devout Christian and founder of Asbury Park, committed the community to temperance by requiring alcohol prohibition clauses in all commercial deeds.[35] In the late nineteenth century, the town became the local stronghold for progressive Republicans who espoused political reform and Protestant "blue laws."[36] Between 1880 and 1940, the dominant attitudes of white Protestant supremacy crossed partisan political lines in central New Jersey as they did across the country. Meanwhile, Asbury Park's tourism economy suffered a slow decline between 1930 and 1960, losing many Philadelphians and New Yorkers to Atlantic City, with its thriving boardwalk and hotels.[37] As one local writer commented in 1945, "Originally established for healthy recreation, [Asbury Park] has now become a congested resort with no real character of its own. . . . It has been transformed from a proper and popular facility to a hodgepodge of catchpenny devices and competitive bazaars."[38]

After decades of population growth, Asbury Park experienced a loss of residents after 1930.[39] World War II brought renewed economic opportunity to Asbury Park. Fort Monmouth and Earle Naval Ammunition Depot offered new jobs in eastern Monmouth County between 1940 and 1960. In Asbury Park, the federal government purchased the convention hall, the YMCA, and several hotels for military use.[40] As a result of hurricane and storm damage to the Asbury Park boardwalk in 1945, these military bases supplanted tourism as the foundation of Asbury Park's economy.[41] Unemployment reached nearly 10 percent by 1950 and remained steady through 1990.[42] By the end of the twentieth century, Asbury Park no longer attracted fashionable visitors and vacationing families. The town had become the shame of central Jersey's suburban paradise.

The black community in Asbury Park faced an intolerant social and political atmosphere throughout the twentieth century. Despite these obstacles, by 1910, more African Americans lived in Asbury Park than in any other municipality in Monmouth County.[43] By 1940, African Americans had founded local chapters of the UNIA and the NAACP, and had established several large churches, like Saint Augustine's Episcopal, Mount Pisgah Baptist, and Bethel AME.[44] A small group of African American professionals (mainly preachers, educators, and morticians) coalesced to serve the larger group of black workers. Fort Monmouth and Earle Naval Depot attracted so many African American scientists that the area became known as the "Black Brain Center."[45] African Americans continued to enjoy Asbury Park's newly desegregated beaches and attractions as their local population surged between 1940 and 1960. Asbury

Park's population stabilized through the second half of the twentieth century, hovering around seventeen thousand. Income levels, property values, commercial development, and employment opportunities, on the other hand, declined. While the neighboring municipality of Ocean City experienced dramatic population increases, especially among second-generation, middle-class Latino, Asian, and Middle Eastern migrants, Asbury Park became increasingly working class and black.[46] In fact, this was the only municipality in the county with a majority black population after 1980. Asbury Park residents argued that the city had been "redlined for commerce." A growing population of "deinstitutionalized people," welfare recipients, and parolees repelled prospective local investors. Furthermore, two-thirds of Asbury Park residents did not own a car, so they were unable to seek employment outside of the city.[47] There is no public transportation connecting the towns in Monmouth County, a limitation that maintained the high unemployment and poverty rates in Asbury Park. By 1990, 30 percent of African Americans lived below the poverty line, and 14 percent were unemployed (compared with a 22 percent poverty rate and 13 percent unemployment rate in 1960).[48] Poor families from throughout the region increasingly found their homes in Asbury Park as the end of the twentieth century approached.

As surrounding suburban areas developed into some of the most desirable communities in the nation, Asbury Park took on characteristics of an inner city.[49] The local patterns of uneven metropolitan development reflected the national trends regarding suburban racial transition. As the rural corridor in New Jersey connected the metropolitan regions of New York and Philadelphia, black farming communities either vanished under the bulldozer's plow or moved into impoverished suburbs. These patterns unfolded in many states, especially in the Northeast and Midwest. The combination of poverty, racism, and physical isolation created an experience of oppression that resembled the worst aspects of segregation and sharecropping in the rural South.[50] The final blow to the prosperous resorts along the central Jersey shore was the race riots that swept through Asbury Park and Red Bank in 1969 and 1970. These violent eruptions bore similarities to the conflagrations that consumed major American cities between 1960 and 1970. Protests over inadequate housing, police brutality, and joblessness sparked tensions between African Americans and local authorities. The worst conflicts occurred during the second week of July 1970, when Asbury Park and Red Bank burned. Official estimates placed fewer than one hundred young rioters in each city, but local residents (especially in Asbury Park) claimed the crowds were larger.[51] In Asbury Park, the Monmouth Community Action Program (MCAP) met with white mayor Joseph Mattice in the days following the riot to address community demands, ranging from youth employment to increased low-income housing to hiring black police officers. Mattice ignored eyewitness accounts that civilian peacekeepers (requested by local authorities) were arrested and overlooked MCAP leaders' demands for urban renewal to construct new low-income housing, new schools, and a revitalized business district.[52] In Red Bank, noncompliance with the demands made by the NAACP Youth Council after the 1969 riot led to the resurgence of violence in 1970. After one year, Red Bank officials had rejected a three-million-dollar renewal project because they did not want to increase the number of multifamily units in the town, and police complained openly about community oversight of their activities.[53] Following these upheavals, white flight accelerated, and county planners surrendered their hopes of revitalizing these communities.[54] This abandonment of civil engagement through the 1970s and 1980s exacerbated the problems of unemployment, poverty, and crime in these areas. In small communities, the tragedies of rigid racial boundaries in both public discourse and residential space were perhaps more profound than in the major cities. Just as these communities' residents needed to rally together to maintain their local economies in a globalizing context, the painful, personal repercussions of rioting and the backlash of law enforcement drove people apart.[55] As historians consider the connections among the towns that constitute metropolitan regions, the resistance to break down racial barriers becomes clearer.

COMMON THEMES

These three formerly golden resorts languished between 1971 and 1991. De facto segregation and enormous drug crises expanded through the African American communities on the west side of each town. White families moved out of the towns and into neighboring municipalities in droves and organized to prevent tax increases to support school construction, welfare programs, and hospital staffing under the "home rule" provisions of the New Jersey Constitution. The flight of white families from older suburban resorts and the concentration of rural black families within their decaying boundaries revealed the bankruptcy of any optimism regarding American race relations in this period. The collapse of the resort economies as a result of highway and air travel merely sealed the local residents' sense of collective doom.[56] Upper- and upper-middle-class residents of New York and Philadelphia no longer planned weekend getaways to the Jersey shore, especially not to Asbury Park or Red Bank. If a family could afford it, Florida, California, Europe, Australia, and South America beckoned. Even the less affluent did not settle for less than Atlantic City or Las Vegas. In the era of integration, only the white poor and working class continued to visit the deteriorating catchpenny towns in central New Jersey. The remains of the black middle class that had grown in these towns steadily drifted into the older suburbs of the region like Montclair, Haddonfield, and Franklin.

The collapse of Asbury Park as a rural resort was a result of the concentration of poverty among its remaining residents after 1970. Several small towns throughout New Jersey experienced similar economic contractions to one degree or another. This process resembled the deindustrialization that swept through larger northeastern and midwestern cities during the same period. However, the demise of the recreational economy destroyed the foundation of the Black Freedom Movement and the possibility of a racially just society in New Jersey at the end of the twentieth century. Where large, industrial communities often experienced severe tensions between racial groups from the beginning of their economic growth, black and white Americans in rural communities often shared an inconsistent and uneasy intimacy. The negotiations over segregation and the absence of major outbreaks of violence (such as the lynching tradition in the South or the massive, urban riots of the North) allowed a sense of steady transformation toward a more egalitarian society, especially in the eyes of many black middle-class families and leaders.

Hypersegregation describes the process of urban isolation of chronically unemployed people of color in America's largest cities. Douglas Massey and Nancy Denton provide clear evidence of this recurring pattern in the context of deindustrialization across the country.[57] In New Jersey, these patterns emerged as the rural communities became part of the metropolitan tapestries outside of New York and Philadelphia. The riots targeting white-owned properties in New Jersey's rural corridor expressed the frustration of young African Americans who had been taught to cooperate with authorities in exchange for small improvements in their social status. As hypersegregation effectively transformed whole towns into prisons without any opportunity for communication, transportation, or wealth accumulation, civil rights leaders like Ermon Jones struggled to convince young people that the Black Freedom Movement still had meaning in their lives.[58] The processes of uneven metropolitan development abandoned the people and institutions that had done the most to prove that American democracy was truly based on the promise of equality for all people.

CONCLUSION

The burgeoning black middle class that formed after 1940 failed in their efforts to sustain these towns. Where there had been only maids, ditch diggers, and the occasional waiter or porter in the early twentieth century, a new generation of doctors, dentists, and engineers arrived. Attracted to the rural North by the slower pace of its lifestyle, the possibilities of owning both land and businesses, and the negotiable status of racial segregation in public facilities, jazz-generation African Americans held debutante cotillions, organized assertive chapters of the National Associa-

Figure 10.1.   New Horizons Development Just outside Englishtown, low-income housing resembled single-family, middle-class suburbanization in other parts of the area. The irony is that the community was built on the land that had been one of the largest migrant labor camps in the rural corridor before 1960—Pergolaville.

tion for the Advancement of Colored People, and financed ambitious capital projects for community improvement through their churches. These families participated in the national Double V campaign in World War II through black newspapers like the *Pittsburgh Courier* and the *New Jersey Afro-American*.[59] They pressured local white politicians to allow access to secondary education for their children. They worked high-profile, white-collar jobs at the military signal lab and weapons depot. These communities represented a moment in American history when the possibility of racially inclusive suburbs was not an ideal, but a reality. After 1970, pockets of uneven development stretched from Somerset County to Gloucester County. Suburban poverty and residential overcrowding resulted from the failures of planning policy, service economics, and conglomerate consumerism to recognize the achievements of black community institutions over the previous fifty years. (See Figure 10.1.) African Americans and Latino immigrants who enjoyed the good fortune to secure public employment at the county or state level in these exurbs scarcely impacted the lives of the suburban poor.

Metropolitanization destroyed the possibility of survival for integrated northern suburbs. As private-sector industrial jobs moved first to the undeveloped land surrounding these rural resorts and then overseas to countries seeking manufacturing investment, the black working class (that had built the economic foundation for middle-class achievement between 1920 and 1940) collapsed under the spatial isolation of hypersegregation. Despite the limited agency of the emerging black middle class in the North, the emigration of white working-class families and the wholesale loss of the resort and industrial job opportunities for the black working class combined to transform thriving rural resorts into impoverished suburbs. Increasingly after 1960, people who had been productive, educated workers found their children's opportunities for success circumscribed. By 1973, the dreams of unlimited opportunity that were rooted in the *Brown* decision were dashed. Instead, drugs, crime, and violence became the hallmarks of life in these empty resorts. The social instability fueled a cycle of cultural and economic isolation that persisted through the end of the twentieth century.

NOTES

1. Becky Nicolaides and Andrew Wiese, eds., *The Suburb Reader* (New York: Routledge, 2006), 8.
2. Myron Orfield, *American Metropolitics: The New Suburban Reality* (Washington, DC: Brookings Institution, 2002), 49–53.
3. Andrew Wiese, *Places of Their Own: African American Suburbanization in the Twentieth Century* (Chicago: University of Chicago Press, 2004), 25–28.
4. Jeanne Theoharis and Komozi Woodard, *Freedom North: Black Freedom Struggles outside the South, 1940–1980* (New York: Palgrave McMillan, 2003), 302–7.
5. Alan J. Karcher, *New Jersey's Multiple Municipal Madness* (New Brunswick, NJ: Rutgers University Press, 1998), 205.
6. Randall Gabrielan, *Red Bank in the Twentieth Century* (Charleston, SC: Arcadia Publishing, 1997), 8–9, 18–19, 23–28, 51, 74; Maurice Mustin, ed., *A Sketch of Monmouth County, New Jersey, 1683–1929* (Camden, NJ: M. Mustin Co., 1929), 43; Mary B. Sim, *Commercial Canning in New Jersey: History and Early Development* (Trenton: New Jersey Agricultural Society, 1951), 41–57, 72–73, 247–49.
7. New Jersey Bureau of the Census (NJBC), *New Jersey State Census— 1895* (ms.) (Manalapan), schedule 1; NJBC, *New Jersey State Census—1915* (ms.) (Manalapan), schedule 1.
8. Herbert J. Gans, excerpt from *The Levittowners*, in *The Suburb Reader*, ed. Weise and Nicolaides, 318–20.
9. Henry Jensen, "Klan to Parade Today," *Red Bank Register*, 11 November 1925, 13.
10. Hudson Dispatch, *The Industrial Directory of New Jersey—1946–47* (Union City, NJ: Hudson Dispatch, 1946), 525–26; Hudson Dispatch, *New Jersey Industrial Directory—1954–55* (Union City, NJ: Hudson Dispatch, 1954), B270–B272.
11. John R. Logan and Harvey L. Molotch, *Urban Fortunes: The Political Economy of Place* (Berkeley: University of California Press, 1987), 135.
12. "A Monmouth County League," *Red Bank Register*, 24 October 1888.
13. "Monmouth County Afro-Republican League," *Red Bank Register*, 3 September 1902, 10; "National Negro Business League," *Red Bank Register*, 20 March 1907, 1.
14. Lenora W. McKay, *The Blacks of Monmouth County* (privately published, 1976), 45–47; Gabrielan, *Red Bank in the Twentieth Century*, 56.
15. Ibid.
16. Wiese, *Places of Their Own*, 156–57.
17. Myra B. Young Armstead, *"Lord, Please Don't Take Me in August": African Americans in Newport and Saratoga Springs, 1870–1930* (Urbana: University of Illinois Press, 1999), 83. Armstead asserts that resort employers in her cases shifted to immigrant service workers at the end of the nineteenth century, but Jersey resorts like Long Branch, Asbury Park, and Red Bank continued to rely on African American service workers as late as 1950.
18. George M. Fredrickson, *The Black Image in the White Mind: The Debate on Afro-American Character and Destiny, 1817–1914* (Hanover, NH: Wesleyan University Press, 1971), 285–90.
19. Bruce D. Haynes, *Red Lines, Black Spaces: The Politics of Race and Space in a Black Middle Class Suburb* (New Haven, CT: Yale University Press, 2001), 5.
20. Cleveland Armory, *The Last Resorts* (New York: Harper and Bros., 1948), 19, 282.

21. MCPB, *MCD&E Updates, Estimates, and Projections*, 8. Oceanport was not organized until 1930. In 1940, Oceanport's population numbered nearly 3,200.

22. Ibid.; MCPB, *Monmouth County Profile 1997*, 18.

23. Sim, *Commercial Canning in New Jersey*, 217; Mustin, ed., *A Sketch of Monmouth County*, 37; Egerton E. Hall, *The Negro Wage Earner in New Jersey: A Study of Occupational Trends in New Jersey, of the Effect of Unequal Racial Distribution in the Occupations, and of the Implications for Education and Guidance* (New Brunswick, NJ: Rutgers University Press, 1935), 37.

24. Randall Gabrielan, *Images of America: Long Branch, People and Places* (Charleston, SC: Arcadia Publishing, 1998), 126; McKay, *The Blacks of Monmouth County*, 45; New Jersey Writers Project, *Entertaining a Nation* (Bayonne, NJ: Jersey Printing Company, 1940), 174, 181, 189.

25. Wright, *Afro-Americans in New Jersey*, 71.

26. C. P. Williams, ed., *Second Baptist Church 100th Anniversary Booklet* (privately published, 1987), not paginated.

27. Vyeta Walker, interview transcript, 5 December 2000.

28. *Annual Report, NAACP* (1939), 21–22.

29. Williams, ed., *Second Baptist Church 100th Anniversary Booklet*, not paginated; John P. Mulligan, "Perspective on Civil Rights in New Jersey," *New Jersey Education Association Review*, 29, no. 7 (March 1956), 295; "Long Branch Unit NAACP," 30 August 1940, box C: 108, file "Long Branch, 1940–1944," group II, NAACP, LOC; "Long Branch NAACP Chartered," 8 December 1940, box C: 108, file "Long Branch, 1940–1944," group II, NAACP, LOC.

30. "Long Branch NAACP Chartered," 8 December 1940, box C: 108, file "Long Branch, 1940–1944," group II, NAACP, LOC; NAACP to McKelvie, 14 April 1942, box C: 108, file "Long Branch, 1940–1944," group II, NAACP, LOC; Barnett J. W. Grier to Ella Baker, 27 March 1944, box C: 108, file "Long Branch, 1940–1944," group II, NAACP, LOC.

31. Wiese, *Places of Their Own*, 75–82.

32. John P. Jackson Jr. and Nadine M. Weidman, *Race, Racism, and Science: Social Impact and Interaction* (New Brunswick, NJ: Rutgers University Press, 2006), 183–88.

33. Jonathan Birnbaum and Clarence Taylor, eds., *Civil Rights since 1787: A Reader on the Black Struggle* (New York: New York University Press, 2000), 307–8, 388–95.

34. Charles M. Lamb, *Housing Segregation in Suburban America since 1960: Presidential and Judicial Politics* (New York: Cambridge University Press, 2005), 2–4.

35. Women's Club of Asbury Park, *An Historical Review of Business and Other Organizations Operating in Asbury Park* (Asbury Park: City Publication, 1929), 2.

36. Ransome E. Noble, *New Jersey Progressivism before Wilson* (Princeton, NJ: Princeton University Press, 1946), 69. Although Noble cites the formation of a formal "New Idea" progressive organization in Monmouth County in 1906, the values and attitudes which led to the creation of that county organization manifested in Asbury Park from its founding in 1879.

37. Thomas Fleming, *New Jersey: A Bicentennial History* (New York: W. W. Norton and Company, Inc., 1977), 143–44.

38. W. Earle Andrews, *Asbury Park Beachfront Improvement* (New York: privately published, 1945), 12.

39. Monmouth County Planning Board (MCPB), *Monmouth County Demographic and Economic (MCD&E) Updates, Estimates, and Projections* (Freehold, NJ: Monmouth County Planning Board, 1997), 8.

40. McKay, *The Blacks of Monmouth County*, 34–38. Signal labs in Long Branch, Asbury Park, and Red Bank all attracted African American workers. Many of these workers were migrants from Virginia, North Carolina, South Carolina, and Georgia.

41. Andrews, *Asbury Park Beachfront Improvement*, 12, 20.

42. USBC, *1950 Census of Population, Volume 2*, 86, table 36; USBC, *Census Tracts—Monmouth County, 1990*, table 8.

43. United States Bureau of the Census (USBC), *Negro Population in the United States, 1790–1915* (New York: Arno Press, 1968), 771, table 1.

44. Pike, *Images of America: Asbury Park*, 62; WCAP, *An Historical Review of Business*, 52, 55; McKay, *The Blacks of Monmouth County*, 45, 46, 98.

45. McKay, *The Blacks of Monmouth County*, 38.

46. MCPB, *MCD&E Updates, Estimates, and Projections*, 8; USBC, *Census Tracts— Monmouth County, 1980*, tables P-7, P-14, and P-15.

47. State Redevelopment Office, *Focus Group: Urban Problems in Asbury Park* (Shrewsbury, NJ: Monmouth County Library, Eastern Branch, September 27, 1994), 21–22, 31–33, 51; MCPB, *MCD&E Profile*, 1:40.

48. USBC, *Census Tracts—Monmouth County, 1990*, tables 22, 23, 28, and 29; USBC, *1960 Census of Population*, vol. 2, part 32 (Washington, DC: Government Printing Office, 1962), 250, 264, tables 76 and 77.

49. Arnold R. Hirsch, "Less than Plessy: The Inner City, Suburbs, and the State-Sanctioned Residential Segregation in the Age of *Brown*," in *The New Suburban History*, ed. Kevin M. Kruse and Thomas J. Sugrue (Chicago: University of Chicago Press, 2006), 51–53.

50. Thomas J. Phelan and Mark Schneider, "Race, Ethnicity, and Class in American Suburbs," *Urban Affairs Review* 31, no. 5 (May 1996): 665–67.

51. "Disorders Wrack City; Mayor Orders Curfews," *Asbury Park Evening News*, 6 July 1970, 1, 3–4; "State, Local Policemen Guard West Side Ruins," *Asbury Park Evening Press*, 7 July 1970, 1, 3–4; "Mobs Halted in City; Red Bank, Freehold Hit," *Asbury Park Evening Press*, 8 July 1970, 1, 6.

52. "Demands Not Met, Negroes Maintain," *Asbury Park Evening Press*, 8 July 1970, 1, 4.

53. "Red Bank Officials Puzzled as New Disturbances Flare," *Asbury Park Evening Press*, 8 July 1970, 6.

54. MCPB, *The Urban Communities Study Series: Red Bank, New Jersey* (Freehold: MCPB Publication, 1977), 7.

55. Thomas J. Sugrue and Andrew P. Goodman, "Plainfield Burning: Black Rebellion in the Suburban North," *Journal of Urban History* 33, no. 4 (May 2007), 591–93.

56. Clay McShane, *Down the Asphalt Path: The Automobile and the American City* (New York: Columbia University Press, 1994), 123. While emphasizing the middle class's audacious optimism about cars and "flying machines," the inverse effect occurred among the working classes and poor people in rural New Jersey.

57. Douglas Massey and Nancy Denton, *American Apartheid: Segregation and the Making of an Underclass* (Cambridge, MA: Harvard University Press, 1998), 74.

58. Ermon Jones, "Housing and Head Start Issues," Court Street School Education Community Center file, Freehold, NJ, 2009.

59. Kevin Mumford, *Newark: A History of Race, Rights, and Riots in America* (New York: New York University Press, 2007), 33.

ELEVEN

Metropolitan Growth and Exclusion

Suburbanization offered many improvements in terms of access to water, electricity, and efficient waste disposal that rural areas could not provide without better roads systems and energy infrastructure. Technology improved health care, work conditions, and residential architecture by connecting New Jersey's farms more directly into the world economy. The rural corridor ceased to be an isolated region within the megapolitan—it became the heart of the metropolitan region. The cost of this incorporation was the acceptance of uneven development that reproduced the racial segregation and discrimination that shaped the resort and agricultural spaces. Uneven development operated in at least two dimensions, spatially and economically.[1] While the most prosperous residential communities in Moorestown, Princeton, and Rumson expanded their wealth during the suburban explosion, several communities, like Willingboro, Glassboro, and Asbury Park, became impoverished suburbs as part of the same process. Assets, jobs, and education were readily accessible on one side of the equation, while racial minorities, immigrants, and the poor found fewer chances than their parents to avoid jail and improve their living conditions.

In contrast to Red Bank, Long Branch, and Asbury Park, three farming towns demonstrate the transformations of New Jersey from the Garden State to the Suburban State. Manalapan shows how the fruit orchards of the state changed and the rapid displacement of the migrant workers who tended the fields. Freehold reveals the concentration of lower-income families in a smaller geographic area, while surrounded by massive residential and commercial expansion. Howell experienced massive overdevelopment after 1940, leading to significant challenges to the traditional ideas about limited government influences in small towns. The exclusion of working-class families of color from the mechanisms of metropolitan development betrayed the possibility of color-blind democracy in the twenty-first century. Instead, suburban municipalities in New Jersey competed against each other with greater ferocity over the last three decades of the twentieth century, driving tax rates inexorably higher for everyone. Multiple municipal madness was the end result of an uncritical resistance to racial and socioeconomic integration under the guise of fiscal responsibility and meritocracy.

MANALAPAN

Manalapan Township maintained its rural atmosphere and agricultural economy longer than most towns in the rural corridor. Manalapan was a tiny municipality among the most rural areas through the first half of the twentieth century. It did not begin its suburban, residential transformation until the late 1960s.[2] Once it started, commercial developers followed quickly, hoping for a population explosion in Manalapan akin to those in other parts of the state. They were not disappointed. The Great Depression's effect on Manalapan greatly reduced living standards for local farmers. As one local historian noted, "The Great Depression . . . was especially devastating and many farmers were forced out of business and lost family farms owned for generations."[3] While older urban centers like Newark collapsed and early suburbs like Pasadena, California, slowed, rural life in these towns nearly stopped.[4] However, competition from farms in the Midwest intensified after 1950, rendering local farms obsolete. This agricultural decline stymied the growth of an African American community that approached one thousand residents for the first time in 1960.

Between 1960 and 1970, Manalapan's total population increased nearly fivefold as the residential development wave swept across the area's farms.[5] White residents from New York and Philadelphia fled from the ongoing legal changes in response to the civil rights movement to the safety and isolation of rural New Jersey. This pattern repeated itself throughout the second half of the twentieth century. Numerous developers made fortunes selling homes on land that had provided jobs just ten years earlier. New recreational parks and Revolutionary War battlefield memorials replaced the various farms and orchards of the previous period. Instead, a nationally known raceway and regional outdoor auction (both located in Manalapan) represented the area through the second half of the twentieth century.[6] Without the jobs to support themselves, working-class African Americans did not contribute to the population boom between 1960 and 1990. The overall black population in the area declined every decade during the period as the in-migration of commuting, middle-class families did not offset the departure of older residents. Latino and Asian communities also grew significantly in Manalapan.[7]

The influx of commercial and residential developments occurred later in Manalapan because the local planning boards and real estate developers focused on the more accessible towns along state highways. However, the developments in Manalapan also revealed black working-class enclaves that struggled to maintain their homes and property against this postindustrial progression. The consequences of suburban development for the borough center and African American workers loomed ominously through the 1980s. The small town effectively became a playground for suburban families, while working-class black families left the surrounding area. The stories of many black families, forced out of migrant laborer housing in Manalapan, lack the letters and diaries to document their pain and determination. Still, the racially diverse and growing community of middle-class families in Manalapan faced a turning point by 1990—duplicate the prior patterns of suburban assimilation or create a new standard for multicultural, multiclass residential living.

Grains like corn and barley provided the stable base for farms in these towns as early as the late nineteenth century. However, as farms in the Midwest moved into that market around the turn of the century, Manalapan and Englishtown production shifted to egg farming, as well as apples, pears, barley, and strawberries.[8] Englishtown served as the commercial hub for Manalapan with both a train station for the Freehold–Jamesburg Agricultural Railroad Company and the Monmouth County Farmers' Exchange.[9] With few roads and a peripheral location at the county's western boundary, Englishtown and Manalapan never became a significant political center. The area followed the overall shift in the region by becoming moderately Republican after World War I.[10] Though the Depression set many farmers back, agriculture remained the leading economic force in the area into the 1960s.[11] Many of the local white families traced their roots back through this soil for several generations.[12] Rural life constituted the existence they knew best and preferred most.

The formula for economic success in these municipalities between 1930 and 1960 was simple. Grow the products that will sell in the fall, put them on the train to markets across the Northeast region, and watch the money return the next year. The Freehold–Jamesburg Agricultural Railroad connected Middlesex County farms (like Seabrook) out to ports at the shore, starting in 1853.[13] Locally, it collected grain and corn during the nineteenth century, then eggs, potatoes, tomatoes, and cucumbers through the first half of the twentieth century.[14] Even as late as 1940, Manalapan led farming-heavy Monmouth County in the production of fruit, and it also stood among the area leaders in barley, wheat, egg, corn, soybean, and tomato production.[15] The Monmouth County Farmers' Exchange operated in Manalapan starting in 1912. They coordinated discount prices for farm supplies for local growers in conjunction with the North Shore Market Growers Association.[16] The only local industrial plant in the early twentieth century consisted of the Evans Tomato Facto-ry, which closed before World War I. [17] Its failure signified the dominance of agriculture for municipal economic success over the next five decades.

After World War I, local Republicans seized control of municipal poli-tics. Mayor A. T. Applegate guided the Englishtown borough council, while other major Englishtown farmers like Edward Hendrickson served on Manalapan's township committee, despite the ostensible separation of the two municipalities in 1888. [18] These politicians were not supporters of racial equality by any means. Still, they did acknowledge the utility of black political support through the early twentieth century. Manalapan did not systematically exclude black voters. However, a dozen black votes in a close election could have conceivably affected the outcome. The local population changed little between 1880 and 1930, hovering between 1,500 and 2,000 people. [19] Over the following three decades, the towns' total population increased from approximately 2,200 to 5,100 people. [20]

Jewish migrants to the area during this period settled on the fringes of the township and organized mutual loan societies to assist home owners. Jews in Manalapan formed a smaller portion of the local population than in neighboring communities, but they worked as egg farmers in the same tradition as the larger Jewish settlements. As in the rest of the rural corri-dor, they faced anti-Semitism in the form of business loan discrimination and social ostracism, but overcame it after World War II through military service, cultural assimilation, and improvements in their economic posi-tion. The Manalapan Township Committee turned down Kervork Hov-nanian's application to build housing developments twice with mention of his Jewish heritage as part of the reasoning after 1960. However, by 1970, the committee recognized the enormous tax income these develop-ments would generate and approved his application. [21] This increasing diversity of the white community in Manalapan coincided with the fun-damental economic shift that would change the area for the remainder of the twentieth century.

This town in rural New Jersey formed a major portion of the area's agricultural production between 1930 and 1960. Shifts in the farm prod-ucts grown in the area in the 1920s and 1940s did not affect the political atmosphere in these towns. As apples and eggs surpassed potatoes as the most profitable products in the area, local farmers and politicians adapted to these changes without any recorded problems. Socially con-servative and economically moderate, the local Republican Party held the local farmers' loyalties throughout the period. Maintaining racial segre-gation in schools and public facilities as well as establishing low costs for shipping farm goods on the local railroad satisfied the expectations of white residents, who showed their support by voting Republican. The next two decades brought a fundamental economic transformation that restructured the local social order in ways unimagined prior to the Sec-ond World War.

Over the horizon, a more voracious consumer approached, and then landed in, Manalapan—the suburban commuter. Real estate developers like Levitt and Sons transformed the fields and orchards in the northern portion of the township into congested cul-de-sacs with American Indian and colonial names.[22] Between 1970 and 1980, several residential communities sprang up and the total local population grew from 3,990 to 14,049. By 1990, over 26,000 people lived in Manalapan.[23] The spread of real estate development and highway construction enabled rapid settlement in this area. The geographic center of the township became a recreational area with parks and athletic fields for a family's weekend entertainment. Lacking sufficient schools, roads, and water services for the growing population, municipal politics changed rapidly after 1970, and Democrats seized a political majority through the following decade. Younger, middle-class families from New York believed in a stronger federal and state government with sweeping protections for racial and religious minorities like the 1964 Civil Rights Act and the 1968 Federal Housing Act. These perspectives all supported the Democratic Party's platform after 1980. For the local white population, the transformation was sudden, but it only changed the economic dominance of the region from the hands of farmers to the real estate developers.

Similar to other towns, Manalapan experienced a percentage population increase that placed it within the top five municipalities in its county.[24] Furthermore, it stood among the top three with the increasing number of housing units.[25] These new housing units sold at prices ranging between 150,000 dollars and 250,000 dollars in the county during the 1980s.[26] Local developers saw the success lower-middle and middle-class residential communities experienced in other suburban towns. Now, the most prosperous entrepreneurs invested in the creation of vast upper-middle-class communities, complete with suburban mansions that would fill half-acre lots. Yet, despite the high cost, only Manalapan, among its surrounding municipalities, had a home ownership rate of above 90 percent among its residents.[27] The new suburbanites in the township clearly liked the homes being offered to them and possessed sufficient income to purchase these houses. By 1990, farmers who had earned thirty thousand dollars ten years earlier were no longer the local aristocrats.

Residential developers like Kervork Hovnanian, who built communities like Holiday Park in the 1970s, now stood atop the local economy.[28] There were fewer than ten industries in Manalapan through the 1980s. These were declining agricultural affiliates like Reed and Perrine or small, private service shops for office and electronic needs.[29] Manalapan's departure from agriculture constituted the end of a statewide trend away from farming. Between 1950 and 1971, the number of farms in New Jersey dropped from 28,838 to 8,400. Half of the state was farmland in 1950, but only one-fifth remained tilled in 1971.[30] This pattern reflected many areas in the Northeast, including northern New York, central Mas-

sachusetts, and Connecticut. In the 1990s, Manalapan's residential developments were symbols of the state's status as a premier northeastern
suburb. Housing developments, strip malls, and retirement communities
replaced the orchards and vegetable farms in Manalapan.[31]

One structural side effect of this rapid population growth in the rural
corridor was the choking of the major roadways. State Route 9, which
had fueled the residential explosion in other towns, suffocated under the
daily commuter traffic that resulted as Manalapan developed. Ted Narozanick, mayor of Manalapan from 1954 to 1957 and holder of various
elected offices through the following decades, studied the transportation
problem in the area between 1970 and 1990. "There [was] such a situation
with commuter transportation and the impatience of people dealing with
congestion. It [was] not getting any better. Highway 9 [was] our main
line into North Jersey and [New York] City, and you just [couldn't] get
any more vehicles on it!"[32] Thus, an irony for emerging suburbs arose.
Every new resident wanted to try to preserve the isolated atmosphere
they had observed when buying property in the area. Yet their very
presence eliminated the possibility of maintaining the rural paradise they
imagined.

Two groups formed the bulk of the movement to Manalapan after
1960—middle-class families and retirees. Their arrival signaled a change
in the political atmosphere as both parties' registration numbers increased, but Democrats outnumbered Republicans in 1990—5,288 to
1,644.[33] Unlike other high-income areas in the county that powered the
area's Republican majority, Manalapan's Democratic base partly
stemmed from the activism of new Jewish residents through the 1980s.
Jewish voters traditionally voted as Democrats from their roots as immigrant voters in major cities. The Republican Party had also campaigned
on anti-Semitic platforms between 1920 and 1940. When the Democratic
Party supported antidiscrimination legislation after 1960, it strengthened
Jewish support for the organization.[34] Republican Party politics favored
reduced federal authority by cutting government spending and reducing
taxes, especially on the wealthy. However, the white ethnic families who
were moving to Manalapan recognized that reduced federal power allowed for the abuse of religious and racial minorities' civil rights. Thus,
while the new residents earned more money than Manalapan's previous
residents, the political dominance of the Republican Party came to an end
after 1980. While total population in Manalapan surged from 5,133 in
1960 to 27,984 in 1990, white per capita income differed significantly
depending on the age and location of the home. More noticeably, poverty
rates for whites in the town center tripled the rates for those on the
fringes.[35] With suburbs replacing farms throughout the area, poverty and
unemployment rose sharply among the most vulnerable.

Sociologists who study the economic and political developments in
Orange County, California, have provided a basis that illustrates the

complexities of suburban development in Englishtown and Manalapan. One study shows how the Irvine Company real estate developers conceived a suburban community centered around a university with emphasis on highway development to facilitate commuter access and egress.[36] In rural New Jersey, highways themselves provided the center for suburban communities as commercial development along the roads served residences built on formerly secluded farms. Another analysis reveals the use of council-manager municipal governments by corporate interests to control growth patterns and land usage.[37] More traditional mayors and city councils in large urban areas often tightly controlled the terms of economic development in their cities. Suburban committees typically allowed corporate interests to dictate settlement patterns, zoning regulations, and municipal needs. There is also an emphasis on the importance of local "commercial-civic" elites to the development of an area, but the use of zoning regulations was also used to maintain racial segregation.[38] Manalapan possessed a municipal committee-manager format, leaving it vulnerable to such manipulation through the 1980s. The suburbanization of Manalapan followed these patterns through its early stages between 1970 and 1990, with better consequences for wealthy and middle-class commuters. Democratic congressman James Howard sponsored major expansions of State Highway 33 and Route 9, which promoted an enormous residential housing boom in Manalapan for middle-class commuters during this period.[39] The sudden influx of people and dollars raised the local standards of living, but also intensified concerns about land preservation and the development of basic public services like schools, sewers, and roads.[40] Equally pressing, but often unmentioned, were concerns about the processes of economic and cultural inclusion in the area. By 2000, it was still possible to adjust zoning policies to address these matters in this suburban township.

Many city residents envisioned the countryside as empty space. Their mistaken perception shaped the business plans of developers, the policies of urban state politicians, and historians of metropolitan development. As thousands of people purchased new homes and adopted new lifestyles based on the automobile, the slower pace of rural life receded into smaller geographic spaces within the Garden State. Manalapan residents experienced the traffic congestion of larger suburbs like New Brunswick or Montclair by the end of the twentieth century. The gridlock commute along Route 9 every day became an environmental hazard that required massive public reinvestment to ameliorate. Only the few neighbors who lived in the area their whole lives understood what had been lost. Newcomers had some sense of disappointment that their dreams of suburban living were more crowded and hectic than they had imagined. The rush to fulfill hundreds of thousands of individual dreams of home ownership yielded a chaotic mass of metropolitan sprawl that consumed the rural corridor.

The sounds of animals and streams had filled the night air for most of the twentieth century in rural New Jersey. On major roadways, the occasional rumble of an engine or blaring horn from a locomotive could be expected. There was no cacophony of mechanical sound like the grinding of brakes in traffic, the shouts of a thousand children running through a mall, or the incessant chatter of keyboards within acres of commercial office spaces. Metropolitan growth carried with it a new sensory vocabulary for work and recreation. The only silent spaces were the individual rooms within hermetically sealed homes once their occupants surrendered to sleep. New York's identity as the city that never slept spread across the entire Northeast. There was no longer any place for the rural people who balanced nature and technology, productivity and recreation, or family and community. The politics of suburbanization left no room for the deference and deliberation of rural society, because the speed of change demanded an infinite amount of individual satisfaction in zoning, construction, and commerce. Managing these demands was a responsibility beyond the capability of any municipal or county planning board. Uneven development shaped the spread of an incoherent metropolitan policy.

FREEHOLD

A sleepy village served as the center of the rural corridor through the first half of the twentieth century. Freehold was the name shared by both a township and a borough in Monmouth County. Formally separated into two municipalities in 1919, Freehold Borough served as the center for county politics and local farmers' markets, while Freehold Township produced most of the county's potatoes.[41] The presence of the county courthouse, jail, and hall of records added another dimension to the connections between the township and the borough. These institutions made the borough important both politically and economically within the county and the state.[42] This importance changed when the economic base shifted after 1960 as the Monmouth County Planning Board oversaw the process from Freehold Borough. Real estate developers from the township changed land-use and zoning regulations through frequent negotiations with the county planning board. As a result, the township benefited most from the influx of middle-class suburban residents (in the form of better roads and schools), while the borough's workers experienced less economic hardship as public funding promoted an economic revival on Main Street in the late 1980s. However, the general trend toward the formation of a middle-class suburb surrounding a working-class town remained the same.

Both towns prospered between 1920 and 1950. Karagheusian Rug Mill and Brakeley Canning Factory served as the respective leading employers in the borough and the township.[43] Both plants contributed to the local culture and economy by providing jobs, hosting picnics in the summers between 1940 and 1960, and sponsoring local athletic teams like the Lady Cagers. With a solid foundation of economic success, a socially liberal coalition of Republicans held most local and county offices throughout this period. Politicians like Joseph McDermott (county clerk) and John Enright (New Jersey's assistant commissioner of education) generally opposed strict racial segregation in education and supported gradual reforms in public accommodations that would lead to racial integration.[44] This combination attracted greater numbers of African American migrants to these small towns than to any other municipality in western Monmouth County. This was the beginning of a new era in race relations in the Freeholds—the first major change since slavery had ended over seventy years earlier. The growing black community sought jobs on the area's farms and also developed religious organizations to structure their leisure time. These groups had no precedent in the nineteenth century. Their creation marked the beginning of the largest African American community in western Monmouth County.

In the first half of the twentieth century, Freehold Township led the county in agricultural production. Local farmers cultivated over one thousand acres of potatoes annually. It also produced the most strawberries, wheat, and corn in the county.[45] Meanwhile, Freehold Borough served as the hub of political discussion and decision making as the county seat. The borough's population remained several times larger than the township's until 1950.[46] With the advent of residential subdivision, Freehold Township's population began to grow rapidly. However, much of the political power embodied by the borough rested upon the economic strength of the township's farms before 1950. This political-economic relationship remained the same through the following four decades. In both the agricultural and commercial-housing economies, the township generated the products that attracted investors, consumers, and workers to the area. The borough, on the other hand, collected taxes on these products and services throughout the twentieth century. Revenues from potato shipments on the Jamesburg–Freehold Railroad before 1950 and licensing fees on shops in the Freehold Raceway Mall after 1990 (both in Freehold Township) kept the roads paved and the schools open in Freehold Borough. Freehold Borough served as the commercial center for agricultural produce from Freehold Township. In fact, the Raceway Mall of the 1990s produced far more municipal revenue for the borough than the largest farms in the township's history. In the township, farmers like John DuBois, the Lazinger family, and Joseph Smith produced potatoes, eggs, and corn between 1900 and 1960.[47] Yet, two of the larger industrial employers also resided in Freehold. Joseph Brakeley's factory canned tomatoes, spinach, peas, and beans in Freehold Township, while A. M. Karagheusian's Rug Mill offered the most jobs in the borough throughout the first half of the twentieth century.[48] When the farms and canning factories in Freehold Township closed during the 1950s and 1960s, Karagheusian Rug Mill also moved away.[49] Both towns faced major decisions about their economic futures after 1970.

The difference between the two towns was the amount of unimproved land. Freehold Township's farmers sold their land to real estate developers, who built hundreds of suburban homes between 1960 and 1990.[50] The borough, lacking the open space to duplicate this process, strengthened the ties between municipal and county government. The functions of county administration and services replaced the farmers' markets and agricultural railroad that characterized the previous period. African Americans who relied on the farms for their income found few opportunities. They now found cheaper homes in Freehold Borough, and their children found jobs in various municipal and county services (mainly welfare administration and paralegal work). In the 1970s and 1980s, Latino immigrants also started new lives in the borough. Latino migrants obtained work in the restaurants, movie theaters, and retail outlets that emerged in the area. Meanwhile, in Freehold Township, several groups representing a diversity of African, Asian, and Latino American backgrounds established small communities during the 1980s.[51] These economic and demographic changes produced a sharp reversal in the relationship between the two towns. By 1990, locals perceived the borough as a dilapidated urban center and the township as the desirable suburban enclave. These perceptions were based on the numbers of new housing units built and the percentage of owner- or renter-occupied structures in each area. Between 1980 and 1990 alone, nearly 2,700 new homes were built in Freehold Township, while only 325 rose in the borough. During the same period, 84 percent of the township residents owned their homes, compared to 59 percent of borough inhabitants. Renters comprised a larger percentage of Freehold Borough's residents compared to the township (41 percent versus 16 percent).[52] With the towns no longer interdependent politically and economically, tensions around race and class issues simmered just beneath the surface. Youth gangs from both Latino and African American communities engaged in sporadic violence, often targeting working people from the other community for muggings and petty theft. This violence was often an expression of frustration with the lack of jobs for young people of color as well as the limited opportunities for educational achievement at the local high school.

Reflecting the overall commercial/agricultural split between the borough and the township in the early twentieth century, Freehold Borough's total population outstripped Freehold Township's until 1970. However, neither municipality exceeded ten thousand residents until that year.[53] The peripheral location kept the population from reaching this level earlier, while the growing housing market in the 1960s finally succeeded in attracting more suburbanites. The political atmosphere differed between the borough and the township. The residents in the township voted Democratic in the first half of the twentieth century. Borough residents supported Republican candidates who proposed wider roads and increased commercial investment, as did the residents of Asbury Park and Red Bank. Democrat Joseph McDermott, an advocate for the expansion of the Freehold–Jamesburg Railroad, was the most notable example of this pattern.[54] Local farmers relied on good roads to get their potatoes and eggs to the train station in the borough and also appreciated municipal loan assistance that helped purchase farm tools and fertilizers. Racial attitudes, as in the rest of the county, remained solidly conservative. Most white residents saw racism as a southern problem and rarely questioned the segregation and discrimination that existed in their own community. Driven by the conversion of its farms and orchards into retirement communities, housing developments, and a megamall complex, the township's population grew from just over 3,400 in 1950 to over 24,700 in 1990. Freehold Borough, on the other hand, has seen its population flatten out at approximately ten thousand since 1970.[55] During that period, Puerto Rican, Central American, and African American populations have grown dramatically in Freehold Borough.[56] The unemployment and poverty rates for these communities of color have stayed near twice as high as those for the white population.[57] Racial discrimination, cultural barriers, and less access to quality secondary education all contribute to these disparities. African Americans remained concentrated in domestic and menial occupations in Freehold through the 1950s. None of the major fraternal organizations (such as the Knights of Columbus and the Kiwanis Club) admitted blacks as members until 1970. The concentration of an ethnically and racially diverse, professionally skilled, and middle-class population in Freehold Township reflected the trends of western Monmouth County in the second half of the twentieth century. While all racial groups grew in Freehold Township, poverty rates for blacks (16.3 percent) were nearly three times as high as those for whites (5.6 percent).[58] Freehold Borough, by comparison, resembles the way working-class Latinos and blacks were residentially concentrated in Long Branch, Asbury Park, and Red Bank. African Americans in both the township and the borough were more likely to rent their homes. More black residents also worked in the immediate vicinity than their white counterparts. These statistics reflected the precarious foundation that supported the emerging black middle class.

Political, economic, and cultural conflicts dominated public life in the United States after World War II. In American eyes, the Cold War divided the globe between capitalist and communist ideologies both internationally and domestically. By the early 1960s, African Americans and women had pressed for greater social equality and an end to race- and gender-based discrimination. A burgeoning antiwar movement took root among the largest generation of children born in the history of the United

States during this decade. Assimilative concepts like the American dream came under increasing assault as different groups of people articulated and pursued different agendas for their lives. An educated, organized, national black community rallied to end legalized racial segregation in public facilities, services, and transportation. A resurgent women's movement called for greater access to higher education, equal opportunity in the job market, and a redefinition of traditional gender roles throughout American society by 1970. Young adults protested compulsory military services, sometimes violently, and challenged the notion that the United States government was truly democratic. Freehold was one place where the political and economic consequences of these conflicts played out.

With the decline of the agricultural economy that bound the two municipalities together in the second half of the twentieth century, a stark division between working-class people (many people of color) and middle-class people (mainly white people) manifested between the borough and the township. It was this new generation of suburban families that would dictate the local policies concerning education, housing, and employment. In central New Jersey, the transparent barriers of economic segregation collided with the everyday reality of cultural interaction between suburban and urban populations. Often without conscious effort, local residents reshaped the race relations in this suburb on a daily basis. For earlier generations, racial deprivation and privilege mandated deference from people of color and attitudes of superiority from whites. In suburbs like Freehold during the Cold War, race relations blurred on the surface as a few middle-class Asians, Latinos, and African Americans gained a greater measure of the American dream. As large numbers of Asian and Latino Americans settled in the United States for the first time after 1970, racial stereotypes such as the "model minority" and the "black conservative" gained new acceptance across the country. Life in the borough for the working-class people of color belied this illusion of color-blind equality.

When the potato farmers in Freehold Township loaded their crops onto trucks, they took the long and lumpy spuds into the borough to be weighed and loaded into railway cars for transportation to New York and Philadelphia via the Freehold–Jamesburg Agricultural Railroad.[59] Main Street in Freehold Borough remained the major artery through the area, and many roads away from the center of town were still unpaved as late as the 1940s. This lack of development made transportation over any significant distance difficult. In the commercial center, farmers like Joseph Smith shared conversations with local officials like Edgar VanDerveer. With little political power among municipal authorities and public coffers relying on the commercial success of local farms, VanDerveer was much more accountable to Smith than most politicians in the second half of the twentieth century were.[60] The tight-knit economy produced a personal closeness among the white residents of the area. While Democrats dominated the shore communities through the late nineteenth century, one of the keys to the local Republican emergence in the early twentieth century was the strength of the community in Freehold. Republicans like Joseph McDermott championed a free-market approach to the economy while advocating the use of public monies to reduce expenses for local businessmen. In Freehold, these policies meant subsidies for farmers and tax incentives for the local railroad line. This coalition of business and political interests formed the core of the area's Republican Party and linked its fortunes to the prosperity of the local businesses. The success of the county Republican Party relied on the farms of western Monmouth County between 1920 and 1950.

While potatoes symbolized the economic thrust of the towns during the 1920s, 1930s, and 1940s, string beans and tomatoes from the area fueled the success of Joseph Brakeley's canning factory in Freehold Township. Between 1882 and 1929, the Brakeley factory canned more tomatoes, peas, spinach, and beans than any other plant in Monmouth County.[61] Young white workers from high schools in Newark, Jersey City, and Trenton spent their summers in Brakeley's fields, buildings, and trucks.[62] The A. M. Karagheusian Rug Mill opened in Freehold Borough in 1904, but operated at peak production between 1920 and 1960. With over one thousand workers during this period, the rug mill employed over half of the workers in the borough every year.[63] Through the 1940s, egg farming became more widespread through Freehold Township. One of the leading farmers was Max Lazinger. Lazinger's farm was one of several Jewish egg farms that operated in Freehold as part of the Central Jersey Farmers Cooperative Association until the 1960s.[64] After World War II, potato demand declined, and Freehold farmers supplemented their production with wheat, corn, and fruit.[65]

With many small potato farmers, a vegetable-canning factory, numerous egg farmers, and the largest rug mill in the area, Freehold enjoyed the most diversified economy in western Monmouth County. Economic stability came with an increasing population and the desire for different social and cultural outlets in these small towns. Between 1920 and 1950, the population of the borough alone increased from 4,768 to 7,550. This movement did not reflect national trends, as the majority of Americans were still moving into urban centers. Two factors combined to explain this growth in Freehold Borough. During the Great Depression, some city families moved out to farms in an attempt to find stability in a rural setting. After 1940, the early waves of suburbanites fled the cities looking for quieter surroundings. The township's total population grew more slowly from 1,498 to 3,442 during the same period.[66] The Republican board of commissioners for the borough and municipal committee for the township judiciously raised money for improving roads and schools through these times.[67] It is also likely that local residents demanded these improvements as more people moved to the area, but the municipal records do not disclose these activities. While the Freehold Military School replaced the late-nineteenth-century Young Ladies Seminary, the West Freehold elementary school and Freehold high school benefited the most from these increases.[68] Local residents recognized the economic significance of good roads and the cultural importance of quality education.

Local businessmen also participated in the expansion and promotion of community life in Freehold. A. M. Karagheusian led the way in this regard, sponsoring basketball teams, a marching band, and a first aid squad. Joseph Brakeley even sponsored a women's basketball team for exhibitions.[69] However, the Great Depression brought many of these activities to a close and bankrupted many independent cultural organizations. Freehold's Polish and Russian Jewish communities started several groups for preservation and celebration of their culture during the late nineteenth century. However, only the local Benefit Society and Workmen's Circle survived in the 1930s.[70] Freehold's white community adapted and expanded to include new ethnic groups during the decade after World War II. Kervork Hovnanian was an example of this transformation. A Jewish real estate developer, Hovnanian became one of the wealthiest businessmen in western Monmouth County after 1950. His acceptance and success would not have been possible earlier in the century, when anti-Semitism was more common and public. The creation of a more inclusive white community also responded to the rhetoric of the Second World War. In distancing the United States from the ideology of Nazi Germany, national politicians constructed a "color-blind" democratic ideal that gained social acceptance after 1960. However, the rhetoric of racial denial was only a marginal improvement over the politics of racial denigration.

The consequences of Freehold Township's economic transformation between 1950 and 1980 created a negative perception of Freehold Borough. The borough no longer served as the marketplace for the township's agricultural goods, so the farmers and attorneys stopped sharing the same social spaces on a regular basis. The expansion of State Route 9 and Highway 18 and the development of a regional high school district further developed an independent identity for the township, weakening its relationship to Freehold Borough. When the Monmouth County Planning Board formed in the 1950s, its focus targeted western Monmouth County for commercial and residential development. This organization's success fueled the cultural, political, and economic transformation of the area after World War II.

One of the most diverse economies in the rural corridor simplified during the 1960s and 1970s. Karagheusian rug mill closed operations and moved to North Carolina in 1962.[71] This departure was part of the national movement of manufacturing businesses to the southern United

States. Industrial migration to the Sunbelt region decimated the major cities throughout the northern United States after 1950. For small towns like Freehold Borough, this trend resulted in a crisis that required major changes to adapt to the emerging service economy. Real estate developers converted dozens of chicken farms into residential developments like Stonehurst-at-Freehold and Greentree.[72] The larger potato and vegetable farms in Freehold Township soon followed suit. By the 1980s, a few factories remained in Freehold Borough, notably a Nescafé plant, 3M tape manufacturing, and Brockway Glass. However, these industries employed no more workers than Karagheusian had.[73] The rise of strip malls, supermarkets, and restaurants along the State Route 9 and County Highway 537 in the township further divided the economic identities of the two towns.

Just as the local economy affected the population in the area in the previous period, economics also played a major role in the area's growing Latino and shrinking black population between 1950 and 1980. Freehold Borough's population increased from 7,550 in 1950 to 9,140 in 1960 to 10,545 in 1970, before dipping slightly to 10,020 in 1980. The township's total population increased from 3,442 to 19,202 during the same period.[74] Residential increases in Freehold Township contributed to the regional and national shift towards suburban areas. Whites living in the township earned five thousand dollars more than those in the borough in terms of per capita income, and the white poverty rate in the surrounding town was one-fourth of that in the borough during the 1980s.[75] The construction of a new high school specifically for Freehold Township in 1972 reflected the growth of the suburban community and their perception of "inner-city decay" in the borough.[76] The township's middle-class migrants from larger urban centers likely carried their stereotypes about overcrowded, predominantly black neighborhoods with them and projected those images on the borough. As a result, Freehold Borough gained a stigma in the eyes of these new residents. Furthermore, the area's Republican base became concentrated in the township's retirement communities and residential developments. It became an area where conservatism, masked as "individual political culture," dominated the cultural landscape. The rhetoric of individual effort, meritocracy, and reverse racism became the new vocabulary to justify privileged status for white Americans—in central New Jersey and across the country.[77] Freehold Borough served as the seat of the county's political offices, which were filled with Republican officials through this period. Yet the local government remained solidly Democratic—another symbol of its difference from the rest of the region.[78] Republicans maintained their hold on political power in the township by supporting increased suburban subdivision and a small-scale commercial investment without increasing local tax assessments for road and school improvements. They also consistently opposed proposals for multifamily and low-income housing in these towns. None of these ideas helped the growing working class in Freehold Borough, who now formed the core constituency of the local Democratic Party.

Across the country, similar transformations and divisions have taken place under the auspices of municipal or county planning. Zoning regulations often serve as the primary tools to control the class composition of counties and towns. Human agency is sometimes lost when studying sweeping socioeconomic changes, even in smaller towns. However, the fact that people made everyday decisions to advance this suburban transformation stands out as a powerful lesson. The cultural and political choices that civic leaders and new residents made in Freehold between 1950 and 1980 built the economic wall that distinguished the two municipalities. Wealthy white inhabitants enjoyed comfortable homes in the township, while the working class (disproportionately black, Latino, and Asian) rented older, low-quality houses in the borough. The shape of the suburban, postindustrial future need not conform to its dystopic past.

African Americans and Latino immigrants to New Jersey had greater aspirations for economic success and social inclusion after 1970. The resilience of white assumptions about the geography and politics of acceptable racial interaction still placed severe limits on the realistic accomplishment of those goals. Uneven development illustrates the spatial and economic dimensions of continuing inequality in the wake of the civil rights reforms that took hold in the Garden State between 1950 and 1980. However, the racial justifications for occupational discrimination and residential segregation persisted in ways that the rhetoric of color-blindness ignored completely. The construction of idyllic suburbs throughout the rural corridor established the Boston–Washington corridor as the premier metropolitan region on the planet in the last two decades of the twentieth century. Measuring the cost of such changes relies on a familiarity with the transformation of communities like Manalapan, Freehold, and Howell.

Rural towns did not become metropolitan suburbs without the advances of the civil rights movement. The slow silence and isolation of farming villages reflected a long-standing paternalism—a set of assumptions that all the participants knew their roles and accepted them. Working-class African Americans built organizations and institutions dedicated to interrogating and reinventing those roles in these small towns. Black middle-class families led these groups. Their efforts created the legislative standards for a democracy that promoted racial equality. Their victory advanced on the inclusion of African Americans within local, state, and federal government.[79] However, public employment formed a much larger pillar of support for black professionals in the late twentieth century than it had for any previous racial or ethnic group in American history.[80] Governors like Tom Kean and Christie Whitman dominated the state's political agenda between 1980 and 2000. Their cost-cutting measures frequently focused on the limitation of civil rights programs.[81] When the governmental infrastructure to maintain policies favoring the movement towards racial equality collapsed in New Jersey, so did much of the older, black middle class. At the end of the twentieth century, the gulf between the secure retirements of the civil rights generation and the insecure incarceration of the hip-hop generation widened. The resort and farming economies that sustained these communities a century earlier had little left to offer either group.

HOWELL

A farmer's day begins before dawn and ends long after dark. However, a major aspect of farming labor involves the execution of numerous manual tasks by unskilled workers. Howell Township exemplified the small farming village through the first half of the twentieth century.[82] African American migrants' labor on Howell's farms was essential through the late nineteenth and early twentieth century. A shift towards egg farming after 1920 and the gradual abandonment of local agriculture after World War II changed the relationship between employer and employee in Howell. These transformations undercut the need for black day laborers. Between 1910 and 1940, egg farming formed the basis for the local economy. Jewish farmers organized settlement programs to encourage unhappy urban residents to relocate to the rustic countryside.[83] Native-born whites opposed such efforts initially, but their resistance wavered when they began to emulate the Jewish residents' profitable egg-farming techniques. While egg farming took the lead, fruit and vegetable processing maintained a significant role.[84] As older marl and cranberry farms gave way to chicken farming, the vegetable-canning plants employed many of the day laborers that had lost their jobs.[85] Despite these changes, Howell residents remained politically consistent, electing conservative Democrats like R. J. Estelle, Howard J. Ketcham, Charles Pohlemus, and Edgar O. Murphy to local office throughout the period.[86] Throughout this period, Howell retained a small-town atmosphere. In 1875, just over 4,300 people lived in Howell.[87] By 1920, this number had fallen to approximately 2,500 as many farm workers sought better pay in industrial cities. Yet, by 1950, Howell's population had rebounded to nearly 6,700 people.[88] By the 1950s, changes were sweeping through this area. While the town grew steadily between 1910 and 1940, it experienced unprecedented population growth between 1940 and 1970. Howell, with vast expanses of open land, exploded during this period. As real estate developers purchased large farms and subdivided them into residential lots, Howell's population quintupled between 1940 and 1970.[89] Real estate and retail businesses took the lead as banks, stores, and other small businesses lined both sides of State Route 9 along the western edge of Howell.[90] These two towns had become the model for suburban development in the rural corridor.

African Americans had carved a small niche in this rural setting before World War II. Throughout the late nineteenth century, census records indicate that fewer than twenty black people lived in Howell.[91] Even in the first two decades of the twentieth century, the number of African American residents did not exceed 250 people.[92] Transience among local black workers contributed to the low number of black residents. Unlike seasonal resort laborers along the central New Jersey shore, African Americans in Howell often worked in the area, then walked home to neighboring municipalities. In the segregated culture of early-twentieth-century America, these workers provided essential production for local economic success but found their prospects for cultural and educational participation sorely limited by racial discrimination.

The small black community in Howell dispersed during the residential and commercial transformation that occurred after World War II. African Americans who had previously worked in canning plants, around the egg farms, and at local residents' homes found no jobs. While the number of black residents climbed steadily into the hundreds by 1950, more and more African American laborers worked outside of the area. By 1970, Howell's black population was over one thousand people. African Americans represented less than 5 percent of Howell's total population.[93] African American communities within Howell remained hidden on small, unpaved roads far from the sight of the new developments and an expanding Route 9. Churches like Bethany Baptist maintained a sense of community for African Americans in these two towns.[94] Much like other developing suburbs across the nation, Howell welcomed new residents of all races, as long as they met two criteria—the ability to afford the area's expensive homes and to assimilate into the majority culture upon arrival.[95] This left virtually no place for the working-class black families that had built the community changing rapidly before their eyes.

Swamps and fertilizer have never been known to make millionaires. In Howell's case, however, they did well enough to support a small farming community through the nineteenth century. Cranberry production made for messy collection and processing, but once canned, cranberries sold quickly up and down the East Coast. The Freehold–Jamesburg Agricultural Railroad picked up marl, a moss known for its quality as a fertilizer, from Howell for use in the rest of New Jersey's farms. Until 1920, cranberries and marl provided the foundation for commercial success in Howell.[96] Howell farmers grew corn, potatoes, soybeans, wheat, and barley for the following decades. Then, poultry and egg farming dominated the local economy between 1940 and 1960.[97] The two largest industries in Howell through the first half of the twentieth century were A. C. Soper and Company and I. Rokeach and Sons. Both processed tomatoes and pumpkins for canning and food paste, reflecting the area's emphasis on agricultural production.[98] In these two villages, stability in the economy accompanied a cultural and political atmosphere led by native-born white families who had lived in the area for generations.

The total population for Howell Township in the nineteenth century dropped from 4,393 in 1870 to 3,245 in 1895. It continued to slide through the first two decades of the twentieth century to a low of 2,549 in 1920.[99] Howell elected township and borough officials who advertised the communities to Jewish poultry farmers.[100] After World War I, at a time when small dairy farmers like Hendrick Sayton and John Barkalow still paid approximately eight dollars a week for ten people, agricultural entrepreneurs like Benjamin Peskin began opening increasing numbers of chicken farms.[101] The local poultry industry slowed slightly during the Great Depression, but it still maintained sufficient production for Howell to rank as the state's "egg basket" in 1940.[102] In 1903, A. C. Soper and Company opened a catsup production and bottling plant. The Farmingdale Packing Corporation bought and expanded the plant in 1933, operating it until 1949. Many of the workers who could not find jobs on less labor-intensive chicken farms during this period worked at this factory.[103] While not as diversified as the shore economies during this period, Howell's transformation maintained a degree of prosperity for their communities and attracted new residents to the area.

German Jews constituted the first wave of new migrants to the Howell area after World War I. They founded the Central Jersey Farmers Cooperative Association (CJFCA) almost immediately upon arrival.[104] By 1925, the CJFCA had evolved into the Jewish Agricultural Society, which developed settlement loan programs for prospective Jewish farmers. Many Jews took advantage of these programs to make new homes in rural, central New Jersey. Older Jewish residents opened a cultural center, where courses in literature, language, and history were taught to newer Jewish immigrants. By the 1940s, the younger, more liberal, and professionally educated Jews rejected many of the "old" ways, but still faced rejection from the native-born white community in Howell.[105] Anti-Semitism rose in the area. The Peskin family, in particular, experienced cross burnings on their property and violent threats against their children from Klan sympathizers in the 1920s.[106] Resident Rose Staples offers another perspective on the differences between local native-born whites and Jewish families before the Second World War. She said, "My father was civic minded and very broad-minded. When I was young, I recall, when African Americans came into your house, other people looked at you very strangely. But my father thought nothing of it. Or of going to their houses. Or going to their churches for their church dinners. I didn't think of it as racial tension."[107]

While much of Monmouth County benefited the most from World War II and the subsequent Cold War because of the larger industrial presence there, farming communities also felt an economic surge after 1940. Howell led Monmouth County in corn and poultry production between 1940 and 1960. Residents in these municipalities dedicated over fifteen thousand acres to farming during this period.[108] However, an influx of eastern European Jewish immigrants deflated the market value of local eggs by 1960.[109] This initiated the first major efforts to sell farmland in the area—a harbinger of things to come. The United States Navy also stimulated the local economy with the opening of Earle Naval Ammunition Depot in 1943.[110] The installation remained a leading employer in the rural economy in 2000.[111] The rapidly growing community also had a prosperous asphalt plant to pave the town's major thoroughfares— State Route 9 and State Highway 33.[112] Overall, the postwar period brought a growing prosperity to this small farming area.

In popular memory, the 1960s was a decade of unparalleled change for the United States. This was certainly the case for the economy in Howell. Real estate developers like the Land of Pines Development Corporation built residential communities by purchasing former egg farms, subdividing them into one-acre plots, and reselling them to commuters who desired life outside of urban centers like Newark, Camden, Trenton, New York, and Philadelphia.[113] By 1965, Kervork Hovnanian's Candlewood neighborhood advertised that it housed over twenty thousand residents, nearly twice the residential population counted for the area at the 1960 census.[114] This rural community had become a suburb within a decade, despite the persistence of a few farms, small agricultural-processing plants, and individually owned technical shops over the next two decades.[115] This shift in the local economy wrought a change in the political atmosphere. As residential communities became more common between 1970 and 1990, the increasing number of commuting workers and retirees tipped the towns' political majorities from Democratic to Republican.[116] However, moderation characterized the local political candidates as centrist, and conservative Democrats have won local and county elections since 1960.

The economic and political transformation of Howell during the early decades of the Cold War produced a startling increase in the municipalities' total populations. Howell's population, on the other hand, grew from 6,696 in 1950 to 21,756 in 1970. By 2000, nearly 50,000 people lived in Howell Township.[117] After 1960, the Jewish population in the area declined because the younger generation sought residence closer to urban centers.[118] In the following decade, the home ownership rate in Howell soared to near 90 percent, which was among the highest in the county. Retail strip malls dotted State Route 9 for miles through the center of Howell, attracting middle-class families and filling municipal coffers because commercial and property tax revenue soared.[119] In Howell, prosperity generated a sense of inclusion and municipal pride after 1960. In 1996, a local journalist wrote, "I consider it a blessing to see traditional

African, Asian Indian, Kalmyk, Middle Eastern, and Hasidic clothing . . . in public places from the shopping plazas to Allaire State Park." Local photographs dating from the period showed integrated Brownie troops and high school wrestling teams.[120] However, the statistics show significant economic differences among racial groups. In 1990, white unemployment in Howell stood just beneath 6 percent and white poverty was just over 3 percent.[121] White per capita income significantly outstripped other racial groups in Howell.[122] Poverty rates among blacks (7.6 percent) in Howell were twice as high as those for whites (3.2 percent).[123]

One sociologist describes a dormitory suburb as a community where the predominant land use is residential. Howell meets this criterion because 70 percent of the land there serves as housing.[124] His profile of Franklin Township corresponds most closely to this town. Franklin's sudden population growth after 1950 has caused greater deterioration among its houses and transportation infrastructure than was the case in central New Jersey. Conflicts between new residents and older families were common, especially concerning future municipal development. Many residents lived in Franklin for less than ten years, and this transience limited the possibilities for a cohesive community.[125] Howell faced similar divisions on a smaller scale in the second half of the twentieth century. Mile-long traffic jams, insufficient public sewer and water service, and residential overdevelopment all threatened the suburban tranquility in these towns. A description of "suburbia" applies to the reconstruction of Howell as a residential area. The combination of white migration from urban and rural areas to a consumer-oriented suburb exemplifies the growth of these two municipalities between 1960 and 1990. This analysis of white desire for the "opportunities of a great city, coexisting with revulsion from urban life" would likely have resonated with many people who moved to the rural corridor.[126] Another examination explicitly addresses suburban strategies to exclude the poor and racial minorities from their enclaves. They describe three zoning methods which serve this end—restrictions on the type of dwellings permitted, requirements increasing the cost of building a housing unit, and administrative/procedural delaying tactics.[127] The emphasis on expensive single-family homes combined with bureaucratic obstacles to prevent more equitable neighborhood development. In Howell, the primary conditions that attracted upper-middle-class, white residents to the area included the subdivisions of farmland where migrant families in exchange for their labor and the escalating property taxes that accompanied widespread residential development. Loss of farm land, rising property taxes, and arbitrary zoning ordinances offered ample protection from socioeconomic integration in central New Jersey.[128]

In the space of ten short years, Howell's economic and political relationship changed in ways that predicted similar patterns in the rest of the rural corridor. No longer one of the area's major economic producers,

Howell has become an enormous consumer town attracting restaurants and strip malls along Route 9, which was expanded after 1970. The population explosion brought millions of dollars in new investment to the township. However, all of the new residents carried with them cultural expectations about the municipal services their new neighborhoods would provide. The costs of expanding police protection, emergency services, public water, new schools, and greater electrical infrastructure surged beyond any elected official's wildest projections. Towns throughout the rural corridor created new municipal boundaries in attempts to control the rampant growth in public expenditures. Each new community required a duplication of all these investments. This redundant multiplication of governmental services threatened to bankrupt their entire state in the first decade of the twenty-first century.[129] The cost of wholesale economic and racial isolation—from within the confines of each household to the statewide constraints on the legislature—revealed the fraudulent rhetoric of color-blind politics and economics.

Unthinking reproduction of endless residential and commercial suburban communities betrayed political promises of fiscal responsibility and public fairness at the end of the twentieth century. Town after town throughout the rural corridor repeated the mistakes of its neighbors in a vain pursuit of sufficient private investment to secure enough revenue to meet the demands of thousands of new residents. They adjusted the standard racial exclusion of African Americans and immigrants just enough to create new boundaries of uneven development based on the intersection of wealth and race. Manalapan, Freehold, and Howell revealed the resiliency of white supremacy even as the local and state governments claimed to pursue new policy to rectify the wrongs of segregation. The suburban ideal displayed in magazines, television shows, and movies in the second half of the twentieth century constituted only half of the story about metropolitan growth in the Garden State. Centerless cities made it possible for the computerized service economy to balance management, production, and consumption on a global scale. Were suburban slums where violent crime, unemployment, and poverty increased on a daily basis worth this fundamental reordering of the rural corridor? The greatest orator of the black freedom movement argued otherwise when he said, "Injustice anywhere is a threat to justice everywhere."[130] His claim holds especially true in the tightly connected web of social relationships developing in the twenty-first century.

One of the crucial failings of state and municipal government after 1950 was the exclusion of civil rights leaders from sustained engagement with the various levels of public planning in the rural corridor. New Jersey had the opportunity to engage rural African Americans in the economic development of the state in ways similar to the legislative and political reforms adopted over the previous decade. A combination of public and private entrepreneurship at the midpoint of the twentieth century was the prescription needed to undo the persistent effects of racial segregation. More inclusive engagement was necessary to end the need for judicial rulings like *Mount Laurel* I and II throughout the deeply fragmented state between 1970 and 1990. Black communities caught in the process of metropolitan growth in rural areas offered greater chances for interracial economic engagement after the waves of federal legislative reform than programs like Soul City in North Carolina.[131] Missed opportunities to anticipate spatial change left New Jersey politicians in late twentieth century behind the curve in promoting some form of equitable development. Historians must engage the public process more aggressively to avoid similar oversights in the future.

NOTES

1. John Logan and Mark Schneider, "The Stratification of Metropolitan Suburbs, 1960–1970," *American Sociological Review* 46 (April 1981): 175–77.

2. Monmouth County Planning Board (MCPB), *Monmouth County Demographic and Economic (MCD&E) Profile: Updates, Estimates, and Projections* (Freehold: Monmouth County Planning Board Publication, 1997), 8; James S. Brown, *Manalapan in Three Centuries* (Manalapan: Township of Manalapan Publication, 1991), 54.

3. Brown, *Manalapan in Three Centuries*, 53.

4. Paul A. Stellhorn, "Depression and Decline: Newark, New Jersey, 1929–1941," PhD diss., Rutgers University, New Brunswick, NJ, 1982, iii; Robert M. Fogelson, *The Fragmented Metropolis: Los Angeles, 1850–1930* (Cambridge, MA: Harvard University Press, 1967), 273.

5. MCPB, *MCD&E Updates, Estimates, and Projections*, 8.

6. Richard J. Dalik, *Images of America: Manalapan and Englishtown* (Dover, NH: Arcadia Publishing, 1998), 56.

7. MCPB, *MCD&E Profile*, vol. 1 (Freehold: MCPB Publication, 1993), 49–51.

8. Brown, *Manalapan in Three Centuries*, 53; Extension Service, College of Agriculture, *Census Facts—Monmouth County*, table 2b.

9. Ibid., 48; Dalik, *Manalapan and Englishtown*, 38.

10. Alan Rosenthal and John Blydenburgh, eds., *Politics in New Jersey* (New Brunswick, NJ: Rutgers University, 1975), 130.

11. Extension Service, *Census Facts—Monmouth County*, table 2b.

12. Dalik, *Manalapan and Englishtown*, 65–88.

13. John T. Cunningham, *Railroads in New Jersey: The Formative Years* (Andover, NJ: Afton Publishing Company, Inc., 1997), 206; New Jersey State Emergency Relief Association, *Negroes on the Road: A Survey of the Transient Negro in New Jersey* (privately published, 1934), 22–27.

14. Brown, *Manalapan in Three Centuries*, 53; Dalik, *Manalapan and Englishtown*, 28, 37, 48.

15. Extension Service, *Census Facts—Monmouth County*, table 2b.

16. Maurice Mustin, ed., *A Sketch of Monmouth County, New Jersey, 1683–1929* (Camden, NJ: M. Mustin Company, 1929), 11; Dalik, *Manalapan and Englishtown*, 38.

17. Mary B. Sim, *Commercial Canning in New Jersey: History and Early Development* (Trenton: New Jersey Agricultural Society, 1951), 240.

18. Edgar I. VanDerveer, *County, City, Township, and Borough Officials of Monmouth County (1917)* (Keyport, NJ: The Weekly Print, 1917), 5; Dalik, *Manalapan and Englishtown*, 7.

19. Monmouth County Archives (MCA), *Census Enumeration 1880: Color and Age*, vol. 1, (Manalapan), 1; NJBC, *New Jersey State Census—1895* (ms.), schedule 1; NJBC,

New Jersey New Jersey State Census—1915 (ms.), schedule 1; MCPB, *MCD&E Profile: Updates, Estimates, and Projections,* 8.

20. MCPB, *MCD&E Profile: Updates, Estimates, and Projections,* 8.

21. Pine, Hershenov, and Lefkowitz, *Peddler to Suburbanite,* 99–100, 182.

22. Brown, *Manalapan in Three Centuries,* 69.

23. MCPB, *MCD&E Updates, Estimates, and Projections,* 8.

24. MCPB, *MCD&E Profile,* 1:6.

25. MCPB, *Monmouth County Profile 1997* (Freehold: MCPB Publication, 1997), 2.

26. MCPB, *MCD&E Profile,* 1:26.

27. Martin P. Truscott, *Census Trends, 1970–1980* (Freehold: MCPB Publication, 1984), 55.

28. Pine, Hershenov, and Lefkowitz, *Peddler to Suburbanite,* 144–45.

29. State Industrial Directories Corporation, *1980 New Jersey Industrial Directory* (New York: State Industrial Directories Corporation, 1980), G287, G295; MacRae's Blue Book, Inc., *MacRae's Industrial Directory—New Jersey, 1985* (New York: MacRae's Blue Book, Inc., 1985). The only remaining industry in Manalapan in 1985 was Frank Rust Company, Inc., which arranged trade show displays at area malls.

30. Hubert G. Schmidt, *Agriculture in New Jersey: A Three Hundred-Year History* (New Brunswick, NJ: Rutgers University Press, 1973), 272.

31. MCPB, *Monmouth County Profile 1997,* 10–13.

32. Sherry Conohan, "Interview with Theodore Narozanick," 30 June 2000, in *Remembering the Twentieth Century: An Oral History of Monmouth County,* ed. Flora T. Higgins, http://www.visitmonmouth.com/oralhistory/bios/NarozanickTed.htm

33. 33 Monmouth County Board of Elections (MCBE), *Monmouth County Political Registration Book* (Freehold, NJ: Monmouth County Board of Elections, 1990).

34. Barbara G. Salmore and Stephen A. Salmore, *New Jersey Politics and Government: Suburban Politics Comes of Age* (Lincoln: University of Nebraska Press, 1993), 29, 57, 63; Pine, Hershenov, and Lefkowitz, *Peddler to Suburbanite,* 145.

35. MCPB, *MCD&E Profile: Updates, Estimates, and Projections,* 8; MCPB, *MCD&E Profile,* vol. 2 (Freehold: MCPB Publication, 1993), 44, 53.

36. Martin J. Schiesl, "Designing the Model Community: The Irvine Company and Suburban Development, 1950–1988," in *Postsuburban California: The Transformation of Orange County Since World War II,* ed. Rob Kling, Spencer Olin, and Mark Poster (Los Angeles: University of California Press, 1991), 57, 61–63.

37. Spencer Olin, "Intra-class Conflict and the Politics of a Fragmented Region," in *Postsuburban California,* ed. Kling, Olin, and Poster, 227–29, 234.

38. William N. Black, "Empire of Consensus: City Planning, Zoning, and Annexation in Dallas, 1900–1960," PhD diss., Columbia University, 1982, 5, 325.

39. Salmore and Salmore, *New Jersey Politics and Government,* 225.

40. Brown, *Manalapan in Three Centuries,* 54.

41. Joseph Safia, "Where Farmers and Lawyers Rub Shoulders," *Asbury Park Press,* 16 December 1999, special insert section, 1–2.

42. Lee Ellen Griffith, *Images of America: Freehold* (Dover, NH: Arcadia Publishing, 1996), 7; Lee Ellen Griffith, *Images of America: Freehold, Volume II* (Charleston, SC: Arcadia Publishing, 1999), 10.

43. Maurice Mustin, ed., *A Sketch of Monmouth County, New Jersey, 1683–1929* (Camden, NJ: M. Mustin Company, 1929), 13; Sim, *Commercial Canning in New Jersey,* 270–79.

44. Alan Rosenthal and John Blydenburgh, eds., *Politics in New Jersey* (New Brunswick, NJ: Rutgers University Press, 1975), 130.

45. Extension Service, College of Agriculture, *Census Facts—Monmouth County* (New Brunswick, NJ: Rutgers, The State University, 1954), table 2b.

46. MCPB, *Monmouth County Demographic & Economic Profile: Updates, Estimates, and Projections,* 8.

47. Ibid., 50; Griffith, *Freehold, Volume II,* 48, 58.

48. Sim, *Commercial Canning in New Jersey*, 270–79; Mustin, ed., *A Sketch of Monmouth County*, 13; Griffith, *Freehold, Volume II*, 37.

49. Georgia East, "Old Rug Mill Getting the Red Carpet Treatment," *Asbury Park Press*, special insert section, 9.

50. Pine, Hershenov, and Lefkowitz, *Peddler to Suburbanite*, 142.

51. MCPB, *Monmouth County Demographic and Economic (MCD&E) Profile*, 1:10.

52. Ibid., 64–65.

53. MCPB, *MCD&E Updates, Estimates, and Projections*, 8.

54. Edgar I. Vanderveer, ed., *County, City, Town, Township, and Borough Officials of Monmouth County (1917)* (Keyport, NJ: The Weekly Print, 1917), 5.

55. MCPB, *Monmouth County Profile 1997* (Freehold: MCPB Publication, 1997), 10–13; MCPB, *MCD&E Updates, Estimates, and Projections*, 8.

56. United States Bureau of the Census (USBC), *Census Tracts—Monmouth County (1990)* (Washington: United States Government Printing Office, 1990), table 8.

57. USBC, *Census Tracts—Monmouth County (1990)*, tables 22, 23, 28, 29. The white unemployment rate was 4.9 percent. For African Americans, it was 13.0 percent. For Latinos, the unemployment rate was 11.8 percent, and 17.6 percent lived in poverty.

58. MCPB, *MCD&E Profile*, 1:47, 49, 2:53.

59. Griffith, *Freehold, Volume II*, 7; Griffith, *Freehold*, 55.

60. Griffith, *Freehold*, 50; Griffith, *Freehold, Volume II*, 12.

61. Sim, *Commercial Canning*, 270–79.

62. Griffith, *Freehold, Volume II*, 54–55.

63. Mustin, *A Sketch of Monmouth County*, 13; Griffith, *Freehold*, 57. Griffith, *Freehold, Volume II*, 82–86; East, "Old Rug Mill," *Asbury Park Press*, 16 December 1999, 9.

64. Pine, Hershenov, and Lefkowitz, *Peddler to Suburbanite*, 109; Griffith, *Freehold, Volume II*, 58.

65. Extension Service, *Census Facts—Monmouth County*, table 2b.

66. MCPB, *MCD&E Updates, Estimates, and Projections*, 8.

67. Vanderveer, ed., *County, City, Town, Township, and Borough Officials of Monmouth County (1917)*, 5.

68. Griffith, *Freehold*, 113; Griffith, *Freehold, Volume II*, 66–69.

69. Griffith, *Freehold, Volume II*, 28–29, 37, 39.

70. Pine, Hershenov, and Lefkowitz, *Peddler to Suburbanite*, 94, 98.

71. East, "Old Rug Mill," *Asbury Park Press*, 16 December 1999, 9; Griffith, *Freehold, Volume II*, 85.

72. Pine, Hershenov, and Lefkowitz, *Peddler to Suburbanite*, 142; MCPB, *Municipal Developments and Start Dates* (Freehold: MCPB DataFile, 2000), unpaginated.

73. State Industrial Directories Corporation, *1980 New Jersey Industrial Directory* (New York: State Industrial Directories Corporation Publication, 1980), G290–G291; MacRae's Blue Book, Inc., *MacRae's Industrial Directory—New Jersey, 1985* (New York: MacRae's Blue Book, Inc., 1985), 269–70.

74. MCPB, *MCD&E Updates, Estimates, and Projections*, 8.

75. MCPB, *MCD&E Profile*, 2:44, 53.

76. Brown, *Manalapan in Three Centuries*, 69; Pine, Hershenov, and Lefkowitz, *Peddler to Suburbanite*, 148.

77. Barbara G. Salmore and Stephen A. Salmore, *New Jersey Politics and Government: Suburban Politics Comes of Age* (Lincoln: University of Nebraska Press, 1993), 26–27.

78. Board of Elections, *Monmouth County Political Registration Book* (Freehold, NJ: Monmouth County, Board of Elections, 1990), unpaginated.

79. Linda Faye Williams, "The Civil Rights–Black Power Legacy: Black Women Elected Officials at the Local, State, and National Levels," in *Sisters in the Struggle: African-American Women in the Civil Rights-Black Power Movement*, ed. Bettye Collier-Thomas and V. P. Franklin (New York: New York University Press, 2001), 306–31.

80. Michael B. Katz, Mark J. Stern, and Jamie J. Fader, "The New African American Inequality," *Journal of American History*, June 2005, accessed 12 April 2009, http://

www.historycooperative.org/cgi-bin/justtop.cgi?act=justtop&url=http://
www.historycooperative.org/journals/jah/92.1/katz.html.

81. David L. Kirp and John P. Dwyer, *Our Town: Race, Housing, and the Soul of Suburbia* (New Brunswick, NJ: Rutgers University Press, 1997), 112–36.

82. Maurice Mustin, ed., *A Sketch of Monmouth County, New Jersey, 1683–1929* (Camden, NJ: M. Mustin Company, 1929), 44.

83. Pine, Hershenov, and Lefkowitz, *Peddler to Suburbanite*, 118.

84. Sim, *Commercial Canning in New Jersey*, 448–51.

85. Alma Donahay and 1967 Eighth Grade Class, *History of Howell* (Howell, NJ: Howell Historical Society, 1982), 27, 47–48.

86. Edgar I. Vanderveer, *County, City, Town, Township, and Borough Officials of Monmouth County (1917)* (Keyport, NJ: The Weekly Print, 1917), 5.

87. NJBC, *New Jersey State Census—1875* (ms.), schedule 1.

88. MCPB, *Monmouth County Demographic and Economic (MCD&E) Profile: Updates, Estimates, and Projections*, 8.

89. Ibid.

90. Tova Navarra, *Images of America: Howell and Farmingdale: A Social and Cultural History* (Dover, NH: Arcadia Publishing, 1996), 7.

91. NJBC, *New Jersey State Census—1875* (ms.), schedule 1; Monmouth County Archives (MCA), *Enumeration 1880* (Manalapan), 2–55; Ellen Thorne Morris, *Monmouth County, New Jersey: Families of Color in 1880* (Allenhurst, NJ: privately published, 1991), 65–66; NJBC, *New Jersey State Census—1895* (ms.), schedule 1.

92. NJBC, *New Jersey State Census—1895* (ms.), schedule 1.

93. United States Bureau of the Census (USBC), *United States Census Data for Townships*, 32.6–32.7; Lenora McKay, *The Blacks of Monmouth County: A Bicentennial Tribute* (privately published, 1976), 41.

94. Donahay, et al., *History of Howell*, 40.

95. Leslie Wilson, "Dark Spaces: An Account of Afro-American Suburbanization, 1890–1950," PhD diss., City University of New York, 1992, 406; MCPB, *Monmouth County Profile 1997*, 2.

96. Donahay, et al., *History of Howell*, 27, 47–48.

97. Extension Service, College of Agriculture, *Census Facts: Monmouth County* (New Brunswick, NJ: Rutgers, the State University, 1954), tables 1 and 2b.

98. Sim, *Commercial Canning in New Jersey*, 424, 448–51.

99. USBC, *Ninth Census of the United States, 1870* (ms.), schedule 1; NJBC, *New Jersey State Census—1895* (ms.), schedule 1; Mustin, *A Sketch of Monmouth County*, 38; MCPB, *MCD&E Profile: Updates, Estimates, and Projections*, 8.

100. Vanderveer, ed., *Officials of Monmouth County (1917)*, 5. R. J. Estelle, Howard J. Ketcham, and Charles Pohlemus served on the Howell Township committee at this time. Edgar O. Murphy served as Farmingdale's mayor and coordinated the borough council.

101. NJBC, *New Jersey State Census—1915*, schedule 3; Pine, Hershenov, and Lefkowitz, *Peddler to Suburbanite*, 116. Barbara Cunningham, ed., *The New Jersey Ethnic Experience* (Union City, NJ: William H. Wise and Company, 1977), 303–4.

102. John Cunningham, *New Jersey's Rich Harvest: A 200th Anniversary Tribute to the New Jersey Agricultural Society* (Trenton: New Jersey Agricultural Society Publication, 1981), 26–27.

103. Sim, *Commercial Canning*, 448–51.

104. Pine, Hershenov, and Lefkowitz, *Peddler to Suburbanite*, 109.

105. Ibid., 118–20.

106. Ibid., 182–83.

107. Flora Higgins, "Interview with Rose Staples," 12 July 2000, in *Remembering the Twentieth Century: An Oral History of Monmouth County*, ed. Flora T. Higgins, http://www.visitmonmouth.com/oralhistory/bios/StaplesRose.htm.

108. Extension Service, College of Agriculture, *Census Facts: Monmouth County*, table 2b.

109. Pine, Hershenov, and Lefkowitz, *Peddler to Suburbanite*, 121.

110. Navarra, *Howell and Farmingdale*, 62.

111. Monmouth County Department of Economic Development and Tourism (MCDEDT), *Major Employers List* (Freehold, NJ: MCDEDT Publication, 2000), 2.

112. Navarra, *Howell and Farmingdale*, 125.

113. MCPB, *Municipal Developments and Start Dates* (Freehold, NJ: MCPB DataFile, 2000), unpaginated.

114. Navarra, *Howell and Farmingdale*, 7; MCPB, *MCD&E Profile: Updates, Estimates, and Projections*, 8; Pine, Hershenov, and Lefkowitz, *Peddler to Suburbanite*, 142, 144.

115. State Industrial Directories Corporation, *1980 New Jersey Industrial Directory* (New York: State Industrial Directories Corporation Publication, 1980), G288–G290, G292–G293. Howell and Farmingdale housed 50 industries, including electrics, electronics, road construction, plastics, retail, and sheet metal, in 1980; MacRae's Blue Book, Inc., *MacRae's Industrial Directory—New Jersey, 1985* (New York: MacRae's Blue Book, Inc., 1985), 267–69, 271. Farmingdale and Howell hosted 41 industries, including lubricants, technical education products, metal processing, tubing, insulated steel, and engineering tools.

116. Barbara G. Salmore and Stephen A. Salmore, *New Jersey Politics and Government: Suburban Politics Comes of Age* (Lincoln: University of Nebraska Press, 1993), 54, 57, 176.

117. MCPB, *MCD&E Profile: Updates, Estimates, and Projections*, 9. If Farmingdale was not landlocked by Howell, it is quite likely its population would have continued to grow just like the surrounding township.

118. Pine, Hershenov, and Lefkowitz, *Peddler to Suburbanite*, 148.

119. MCPB, *Monmouth County Profile 1997*, 10–11.

120. Navarra, *Howell and Farmingdale*, 8, 88, 92.

121. USBC, *Census Tracts—Monmouth County (1990)*, tables 20, 21, 26; MCPB, *MCD&E Profile*, 2:53. Figures for black unemployment were not calculated for Howell and Farmingdale because there were fewer than 400 African Americans in any tract.

122. MCPB, *MCD&E Profile*, 2:44.

123. Ibid., 44, 53.

124. MCPB, *MCD&E Profile*, 1:78.

125. Robert W. Lake, *The New Suburbanites: Race and Housing in the Suburbs* (New Brunswick, NJ: Center for Urban Policy Research, 1981), 51, 90–92.

126. Robert Fishman, *Bourgeois Utopias: The Rise and Fall of Suburbia* (New York: Basic Books, Inc., 1987), 8, 10, 26.

127. Paul Davidoff and Mary E. Brooks, "Zoning Out the Poor," in *Suburbia: The American Dream and Dilemma*, ed. Philip C. Dolce (New York: Anchor Books, 1976), 145.

128. Alan J. Karcher, *New Jersey's Multiple Municipal Madness* (New Brunswick, NJ: Rutgers University Press, 1998), 205; David Delaney, *Race, Place and the Law, 1836–1948* (Austin: University of Texas Press, 1998), 9.

129. Peter Siskind, "Suburban Growth and Its Discontents: The Logic and Limits of Reform on the Postwar Northeast Corridor," in *The New Suburban History*, ed. Kevin Kruse and Thomas Sugrue (Chicago: University of Chicago Press, 2006), 174–76.

130. Jonathan Birnbaum and Clarence Taylor, eds., *Civil Rights since 1787: A Reader on the Black Struggle* (New York: New York University Press, 2000), 477–89.

131. Roger Biles, "The Rise and Fall of Soul City: Planning, Politics, and Race in Recent America," *Journal of Planning History* 4, no. 1 (February 2008): 68–70.

Conclusion

White middle-class households in metropolitan areas throughout the United States perpetuated the segregation and discrimination African Americans faced between 1865 and 1965. The preservation of white supremacy after the abolition of slavery entailed a system explicitly designed to provide material and psychological advantages to white Americans. The denial of black institutions and organizations' collective efforts to improve the socioeconomic position of African American families defined the evolution of the nation's laws and economy. Only the limited attempts at reform through the Tuskegee movement, the women's club movement, the black church, and various civil rights or black nationalist organizations offered the chance for African Americans to survive racist violence and create enduring communities in New Jersey. African American success in transforming the legal restrictions facing them in both the North and the South met increasingly sophisticated resistance after 1945. The use of federal executive and judicial authority to undermine and eliminate permanent white advantages in employment, housing, and education engendered supposedly color-blind policies that were actually designed to continue the social and spatial isolation of African Americans. The rural corridor in the Garden State epitomized the processes of metropolitan exclusion between 1950 and 2000 in that middle-class black communities abandoned their historical activism and impoverished black towns became invisible within the emerging global economy and culture.

The election of Barack Obama in 2008 illustrated the tensions between the Black Freedom struggle and global metropolitan development. President Obama (then a senator) spoke in Philadelphia about the urgency of national unity across racial barriers at a moment of national and international crisis. He stood at crossroads for the nation where white resentment and black anger had held the political discourse in stalemate since 1970. His insight guided the electorate to consider the broad economic limitations that conglomerate capitalism generated in all Americans' lives over the previous four decades. "Just as black anger often proved counterproductive, so have these white resentments distracted from the real culprits of the middle class squeeze—a corporate culture rife with inside dealing, questionable accounting practices, and short term greed; a Washington dominated by lobbyists and special interests; economic policies that favor the few over the many."[1] American historians have often reproduced the same easy divisions between African Americans in major cities and white Americans in the surrounding suburbs. The more recent framework for the study of metropolitan regions and their role in the global society turns the page on this oversimplified history of urban divisions.[2] However, the function of race as a social force persisted across the redefinition of geographic, economic, and political spaces as New Jersey's suburbs erased its garden communities. African American activism did not reform New Jersey's economic priorities.

In the first half of the twentieth century, African American migrants built schools, churches, and towns to provide opportunities for their children in a state that denied them equal education, employment, and housing. The audacity of black civil rights organizations gradually eroded the formal and informal racial barriers that fueled the anger in the African American community throughout the twentieth century. Children of European immigrants formed a larger white community that understood the dangers of discrimination from their family histories.[3] Yet, state, regional, and local planning organizations throughout New Jersey still failed to recognize the needs for regional development, especially throughout the rural corridor. Instead, public planning rested on assumptions about the propriety of white control over the state economy as well as the local governance bodies. African American institutions and leaders maintained their calls for greater public engagement and investment, based on their experience in dismantling northern Jim Crow. White elected officials continued to exclude them from the conversations that shaped the first fifty years of the state's planned management. This discrimination nearly guaranteed the continuation of inequality for immigrants, the poor, and racial minorities into the twenty-first century.

African American migrants chose to settle in rural New Jersey because the small towns combined the pace of farm life in the South with freedom from frequent racist violence. Family life among African Americans in the rural corridor made the possibility of the American dream real for generations that had only known oppression in the United States. The discipline of black life in small towns between 1870 and 1930 stemmed from the new lifestyles African Americans enjoyed in these towns. Extended family networks taught moral piety and civic reform as the basis for aspirations to create a better nation. Without the safety of home and stability of employment, the attempts to transform the laws of the land would have been doomed from the start. The decisions to create communities in the rural North changed black families' opportunities for education, employment, and civic engagement by allowing new opportunities for free expression and public assembly.[4] African American ministers, doctors, and teachers motivated working-class and impoverished migrants to create new institutions and organizations dedicated to ending de facto segregation. The responsibilities of black leadership created new expectations for African Americans to organize in defense of their citizenship rights.

Historical memory provided the inspiration in these families and communities. Its influence in the communication of these lessons reinforced the importance of racial uplift in both the home and the church. Florence Spearing Randolph, Marion Thompson Wright, Lenora Walker McKay, and Madonna Carter Jackson preserved evidence of black history to instruct future generations. The consistency of their admonitions to maintain personal discipline and accountability shows that African Americans built their communities around a resilient sense of dignity and history. The church functioned as the core institution committed to the survival of the fledgling black communities in rural New Jersey. The measure of the churches' success in these towns was the education of young people about their spiritual worth. However, the churches also transformed local segregated schools from symbols of racial inferiority into bastions of scholastic achievement.[5]

Civil rights organizations formed in these towns to give voice to the demands of the New Negro movement. These groups emerged from the contexts provided by black churches and schools between 1920 and 1970. African Americans in communities like Red Bank and Long Branch began to use negotiations with local authorities and lawsuits at the state level to overturn previously unchallenged policies of racial segregation.[6] However, their dramatic failures after 1970 in the face of increasing incarceration rates for young black people left African Americans in small towns vulnerable to the massive economic shifts at the end of the twentieth century. The unprecedented imprisonment of young African Americans removed the constituency that pushed for the most dramatic legislative reforms. The politics of race changed at the local and state levels in response to the success of civil rights laws. White supremacy and white privilege differed as the former bitterly resisted racial equality and the latter only appeared to tolerate it. As the public discourse founded on the assumptions of the former concept lost support in New Jersey after 1950, the rhetoric of color blindness became a consistent refrain in denying the legitimacy of African American opinions. White privilege constituted the subconscious denial of any advantages white Americans continued to enjoy despite the adoption of civil rights laws to eliminate racial discrimination. Access to better housing remained one of the most profound manifestations of these advantages between 1970 and 2000 in the rural corridor.

Small black communities struggled to adapt to the forms of racial integration that developed after 1950. The rhetoric of color blindness combined with white financial advantages reinforced limitations on black educational and occupational achievement within the context of the global service economy.[7] American financial and real estate conglomerates relied on the inclusion of African American consumers to finance

metropolitan development and commerce. However, inclusion came at
the cost of public silence on continuing questions about racial inequality
after 1970. Racial integration failed to improve education, employment,
income, and wealth in many of these towns because the spatial separation of the black middle class and the black poor defined metropolitan
consolidation and uneven development. The emergence of a black middle class within the geographic context of suburbanization in New Jersey
provided greater physical and occupational mobility than any previous
generation enjoyed.[8] However, these opportunities for higher income
and more conspicuous consumption masked the collapse of the black
working class in many small towns. Few black professionals attained
elective offices in these suburbs, despite the rhetoric of color blindness
employed by local white residents. The impact of uneven development in
the suburbs on the earlier black settlements in the rural corridor was
devastating. Higher rates of unemployment, poverty, drug addiction,
and crime left them isolated and destitute after 1970. The experience of
towns like Red Bank, Long Branch, and Asbury Park contrasted sharply
with the larger regional patterns of suburban affluence.

    White middle-class diffidence towards black candidates for public of-
fice in rural New Jersey contributed to racial inequalities at the end of the
twentieth century by allowing the material conditions of racial integration to worsen the socioeconomic status of working-class African
Americans between 1970 and 2000.[9] When the culture of white privilege
and the economics of uneven development intersected during this period, exclusive white suburbs emerged where black migrant laborer communities once thrived. Rampant duplication of municipal services
throughout New Jersey under the guise of "home rule" threatened to
bankrupt municipalities. The entire state suffered financially because
these patterns went unchallenged at the end of the twentieth century.

    The southern counties in the rural corridor—Gloucester, Camden, and
Burlington—avoided the most severe fragmentation and taxation problems due to metropolitan growth at the end of the twentieth century. The
city of Camden continued its struggle to find a role in the global economy, but many of the suburbs in the rest of the county continued to attract
new residents. Uneven development was most prevalent in the compari-
sons between small communities like Pennsauken and Collingswood.
Burlington and Gloucester counties, on the other hand, only experienced
the benefits of metropolitan growth over the last two decades of the
century. While places like Woodbury and Mount Holly encountered
some racial tensions when African Americans began to move into the
suburbs, Medford and Woodbury Heights maintained high standards of
living. As a region, the most severe economic disparities along racial lines
reflected the patterns found surrounding Newark and Trenton between
1930 and 1970. These findings may indicate that the more extreme suburbanization of poverty will unfold as metropolitan growth sweeps

through this part of the state over the next few decades, as discussed in chapter 10.[10]

Northern New Jersey suburbs in Monmouth, Middlesex, Somerset, and Morris counties showed the costs of accelerated development in the megapolitan. The highest percentage of African Americans in the suburbs (41 percent) lived in the communities of northeastern New Jersey in 2000, while the lowest percentage (6 percent) lived in the northwestern part of the state. Morristown, Bound Brook, New Brunswick, and Asbury Park experienced the highest rates of African American and Latino migration into the suburbs. Rumson, Chatham, Randolph, and Far Hills remained the most racially exclusive communities during the period of metropolitan expansion. The municipal boundaries that defined racially integrated suburban communities within the context of a growing service economy became more rigid in these northern counties. At the start of the twenty-first century, the persistent residential segregation in the towns of northern New Jersey represented a considerable obstacle to economic growth and social stability.[11] Continuing racial inequality as commercial and residential sprawl consumes the green spaces at the metropolitan fringe counteracts the formation of a more cohesive global society in service to white middle-class consumption.

Growth management is a critical aspect of any process to dismantle persistent forms of racial segregation in a metropolitan region. Stuart Meck and Rebecca Retzlaff documented one of the defining legal precedents regarding sprawl and residential development in the 1972 *Golden v. Planning Board of Town of Ramapo* (New York) case. The town developed an eighteen-year capital development plan that prioritized residential construction approval for developers who provided funding for public infrastructure. As individual home owners and local developers challenged the requirements of the plan in court, the effects of the policy became apparent. Low-income and multifamily housing units could not compete with single-family home developers in the provision of new water lines and electrical systems. Ultimately, the system facilitated slow growth residential development that limited the economic prosperity of the Ramapo region. Local authorities abandoned the specific development system, while preserving the assumptions about residential homogeneity that created it.[12]

The inclusion of low-income and multifamily residential units took priority in New Jersey because the state Supreme Court ordered the real-estate construction industry to cease its discrimination against metropolitan inclusion. William Baer considered the process of unfettered metropolitan expansion under private investment in California between 1967 and 2004. Long-standing appeals to "home rule" received considerable scrutiny from state authorities between 1980 and 2000. As a result, local officials, home owners, and developers adapted the vocabulary of regional planning to resist the future inclusion of more affordable housing. The early stages of metropolitan development plans in California survived because they could not be effectively enforced. As enforcement improved over a period of decades, local compliance with both the goals and the methods of state-guided land use policy increased. Baer closes, "Redistribution [of municipal land use] . . . through planning and the law in both New Jersey and California is turning out to be a marathon, not a 100-meter dash to success."[13] The patience about the transformation of an economic institution like the real estate industry and its supporters in local government combines with the chronological scope planning professionals use to frame development plans to offer important perspectives on the ways the Black Freedom struggle can contribute to metropolitan growth in the twenty-first century.

When African American migrants moved to New Jersey at the start of the twentieth century, they entertained no expectation that racial equality would be realized in their lifetimes. Their approach was circumspect. The visceral experiences of racial terrorism mandated a careful strategy, even from the most strident voices for integration. Leaders like Florence Randolph and George White employed a long-term perspective in their pursuit of racial justice. Their sense of civil rights planning stretched beyond a twenty-year or forty-year time line. More recent advocates for black equality like Ollievita Williams and Ermon Jones did not engage the institutions of regional planning in the language of development employed in places like Ramapo, New York, and Modoc County, California. Constructing proposals that award points for specific municipal, county, and regional benchmarks for dismantling the processes of segregation and discrimination carries the work of inclusive democracy into the twenty-first century. The collaboration of government agencies ranging from human rights commissions to state planning boards with the largest commercial and residential developers in building and marketing profitable, integrated neighborhoods would satisfy the requirements of the *Mount Laurel* I and II rulings.

Prioritizing the involvement of individual home owners and renters in the growth management process would remove the burden of opaque decision making at the state or regional levels. African Americans constructed interactive organizations from the local through the global levels to articulate their agenda for civil rights and racial equality between 1881 and 1977. The political isolation of these organizations from planning boards in New Jersey, especially above the municipal level, only hindered the creation and implementation of new strategies to break down residential segregation and racial discrimination. Race cannot be absent from the discussion of water treatment, architectural design, commercial zoning, or waste management systems. The historical assumptions about the quality of life different people experience in different neighborhoods must be made explicit in policy discussions at every level. White elected officials and professional staffers need to learn the cultural vocabulary of the people they serve, particularly in the smaller communities on the metropolitan fringe. African American activists and community leaders should draft and develop the financial and scientific plans for the physical manifestation of Martin Luther King Jr.'s beloved community. When the political leadership of the white middle class allows the values of democratic equality to shape the science of regional planning and design, then the nation will have taken a significant step forward in pursuit of its ideals.

Racial segregation probably stretches back to the late seventeenth century, predating the formal creation of the United States in 1789 by one hundred years. Widespread European discrimination against Africans and their descendants may have originated three centuries earlier. The legacies of unspoken decisions that became inarguable traditions between 1500 and 1850 continue to haunt current political, economic, and cultural debates in 2013. The solutions will require more determination from future citizens than any slaveholder or segregationist mustered in the creation and maintenance of inequality over more than sixteen generations of oppression. In 1950, the Garden State's chosen representatives made a choice to move into an uncertain future where race no longer dictated the material conditions of a person's life. Fifty years later, much of the promise of that decision remained unfulfilled for African Americans in the Suburban State. Regional planning was a crucial frontier for civil rights involvement in New Jersey after 1950. While African American leaders focused on the political and cultural aspects of desegregation, the culture of public planning reinforced the traditions of white economic authority at both the state and local levels. Churches, schools, and civil rights organizations missed a crucial opportunity gain a foothold in the process to shape the future of the state between 1960 and 2000. The values of family, history, and leadership held particular importance for the regional planning processes across the state. Principles like accountability and sustainability had been a consistent part of the black freedom struggle from the early twentieth century. Without the voices of African Americans shaping state planning policy, the chances of reducing inequality for immigrants, the poor, and racial minorities shrank as the twenty-first century began.

NOTES

1. Barack Obama, "Obama Race Speech," *Huffington Post*, 17 November 2008, http://www.huffingtonpost.com/2008/03/18/obama-race-speech-read-th_n_92077 .html.

2. Amanda I. Seligman, "The New Suburban History," *Journal of Planning History* 3, no. 4 (November 2004): 313; Matthew D. Lassiter, "The New Suburban History II: Political Culture and Metropolitan Space," *Journal of Planning History* 4, no. 1 (February 2005): 76.

3. Matthew Frye Jacobson, *Whiteness of a Different Color: European Immigrants and the Alchemy of Race* (Cambridge, MA: Harvard University Press, 1998), 82–85.

4. Kevin K. Gaines, *Uplifting the Race: Black Leadership, Politics, and Culture in the Twentieth Century* (Chapel Hill, NC: University of North Carolina Press, 1996), 234–60.

5. C. Eric Lincoln and Lawrence Mamiya, *The Black Church in the African American Experience* (Durham, NC: Duke University Press, 1990), 115–62.

6. Michelle R. Boyd, *Jim Crow Nostalgia: Reconstructing Race in Bronzeville* (Minneapolis: University of Minnesota Press, 2008), 11–24.

7. Kevin M. Kruse, *White Flight: Atlanta and the Making of Modern Conservatism* (Princeton, NJ: Princeton University Press, 2005), 194–95, 200–1.

8. Lizabeth Cohen, *A Consumer's Republic: The Politics of Mass Consumption in Postwar America* (New York: Alfred A. Knopf, 2003), 181–84.

9. Linda Faye Williams, "The Civil Rights–Black Power Legacy: Black Women Elected Officials at the Local, State, and National Levels," in *Sisters in the Struggle: African American Women in the Civil Rights-Black Power Movement*, ed. Bettye Collier-Thomas and V. P. Franklin (New York: New York University Press, 2001), 309, 326–27.

10. Howard Gillette, *Camden after the Fall: Decline and Renewal in a Post-Industrial City* (Philadelphia: University of Pennsylvania Press, 2005), 95–120; Andrew Mangler, "South Jersey Data," Court Street School Education Community Center file, Freehold, NJ, 2009.

11. Kevin J. Mumford, *Newark: A History of Race, Rights, and Riots in America* (New York: New York University Press, 2007), 3, 101–2; Andrew Mangler, "South Jersey Data," Court Street School Education Community Center file.

12. Stuart Meck and Rebecca Retzlaff, "The Emergence of Growth Management Planning in the United States: The Case of *Golden v. Planning Board of Town of Ramapo* and Its Aftermath," *Journal of Planning History* 7, no. 2 (May 2008): 113–57.

13. William C. Baer, "California's Fair-Share Housing 1967–2004: The Planning Approach," *Journal of Planning History* 7, no. 1 (February 2008): 48–71.

Bibliography

PRIMARY SOURCES

Aumack, Douglas. "Interview with David Engebretson." 15 August 2000. In *Remembering the Twentieth Century: An Oral History of Monmouth County*, ed. Flora T. Higgins. http://www.visitmonmouth.com/oralhistory/.

Board of Elections. *Monmouth County Political Registration Book*. Freehold, NJ: Monmouth County Board of Elections, 1990.

Community Planning Associates. Randolph Township Comprehensive Development Plan—Report and Recommendations , 1960.

Conohan, Sherry. "Interview with Theodore J. Narozanick." 30 June 2000.

Cooper, Anna Julia. *A Voice from the South*. Xenia, OH: The Aldine Printing House, 1892.

Elliott, Helen. Recorded interview. 18 December 2000.

Extension Service, College of Agriculture. *Census Facts—Monmouth County*. New Brunswick, NJ: Rutgers, The State University, 1954.

Garcia-Malave, Maria. Recorded interview. 4 December 2000.

Higgins, Flora. "Interview with Rose Staples." 12 July 2000. In *Remembering the Twentieth Century: An Oral History of Monmouth County*, ed. Flora T. Higgins. http://www.visitmonmouth.com/oralhistory/bios/StaplesRose.htm.

Ku Klux Klan. *Tri-State KlonKlave Souvenir Program*. George Moss Collection, Long Branch, NJ, 1924.

———. *Imperial Klaliff's Day Program*. Long Branch, NJ: George Moss Collection, 1925.

———. *Fourth Annual Fourth of July Celebration*. Long Branch, NJ: George Moss Collection, 1926.

Lenox, Alison. "Interview with Renee Swartz." 11 July 2000. In *Remembering the Twentieth Century: An Oral History of Monmouth County*, ed. Flora T. Higgins. http://www.visitmonmouth.com/oralhistory/bios/SwartzRenee.htm.

Monmouth County Archives. *Census Enumeration 1880*. Manalapan, NJ: Monmouth County Library, 1997.

———. *New Jersey State Census—1865*. Manalapan, NJ: Monmouth County Library, 1997.

———. *New Jersey State Census—1875*. Manalapan, NJ: Monmouth County Library, 1997.

———. *New Jersey State Census—1895*. Manalapan, NJ: Monmouth County Library, 1997.

———. *New Jersey State Census—1915*. Manalapan, NJ: Monmouth County Library, 1997.

Monmouth County Department of Economic Development and Tourism. *Major Employers List*. Freehold, NJ: Monmouth County Department of Economic Development and Tourism, 2000.

Monmouth County Planning Board. *1996 Annual Report*. Freehold, NJ: Monmouth County Planning Board, 1996.

———. *Cross Acceptance '97*. Freehold, NJ: Monmouth County Planning Board, 1997.

———. *Housing: Monmouth County—1971*. Freehold, NJ: Monmouth County Planning Board, 1971.

————. *Monmouth County Demographic and Economic Profile.* 2 vols. Freehold, NJ: Monmouth County Planning Board, 1993.

————. *Monmouth County Demographic and Economic Updates, Estimates, and Projections.* Freehold, NJ: Monmouth County Planning Board, 1997.

————. *Monmouth County Population and Employment Estimations.* Freehold, NJ: Monmouth County Planning Board, 1997.

————. *Monmouth County Profile 1997.* Freehold, NJ: Monmouth County Planning Board, 1997.

————. *Municipal Developments and Start Dates.* Freehold, NJ: Monmouth County Planning Board DataFile, 2000.

————. *Proposed Development Activity, Monmouth County, 1994.* Freehold, NJ: Monmouth County Planning Board, 1994.

————. *Proposed Development Activity, Monmouth County, 1994.* Freehold, NJ: Monmouth County Planning Board, 1995.

————. *Proposed Development Activity, Monmouth County, 1994.* Freehold, NJ: Monmouth County Planning Board, 1996.

————. *Monmouth County Transportation: Trends and Issues.* Freehold, NJ: Monmouth County Planning Board, 1995.

————. *The Urban Communities Study Series: Red Bank, New Jersey.* Freehold, NJ: Monmouth County Planning Board, 1977.

New Jersey Local Government Services Division. *Census Data for New Jersey Townships.* Trenton: State of New Jersey Publication, 1970.

Oates, Reverend Caleb. Recorded interview. 27 June 2000.

Parker, Dr. James. Recorded interview. 22 June 2001.

Parker, Dr. Margaret. Recorded interview. 16 June 2000.

Paul, Connie. "Interview with Lillie Hendry and Marion Russell." 28 August 2000. In *Remembering the Twentieth Century: An Oral History of Monmouth County,* ed. Flora T. Higgins. http://www.visitmonmouth.com/oralhistory/.

Russell, Nicy, M. H. Recorded interview. 8 January 1998. 2 tapes.

Southern Poverty Law Center. "Guarding against Hate." *Intelligence Report* (Fall 2000), accessed 8 April 2008, http://www.splcenter.org/intel/intelreport/article.jsp?aid=227.

State Redevelopment Office. *Focus Group: Urban Problems in Asbury Park.* Shrewsbury, NJ: Monmouth County Library, Eastern Branch, 1994.

Stevenson, Lila. Recorded interview. 17 June 2001.

Township of Franklin. Comprehensive Plan Township of Franklin Somerset County, New Jersey . 1982.

Township of Randolph, "Getting to Know Us: History, Our Grand Hotels." Randolph Township Online, 2006. http://www.randolphnj.org/ get_to_know_us/ grand_hotels.

Truscott, Martin P. *Monmouth County Census Trends, 1970–1980.* Freehold, NJ: Monmouth County Planning Board Publication, 1984.

United States Bureau of the Census. *1950 Census of Population.* Vol. 2, *Characteristics of Population, Part 30 (NJ).* Washington, DC: United States Government Printing Office, 1952.

————. *Census Tracts—Monmouth County (1980).* Washington, DC: United States Government Printing Office, 1980.

————. *Census Tracts—Monmouth County (1990).* Washington, DC: United States Government Printing Office, 1990.

————. *Fifteenth Census of the United States—1930.* Washington, DC: United States Government Printing Office, 2003.

————. *Negro Population in the United States, 1790–1915.* Washington, DC: United States Government Printing Office, 1918; Kraus reprint, 1960.

————. *Negroes in the United States, 1920–1932.* New York: Kraus Reprint Co., 1969.

————. *Ninth Census of the United States—1870.* Washington, DC: United States Government Printing Office, 1943.

Urban Colored Population Commission. *New Jersey Negro in World War II: Contributions and Activities.* Trenton: State of New Jersey, 1945.

Walker, Vyeta. Recorded interview. 5 December 2000.

West, June. "Interview with Ada Bryan." In *Remembering the Twentieth Century: An Oral History of Monmouth County,* ed. Flora T. Higgins. http://www.visitmonmouth.com/oralhistory/bios/BryanAda.htm.

OTHER PRINTED PRIMARY SOURCES

Andrews, W. Earle. *Asbury Park Beachfront Improvement.* New York: privately published, 1945.

Asbury Park Evening Press

Asbury Park Press

Asbury Park Sunday Press

Ashby, William M. *Tales without Hate.* Newark, NJ: Newark Preservation and Landmarks Committee, 1980.

Bittle, Holly. "Pennsville Township in Salem County, NJ: History, Present Time, and an Optimistic Future." Online archive for Race and the Suburbs discussion group. http://groups.yahoo.com/ group/Race_Suburbs.

Bledsoe, M. Geraldine Neal. *Ferdinand G. Ferguson: A Great Humanitarian, A Great American.* Privately published, 1976.

Boyd, Julian. *Fundamental Laws and Constitutions of New Jersey, 1664–1964.* Princeton, NJ: Van Nostrand, 1964.

Bureau of Industrial Statistics of New Jersey. *The Industrial Directory of New Jersey—1915.* Camden, NJ: S. Chew and Sons, Co., 1915.

Bureau of Industrial Statistics of New Jersey. *The Industrial Directory of New Jersey—1934.* Trenton: New Jersey Industrial Directory Publishing Company, 1934.

Bureau of Statistics and Records, New Jersey State Department of Labor. *The Industrial Directory of New Jersey—1938.* Trenton: New Jersey Industrial Directory Publishing Company, 1938.

Calvary Baptist Church. *1895–1995, 100th Anniversary Pictorial History of Calvary Baptist Church.* Privately published, 1995.

Center for Community Arts. "Community History Program." Center for Community Arts—Cape May, New Jersey. http://www.centerforcommunityarts.org/history.htm.

Color Lines Project. Rowan University, Glassboro, NJ, 2002.

Colorlines

Correspondence of the National Association for the Advancement of Colored People. Manuscript Division, Library of Congress, Washington, DC. 1928–1955.

Crisis

"East Jersey State Prison," http://prisonplace.com.

The Echo

Freehold News-Transcript

Higgins, Flora T., ed. *Remembering the Twentieth Century: An Oral History of Monmouth County, New Jersey,* accessed 6 June 2002, http://www.visitmonmouth.com/oralhistory/.

Howell Booster

Hudson Dispatch. *The Industrial Directory of New Jersey—1946–47.* Union City, NJ: Hudson Dispatch, 1946.

Hudson Dispatch. *The Industrial Directory of New Jersey—1954–55.* Union City, NJ: Hudson Dispatch, 1954.

The Intelligence Report

Jones, Ermon. "Housing and Head Start Issues." Court Street School Education Community Center file. Freehold, NJ, 2009.

Journal of Blacks in Higher Education. "Blacks Remain a Small Fraction of Fulbright Scholars." 48 (Summer 2005).

Lamond, James. "Development of East Brunswick, NJ." Online archive for Race and the Suburbs discussion group. http://groups.yahoo.com/group/Race_Suburbs.

Long Branch Daily Record

MacRae's Blue Book, Inc. *MacRae's Industrial Directory—New Jersey, 1985*. New York: MacRae's Blue Book, Inc., 1985.

Mandel, Seth. "Training School Memories on Display at Lakeview." *The Sentinel*, 26 January 2006.

Mangler, Andrew. "South Jersey Data." Court Street School Education Community Center file. Freehold, NJ, 2009.Martin, George C. *History of Asbury Park and Long Branch*. West Long Branch, NJ: privately published, 1902.

Monmouth Democrat

Monmouth Inquirer

Monmouth Press

Morris, Ellen Thorne. *Monmouth County, New Jersey: Families of Color in 1880*. Allenhurst, NJ: privately published, 1991.

Mustin, Maurice, ed. *A Sketch of Monmouth County, New Jersey, 1683–1929*. Camden, NJ: M. Mustin Co., 1929.

Newark News

Newark Star-Ledger

New Jersey Afro-American

New Jersey Journal

New York Sun

New York Times

Obama, Barack. "Obama Race Speech." *Huffington Post*, 17 November 2008, http://www.huffingtonpost.com/2008/03/18/obama-race-speech-read-th_n_92077.html.

Olde Monmouth Times

Red Bank Register

The Sentinel

Shore Press

The Star Ledger

State Industrial Directories Corporation. *1980 New Jersey Industrial Directory*. New York: State Industrial Directories Corporation Publication, 1980.

Trentonian

Vanderveer, Edgar I. *County, City, Town, Township, and Borough Officials of Monmouth County, 1917*. Keyport, NJ: The Weekly Print, 1917.

Williams, C. P. *Second Baptist Church 100th Anniversary Booklet*. Privately published, 1987.

Williams, Fannie Barrier. "The Problem of Employment for Negro Women." *Southern Workman* 32 (1903): 432–37.

Women's Club of Asbury Park. *An Historical Review of Business and Other Organizations Operating in Asbury Park*. Asbury Park: City Publication, 1929.

SECONDARY SOURCES

Adamson, Christopher. "Defensive Localism in White and Black: A Comparative History of European-American and African-American Youth Gangs." *Ethnic and Racial Studies* 23, no. 2 (March 2000): 272–98.

Allen, Ernest, Jr. "Making the Strong Survive: The Contours and Contradictions of Message Rap." In *Droppin' Science: Critical Essays on Rap Music and Hip Hop Culture*, edited by William Eric Perkins. Philadelphia: Temple University Press, 1996.

American Social History Project. *Who Built America? Working People and the Nation's Economy, Politics, Culture, and Society.* Vol. 2, *1877 to the Present.* New York: American Social History Productions, Inc., 2000.

Anderson, Claud. *PowerNomics: The National Plan to Empower Black America.* Bethesda, MD: PowerNomics Corporation, 2001.

Anderson, James. *The Education of Blacks in the South, 1860–1935.* Chapel Hill, NC: University of North Carolina Press, 1988.

Armory, Cleveland. *The Last Resorts.* New York: Harper and Bros., 1948.

Armstead, Myra B. Young. *"Lord, Please Don't Take Me in August": African Americans in Newport and Saratoga Springs, 1870–1930.* Chicago: University of Illinois Press, 1999.

Baer, William C. "California's Fair-Share Housing 1967–2004: The Planning Approach." *Journal of Planning History* 7, no. 1 (February 2008): 48–71.

Baldassare, Mark, and Georjeanna Wilson. "More Trouble in Paradise." *Urban Affairs Review* 30, no. 5 (1995): 690–708.

Basie, Count, and Albert Murray. *Good Morning Blues: The Autobiography of Count Basie.* New York: Random House, 1985.

Beale, David, and Andy Schneider. *Juvenile Justice in New Jersey.* Princeton, NJ: Center for Analysis of Public Issues, 1973.

Bebout, John C., and Ronald J. Grele. *Where Cities Meet: The Urbanization of New Jersey.* Princeton, NJ: D. Van Nostrand Company, Inc., 1964.

Bederman, Gail. *Manliness and Civilization: A Cultural History of Gender and Race in the United States, 1880–1917.* Chicago: University of Chicago Press, 1995.

Bennett, Lerone, Jr. *The Shaping of Black America.* Chicago: Johnson, 1975.

Bertman, Stephen. *Vital Speeches of the Day.* Mount Pleasant, SC: City News Publishing, 2000.

Biles, Roger. "The Rise and Fall of Soul City: Planning, Politics, and Race in Recent America." *Journal of Planning History* 4, no. 1 (February 2008): 68–70.

Binford, Henry. *The First Suburbs: Residential Communities on the Boston Periphery, 1815–1860.* Chicago: University of Chicago Press, 1985.

Birnbaum, Jonathan, and Clarence Taylor, eds. *Civil Rights since 1787.* New York: New York University Press, 2000.

Black, William. "Empire of Consensus: City Planning, Zoning, and Annexation in Dallas, 1900–1960." PhD diss., Columbia University, 1982.

Blackmon, Douglas A. *Slavery by Another Name: The Re-enslavement of Black Americans from the Civil War to World War II.* New York: Doubleday, 2008.

Blassingame, John W. "Before the Ghetto: The Making of a Black Community in Savannah, Georgia, 1865–1880." *Journal of Social History* 6 (Summer 1973): 463–88.

Blassingame, John W., and John R. McKivigan, eds. *The Frederick Douglass Papers Series One: Speeches, Debates, and Interviews.* Vol. 15, *1881–1895.* New Haven, CT: Yale University Press, 1992.

Blee, Kathleen M. *Women of the Klan: Racism and Gender in the 1920s.* Berkeley: University of California Press, 1991.

Bluestone, Barry, and Bennett Harrison. *The Deindustrialization of America: Plant Closings, Community Abandonment, and the Dismantling of Basic Industry.* New York: Basic Books, 1982.

Blumberg, Leonard, and Michael Lalli. "Little Ghettoes: A Study of Negroes in the Suburbs." *Phylon* 27 (Summer 1966): 117–31.

Bonilla-Silva, Eduardo. *Racism without Racists: Color-Blind Racism and the Persistence of Racial Inequality in the United States.* New York: Rowman and Littlefield, 2006.

Borchert, James. *Alley Life in Washington: Family, Community, Religion, and Folklife in the City, 1850–1970.* Chicago: University of Illinois Press, 1980.

Boyd, Michelle R. *Jim Crow Nostalgia: Reconstructing Race in Bronzeville.* Minneapolis: University of Minnesota Press, 2008.

Boynton, Maria. "Springtown, NJ. Explorations in the History and Culture of a Black Community." PhD diss., University of Pennsylvania, 1986 (DA 8614769).

Brodkin, Karen. *How Jews Became White Folks and What That Says about Race in America.* New Brunswick, NJ: Rutgers University Press, 1999.

Brown, James S. *Manalapan in Three Centuries.* Manalapan, NJ: privately published, 1991.

Burns, Allan F. *Maya in Exile: Guatemalans in Florida.* Philadelphia: Temple University Press, 1993.

Burton-Rose, Daniel, Dan Pens, and Paul Wright, eds. *The Celling of America: An Inside Look at the United States Prison Industry.* Monroe, ME: Common Courage Press, 1998.

Camden County Historical Society. *The Black Experience in Southern New Jersey.* Camden, NJ: Camden County Historical Society Publication, 1985.

Carmack, Robert M., ed. *Harvest of Violence: The Maya Indians and the Guatemalan Crisis.* Norman: University of Oklahoma Press, 1988.

Carrigan, William D. *The Making of a Lynching Culture: Violence and Vigilantism in Central Texas, 1836–1916.* Chicago: University of Illinois, 2006.

Cha-Jua, Sundiata, and Clarence Lang. "The 'Long Movement' as Vampire: Temporal and Spatial Fallacies in Recent Black Freedom Studies." *Journal of African American History* 92, no. 2 (Spring 2007): 265–88.

Chalmers, David. *Hooded Americanism: The History of the Ku Klux Klan.* Durham, NC: Duke University Press, 1987.

Chang, Jeff. *Can't Stop, Won't Stop: A History of the Hip Hop Generation.* New York: Picador, 2005.

Church of Saint Rose of Lima. *St. Rose of Lima Centennial.* Freehold, NJ: Andersen Graphics, 1971.

Cohen, Lizabeth. *A Consumer's Republic: The Politics of Mass Consumption in Postwar America.* New York: Vintage Books, 2003.

———. *Making a New Deal: Industrial Workers in Chicago, 1919–1939.* New York: Cambridge University Press, 1990.

Collier-Thomas, Bettye. *Daughters of Thunder: Black Women Preachers and Their Sermons, 1850–1979.* San Francisco: Jossey-Bass Publishers, 1998.

———. *Jesus, Jobs, and Justice: African American Women and Religion.* New York: Knopf, 2010.

Collier-Thomas, Bettye, and V. P. Franklin. *Sisters in the Struggle: African American Women in the Civil Rights–Black Power Movement.* New York: New York University Press, 2001.

Collins, Chuck, and Felice Yeskel, eds. *Economic Apartheid in America: A Primer on Economic Inequality and Insecurity.* New York: The New Press, 2005.

Collins, Patricia Hill. *Black Feminist Thought: Knowledge, Consciousness, and the Politics of Empowerment.* New York: Routledge, 2000.

Conkin, Paul K. "Jersey Homesteads—A Triple Cooperative." In *Tomorrow a New World: The New Deal Community Program.* Ithaca, NY: Cornell University Press, 1959.

Conley, Dalton. *Being Black, Living in the Red: Race, Wealth, and Social Policy in America.* Los Angeles: University of California Press, 1999.

Connelly, George J. "Progressive Education between the Wars: The Matawan, New Jersey School District, 1918–1940." PhD diss., Rutgers University, New Brunswick, NJ, 1985.

Contosta, David R. *Lancaster, Ohio, 1800–2000: Frontier Town to Edge City.* Columbus: Ohio State University Press, 1999.

Countryman, Matthew. *Up South: Civil Rights and Black Power in Philadelphia.* Philadelphia: University of Pennsylvania Press, 2007.

Coyle, Andrew, Alison Campbell, and Rodney Neufeld, eds. *Capitalist Punishment: Prison Privatization and Human Rights.* Atlanta: Clarity Press, 2003.

Cranmer, H. Jerome. *New Jersey in the Automobile Age: A History of Transportation.* Princeton, NJ: D. Van Nostrand Company, Inc., 1964.

Crew, Spencer R. *Black Life in Secondary Cities: A Comparative Analysis of the Black Communities of Camden and Elizabeth, New Jersey, 1860–1920.* New York: Garland Publishing, Inc., 1993.

Cunningham, Barbara, ed. *The New Jersey Ethnic Experience*. Union City, NJ: Wise, 1977.
Cunningham, John T. *New Jersey's Rich Harvest: A 200th Anniversary Tribute to the New Jersey Agricultural Society*. Trenton: New Jersey Agricultural Society Publication, 1981.
———. *Railroads in New Jersey: The Formative Years*. Andover, NJ: Afton Publishing Company, 1997.
———. *This Is New Jersey*. New Brunswick, NJ: Rutgers University Press, 1953.
Daines, Marvel. *Be It Ever So Tumbled: A Story of a Suburban Slum*. Detroit: Rackham Fund, 1940.
Dalik, Richard. *Images of America: Manalapan and Englishtown*. Dover, NH: Arcadia Publishing, 1998.
Davidoff, Paul, and Mary E. Brooks. "Zoning Out the Poor." In *Suburbia: The American Dream and Dilemma*, edited by Philip C. Dolce. New York: Anchor Books, 1976.
Delaney, David. *Race, Place and the Law, 1836–1948*. Austin: University of Texas Press, 1998.
Delgado, Richard, and Jean Stefancic, eds. *Critical White Studies: Looking Behind the Mirror*. Philadelphia: Temple University Press, 1997.
Des Jardins, Julie. *Women and the Historical Enterprise in America: Gender, Race, and the Politics of Memory, 1880–1945*. Chapel Hill: University of North Carolina Press, 2002.
Deskins, Donald R. "Race, Residence, and Workplace in Detroit, 1880–1965." *Economic Geography* 48 (January 1972): 79–94.
Donahay, Alma, and the 1967 Eighth Grade Class. *History of Howell*. Howell, NJ: Howell Historical Society, 1982.
Dray, Philip. *At the Hands of Persons Unknown: The Lynching of Black America*. New York: Random House, 2002.
Du Bois, W. E. B. *The Philadelphia Negro*. Philadelphia: University of Pennsylvania Press, 1996.
Duck, Evelyn Blackmore. "An Historical Study of a Racially Segregated School in New Jersey from 1886–1955." PhD diss., Rutgers University, New Brunswick, NJ, 1984.
Dunaway, Wilma A. *The African American Family in Slavery and Emancipation*. New York: Cambridge University Press, 2003.
Englander, Valerie, and Fred Englander. "Workfare in New Jersey: A Five Year Assessment." *Policy Studies Review* 5, no. 1 (1985): 33–41.
Entman, Robert M., and Andrew Rojecki. *The Black Image in the White Mind: Media and Race in America*. Chicago: University of Chicago Press, 2001.
Fader, Jaime J., Michael B. Katz, and Mark J. Stern. "The New African American Inequality." *Journal of American History* 92, no. 1 (June 2005): 75–108.
Fishman, George. *The African-American Struggle for Freedom and Equality: The Development of a People's Identity, New Jersey, 1624–1850*. New York: Garland Publishing, 1997.
Fishman, Robert. *Bourgeois Utopias: The Rise and Fall of Suburbia*. New York: Basic Books, Inc., 1987.
Fleming, Thomas. *New Jersey: A Bicentennial History*. New York: W. W. Norton and Company, Inc., 1977.
Fletcher, Lehman B., et al. *Guatemala's Economic Development: The Role of Agriculture*. Ames: Iowa State University Press, 1970.
Fogelson, Robert M. *The Fragmented Metropolis: Los Angeles, 1850–1930*. Cambridge, MA: Harvard University Press, 1967.
Foner, Eric. *Reconstruction: America's Unfinished Revolution, 1863–1877*. New York: Harper Perennial, 2002.
Foner, Philip S. *History of Black Americans from Africa to the Emergence*. 3 vols. Westport, CT: Greenwood, 1975.
Foner, Philip S., and Ronald L. Lewis. *The Black Worker: A Documentary History from Colonial Times to Present*. Philadelphia: Temple University Press, 1980.
Foucault, Michel. *The History of Sexuality: An Introduction*. Vol. 1. New York: Vintage Books, Inc., 1978.

Franklin, John Hope. *From Slavery to Freedom: A History of Negro Americans.* New York: Knopf, 1996.

Franklin, Vincent P. *The Education of Black Philadelphia: The Social and Educational History of a Minority Community, 1900–1950.* Philadelphia: University of Pennsylvania Press, 1979.

Frazier, E. Franklin. *The Negro Church in America.* New York: Shocken Books, 1964.

Fredrickson, George. *The Black Image in the White Mind: The Debate on Afro-American Character and Destiny, 1817–1914.* Hanover, NH: Wesleyan University Press, 1971.

Freund, David M. P. *Colored Property: State Policy and White Racial Politics in Suburban America.* Chicago: University of Chicago Press, 2007.

Gabrielan, Randall. *Images of America: Long Branch, People and Places.* Charleston, SC: Arcadia Publishing, 1998.

———. *Images of America: Red Bank.* Dover, NH: Arcadia Publishing, 1995.

———. *Images of America: Red Bank, Volume 2.* Dover, NH: Arcadia Publishing, 1996.

———. *Images of America: Red Bank, Volume 3.* Charleston, SC: Arcadia Publishing, 1998.

———. *Red Bank in the Twentieth Century.* Charleston, SC: Arcadia Publishing, 1997.

Gaines, Kevin K. *Uplifting the Race: Black Leadership, Politics, and Culture in the Twentieth Century.* Chapel Hill: University of North Carolina Press, 1996.

Galeano, Eduardo. *Guatemala: Occupied Country.* New York: Monthly Review Press, 1969.

Giddings, Paula. *When and Where I Enter: The Impact of Black Women on Race and Sex in America.* New York: Perennial, 1984.

Gilje, Paul. *Rioting in America.* Indianapolis: University of Indiana Press, 1999.

Gillette, Howard. *Camden after the Fall: Decline and Renewal in a Post-Industrial City.* Philadelphia: University of Pennsylvania Press, 2005.

Goldberg, David J. "Unmasking the Ku Klux Klan: The Northern Movement against the KKK, 1920–1925." *Journal of American Ethnic History,* Summer 1996:32–48.

Golub, Fred T. *The Puerto Rican Worker in Perth Amboy, New Jersey.* New Brunswick, NJ: Rutgers University Press, 1956.

Goodfellow, Caroline. *How We Played: A History of Childhood Games.* New York: The History Press, 2008.

Gottdeiner, M., and George Kephart. "The Multinucleated Region: A Comparative Analysis." In *Postsuburban California: The Transformation of Orange County since World War II,* edited by Robert Kling, Spencer Olin, and Mark Poster. Los Angeles: University of California Press, 1991.

Gray, Phyllis A. "Economic Development and African Americans in the Mississippi Delta." *Rural Sociology* 56, no. 2 (1991): 238–46.

Greason, Walter D. "From Village to Suburb: Race, Politics, and Economics in Monmouth County, New Jersey, 1890–1990." PhD diss., Temple University, Philadelphia, 2004.

Greene, L. A. "A History of Afro-Americans in New Jersey." *Journal of Rutgers University Libraries* 56, no. 1 (1994): 4–71.

Griffith, Lee Ellen. *Images of America: Freehold.* Charleston, SC: Arcadia Publishing, 1996.

———. *Images of America: Freehold, Volume II.* Charleston, SC: Arcadia Publishing, 1999.

Grimshaw, William J. "Revisiting the Urban Classics." *Policy Studies Journal* 24, no. 2 (1996): 230–44.

Guest, Avery M. "Population Suburbanization in American Metropolitan Areas." *Geographical Analysis* 7 (July 1975): 267–83.

Guglielmo, Jennifer. *Are Italians White? How Race Is Made in America.* New York: Routledge, 2003.

Gutman, Herbert G. *The Black Family in Slavery and Freedom, 1750–1925.* New York: Pantheon Books, 1976.

Hall, Egerton E. "The Negro Wage Earner of New Jersey." *Rutgers University Bulletin* 9, no. 8 (February 1935).

Handy, Jim. *Gift of the Devil: A History of Guatemala*. Boston: South End Press, 1984.

Harding, Vincent. *There Is a River: The Black Struggle for Freedom*. Orlando, FL: Harcourt, Brace, and Company, 1981.

Hardy, Charles A. "Race and Opportunity: Black Philadelphia during the Era of the Great Migration." PhD diss., Temple University, 1989.

Hayden, Dolores. *Building Suburbia*. New York: Random House, 2003.

Haynes, Bruce D. *Red Lines, Black Spaces: The Politics of Race and Space in a Black Middle Class Suburb*. New Haven, CT: Yale University Press, 2001.

Heckscher, August. *Woodrow Wilson*. New York: Charles Scribner's Sons, 1991.

Herivel, Tara, and Paul Wright, eds. *Prison Nation: The Warehousing of America's Poor*. New York: Routledge, 2003.

Heston, Alfred F. *South Jersey, A History, 1664–1924*. New York: Lewis Historical, 1924.

Hine, Darlene Clark, Elsa Barkley Brown, and Rosalyn Terborg-Penn, eds. *Black Women in America: An Historical Encyclopedia*. Vols. 1 and 2. Bloomington: Indiana University Press, 1993.

Hirsch, Arnold. *Making the Second Ghetto: Race and Housing in Chicago, 1940–1960*. New York: Cambridge University Press, 1983.

Hirsch, James S. *Riot and Remembrance: The Tulsa Race War and Its Legacy*. New York: Houghton Mifflin Harcourt, 2002.

Hodges, Graham Russell. *Slavery and Freedom in the Rural North: African Americans in Monmouth County, New Jersey, 1665–1865*. Madison, WI: Madison House, 1997.

Holmdel Historical Society. *Sketchbook of Historic Holmdel*. Holmdel, NJ: HHS Publications, 1976.

hooks, bell. *Feminism Is for Everybody*. Boston: South End Press, 2000.

Hunter, Gary. *Neighborhoods of Color: African American Communities in Southern New Jersey, 1660–1998*. Unpublished, 2002.

Immerman, Richard H. *The CIA in Guatemala: The Foreign Policy of Intervention*. Austin: University of Texas Press, 1982.

Jackson, John P., Jr. and Nadine M. Weidman. *Race, Racism, and Science: Social Impact and Interaction*. New Brunswick, NJ: Rutgers University Press, 2004.

Jackson, Kenneth T. *Crabgrass Frontier: The Suburbanization of the United States*. New York: Oxford University Press, 1985.

———. *The Ku Klux Klan in the City, 1915–1930*. New York: Oxford University Press, 1967.

Jackson, Madonna Carter. *Asbury Park: A West Side Story*. Denver: Outskirts Press, 2007.

Jacobson, Matthew Frye. *Whiteness of a Different Color: European Immigrants and the Alchemy of Race*. Cambridge, MA: Harvard University Press, 1998.

Jelliffe, Thelma K. *Achter Coll to Zoning: Historical Notes on Middletown, NJ*. Middletown, NJ: Academy Press, 1982.

Jensen, Leif, and Martha Tienda. "Nonmetropolitan Minority Families in the United States: Trends in Racial and Ethnic Economic Stratification, 1959–1986." *Rural Sociology* 54, no. 4 (1989): 509–32.

Johnson, Kenneth M. "Recent Population Redistribution Trends in Nonmetropolitan America." *Rural Sociology* 54, no. 3 (1989): 301–26.

Jones, Chester Lloyd. *Guatemala: Past and Present*. Minneapolis: University of Minnesota Press, 1940.

Jonas, Gilbert. *Freedom's Sword: The NAACP and the Struggle against Racism in America, 1909–1969*. New York: Routledge, 2005.

Jones, Jacqueline. *Labor of Love, Labor of Sorrow*. New York: Vintage, 1986.

Jordan, Winthrop. *White over Black: American Attitudes toward the Negro, 1550–1815*. Chapel Hill: University of North Carolina Press, 1968.

Justesen, Benjamin R. *George Henry White: An Even Chance in the Race for Life*. Baton Rouge: Louisiana State University Press, 2001.

Karr, Ronald D. "The Evolution of the Elite Suburb: Community Structure and Control in Brookline, Massachusetts, 1770–1900." PhD diss., Boston University, 1981.

Katzman, David M. *Before the Ghetto: Black Detroit in the Nineteenth Century*. Urbana: University of Illinois Press, 1973.

Katznelson, Ira. *When Affirmative Action Was White: An Untold History of Racial Inequality in Twentieth-Century America*. New York: W. W. Norton, 2006.

Keita, Maghan. *Race and the Writing of History: Riddling the Sphinx*. London: Oxford University Press, 2000.

Keller, Susan Etta. "Jamming on the Jersey Shore: A Community of Rock Musicians in Asbury Park, Its Formation and Traditions." *New Jersey Folklife* 13 (1998): 39–48.

Kelley, Robin D. G. *Race Rebels: Culture, Politics, and the Black Working Class*. New York: The Free Press, 1994.

Kellogg, Charles Flint. *NAACP: A History of the National Association for the Advancement of Colored People*, volume 1, *1909–1920*. Baltimore: The Johns Hopkins Press, 1967.

King, Martin Luther, Jr. "A Revolution of Values" *Spirituality and Practice*. http://www.spiritualityandpractice.com/quotes.

Kirp, David, John Dwyer, and Larry Rosenthal. *Our Town: Race, Housing, and the Soul of Suburbia*. New Brunswick, NJ: Rutgers University Press, 1997.

Kruse, Kevin M. *White Flight: Atlanta and the Making of Modern Conservatism*. Princeton, NJ: Princeton University Press, 2005.

Kruse, Kevin M., and Thomas J. Sugrue, eds. *The New Suburban History*. Chicago: University of Chicago Press, 2006.

Kusmer, Kenneth. *A Ghetto Takes Shape: Black Cleveland, 1870–1930*. Chicago: University of Illinois, 1976.

Lake, Robert W. *The New Suburbanites: Race and Housing in the Suburbs*. New Brunswick, NJ: Rutgers University, 1981.

Lamb, Charles M. *Housing Segregation in Suburban America since 1960: Presidential and Judicial Politics*. New York: Cambridge University Press, 2005.

Lassiter, Matthew D. "The New Suburban History II: Political Culture and Metropolitan Space." *Journal of Planning History* 4, no. 1 (February 2005).

Leonard, Thomas H. *From Indian Trail to Electric Rail, 1609–1909*. Atlantic Highlands, NJ: Atlantic Highlands Journal Publication, 1923.

Lincoln, C. Eric, and Lawrence Mamiya. *The Black Church in the African American Experience*. Durham, NC: Duke University Press, 1990.

Logan, John R., and Harvey L. Molotch. *Urban Fortunes: The Political Economy of Place*. Los Angeles: University of California Press, 1988.

Logan, John, and Mark Schneider. "The Stratification of Metropolitan Suburbs, 1960–1970." *American Sociological Review* 46 (April 1981): 175–77.

MacLean, Nancy K. *Behind the Mask of Chivalry: The Making of the Second Ku Klux Klan*. New York: Oxford University Press, 1995.

"Marion Thompson Wright biography," 7 March 2008, http://65.36.189.169/.

Marsh, Margaret. *Suburban Lives*. New Brunswick, NJ: Rutgers University Press, 1990.

Massey, Douglas S., and Nancy A. Denton. *American Apartheid: Segregation and the Making of the Underclass*. Cambridge, MA: Harvard University Press, 1993.

McGinnis, William. *History of Perth Amboy, 1651–1946*. 4 vols. Perth Amboy, NJ: American, 1958.

McKay, Lenora W. *The Blacks of Monmouth County: A Bicentennial Tribute*. Privately published, 1976.

McKay, Lenora Walker. *Mama and Papa: The Blacks of Monmouth County, Volume II*. Privately published, 1984.

McReynolds, Larkin S., and Gail A. Wasserman. "Risk for Disciplinary Infractions among Incarcerated Male Youth." *Criminal Justice and Behavior* 35, no. 9 (September 2008).

McShane, Clay. *Down the Asphalt Path: The Automobile and the American City*. New York: Columbia University Press, 1994.

Meck, Stuart, and Rebecca Retzlaff. "The Emergence of Growth Management Planning in the United States: The Case of *Golden v. Planning Board of Town of Ramapo* and Its Aftermath." *Journal of Planning History* 7, no. 2 (May 2008): 113–57.

Meier, August. *Negro Thought in America: 1880–1915*. Ann Arbor: University of Michigan Press, 1966.

Meier, August, and Elliott Rudwick. *Black Detroit and the Rise of the UAW*. New York: Oxford University, 1979.

Milligan, John P. "Civil Rights in New Jersey" in *New Jersey Education Association Review* March 1956:291–98.

Morton, Patricia. *Disfigured Images: The Historical Assault on Afro-American Women*. Westport, CT: Praeger Publishers, 1991.

Mullen, Clyde A. *Zanesville Odyssey*. Privately published, 1978.

Mumford, Kevin. "Double V in New Jersey: African American Civil Culture and Rising Consciousness against Jim Crow, 1938–1966." *New Jersey History* Fall 2001:22–56.

———. *Newark: A History of Race, Rights, and Riots in America*. New York: New York University Press, 2007.

Myers, Samuel L., and Tsze Chan. "Racial Discrimination in Housing Markets: Accounting for Bad Credit." *Social Science Quarterly* 76, no. 3 (1995): 543–61.

New Jersey County and Municipal Study Commission. *Housing and Suburbs: Fiscal and Social Impact of Multifamily Development*. 9th report. Trenton: New Jersey County and Municipal Study Commission Publication, 1974.

New Jersey Emergency Relief Association. *Negroes on the Road: A Survey of the Transient Negro in New Jersey*. Privately published, 1934.

New Jersey Writers Project. *Entertaining a Nation: The Career of Long Branch*. Bayonne, NJ: Jersey Printing Company, 1940.

———. *Stories of New Jersey*. New York: Viking Press, 1938.

Nicolaides, Becky, and Andrew Wiese, eds. *The Suburb Reader*. New York: Routledge, 2006.

Noble, Ransome E., *New Jersey Progressivism before Wilson*. Princeton, NJ: Princeton University Press, 1946.

Novarra, Tova. *Images of America: Howell and Farmingdale*. Dover, NH: Arcadia Publishing, 1996.

Novick, Peter. *That Noble Dream: The 'Objectivity Question' and the American Historical Association*. Cambridge: Cambridge University Press, 1995.

O'Connor, Carol. *A Sort of Utopia: Scarsdale, New York, 1891–1981*. Albany, NY: State University of New York–Albany Press, 1983.

Olin, Spencer. "Intraclass Conflict and the Politics of a Fragmented Region." In *Postsuburban California: The Transformation of Orange County since World War II*, edited by Robert

Kling, Spencer Olin, and Mark Poster. Los Angeles: University of California Press, 1991.

Omi, Michael, and Howard Winant. *Racial Formation in the United States: From the 1960s to the 1990s*. New York: Routledge, 1994.

Orfield, Myron. *American Metropolitics: The New Suburban Reality*. Washington, DC: Brookings Institution, 2002.

Osofsky, Gilbert. *Harlem: The Making of a Ghetto, Negro New York, 1890–1930*. New York: Harper and Row, 1966.

Parenti, Christian. *Lockdown America: Police and Prisons in the Age of Crisis*. New York: Verso, 1999.

Patterson, Orlando. *Slavery and Social Death: A Comparative Study*. Cambridge, MA: Harvard University Press, 1985.

Pawley, James E. *The Negro Church in New Jersey*. Hackensack: WPA of New Jersey, 1938.

Phelan, Thomas J., and Mark Schneider. "Race, Ethnicity, and Class in American Suburbs." *Urban Affairs Review* 31, no. 5 (May 1996): 665–67.

Philips, Peter. "A Note on the Apparent Constancy of the Racial Wage Gap in New Jersey Manufacturing, 1902–1979." *Social Research* 51, no. 4 (Winter 1984): 71–76.

Pike, Helen-Chantal. *Images of America: Asbury Park*. Charleston, SC: Arcadia Publishing, 1997.

Pine, Alan S., Jean C. Hershenov, and Aaron H. Lefkowitz. *Peddler to Suburbanite: The History of the Jews of Monmouth County, New Jersey*. Deal Park, NJ: Monmouth Jewish Community Council, 1981.

Price, Clement Alexander. *Freedom Not Too Far Distant. A Documentary History of Afro-Americans in New Jersey*. Newark: New Jersey Historical Society, 1980.

Postman, Neil. *Amusing Ourselves to Death: Public Discourse in the Age of Show Business*. New York: Penguin, 2005.

Putnam, Robert D. "Bowling Alone: America's Declining Social Capital." *Journal of Democracy*, 6, no. 1 (1995): 65–78.

Ransby, Barbara. *Ella Baker and the Black Freedom Movement: A Radical Democratic Vision*. Chapel Hill: University of North Carolina Press, 2005.

Reed, Adolph, Jr. *Stirring in the Jug: Black Politics in the Post-Segregation Era*. Minneapolis: University of Minnesota Press, 1999.

Reed, Ingrid W. "The Life and Death of UDAG: An Assessment Based on Eight Projects in Five New Jersey Cities." *Publius* 19 (Summer 1989): 93–109.

Roberts, Russell, and Richard Youmans. *Down the Jersey Shore*. New Brunswick, NJ: Rutgers University Press, 1993.

Roediger, David R. *Colored White: Transcending the Racial Past*. Los Angeles: University of California Press, 2002.

———. *Working toward Whiteness: How America's Immigrants Became White—The Strange Journey from Ellis Island to the Suburbs*. New York: Basic Books, 2005.

Rose, Harold. *Black Suburbanization: Access to Improved Quality of Life or Maintenance of the Status Quo*. Cambridge, MA: Harvard University Press, 1976.

———. "The All-Black Town: Suburban Prototype or Rural Slum?" *Urban Affairs Annual Review* 6 (1972): 407.

Rosenthal, Alan, and John Blydenburg, eds. *Politics in New Jersey*. New Brunswick, NJ: Rutgers University, 1975.

Sackett, William Edgar. *Modern Battles of Trenton*. Trenton, NJ: John L. Murphy, 1895.

Saenz, Rogelio, and John K. Thomas. "Minority Poverty in Nonmetropolitan Texas." *Rural Sociology* 56, no. 2 (1991): 204–23.

Salmore, Barbara G., and Stephen A. Salmore. *New Jersey Politics and Government: Suburban Politics Comes of Age*. Lincoln: University of Nebraska Press, 1993.

Salter, Edwin. *A History of Monmouth and Ocean Counties*. Bayonne, NJ: Garner, 1890.

Schiesl, Martin J. "Designing the Model Community: The Irvine Company and Suburban Development, 1950–1988." In *Postsuburban California: The Transformation of Orange County since World War II* edited by Robert Kling, Spencer Olin, and Mark Poster. Los Angeles: University of California Press, 1991.

Schmidt, Hubert G. *Agriculture in New Jersey: A Three-Hundred-Year History*. New Brunswick, NJ: Rutgers University Press, 1973.

Schnitzspahn, Karen L. *A Strong Legacy: 125 Years of the Community YMCA*. Red Bank: Community YMCA Publication, 1999.

Scott, James C. *Domination and the Arts of Resistance*. New Haven, CT: Yale University Press, 1992.

Seligman, Amanda I. "The New Suburban History." *Journal of Planning History* 3, no. 4 (November 2004).

Sim, Mary B. *Commercial Canning in New Jersey: History and Early Development*. Trenton: New Jersey Agricultural Society, 1951.

Simon, Bryant. *Boardwalk of Dreams: Atlantic City and the Fate of Urban America*. New Brunswick, NJ: Rutgers University Press, 2006.

Sinclair, Donald. *New Jersey and the Negro: A Bibliography*. Trenton: New Jersey Library Association, 1967.

Sinden, Jeff. "The Problem of Prison Privatization: The United States Experience." In *Capitalist Punishment: Prison Privatization and Human Rights* edited by Andrew Coyle, Allison Campbell, and Rodney Neufield. Atlanta: Clarity Press, 2003.

Singh, Nikhal Pal. *Black Is a Country: Race and the Unfinished Struggle for Democracy*. Cambridge, MA: Harvard University Press, 2004.

Snyder, Eve. "Oral History Archives of WWII Interview with Alice Jennings Archibald." 1997. http://oralhistory.rutgers.edu/Interviews/ archibald_alice.html (25 June 2006).

Society of Colonial Wars in the State of New Jersey. *Historic Roadsides in New Jersey.* Plainfield, NJ: Society of Colonial Wars in the State of New Jersey Publication, 1928.

Soja, Edward. "Inside Exopolis: Scenes from Orange County." In *Variations on a Theme Park: The New American City and the End of Public Space,* edited by Michael Sorkin. New York: Hill and Wang, 1994.

Sowell, Thomas. *Basic Economics: A Common Sense Guide to the Economy.* New York: Basic Books, 2007.

St. John, Craig, Mark Edwards, and Deeann Wenk. "Racial Differences in Intraurban Residential Mobility." *Urban Affairs Review* 30, no. 5 (May 1995): 709–29.

Stansfield, Charles. *A Geography of New Jersey: The City in the Garden.* New Brunswick, NJ: Rutgers University Press, 1998.

Stellhorn, Paul. "Depression and Decline: Newark, New Jersey, 1929–1941." PhD diss., Rutgers University, 1983.

Stilgoe, John. *Borderland: Origins of the American Suburb, 1820–1939.* New Haven, CT: Yale University Press, 1988.

Sugrue, Thomas. *The Origins of the Urban Crisis: Race and Inequality in Postwar Detroit.* Princeton, NJ: Princeton University Press, 1996.

———. *Sweet Land of Liberty: The Forgotten Struggle for Civil Rights in the North.* New York: Random House, 2008.

Sugrue, Thomas J., and Andrew P. Goodman. "Plainfield Burning: Black Rebellion in the Suburban North." *Journal of Urban History* 33, no. 4 (May 2007): 591–93.

Summers, Gene F. "Minorities in Rural Society." *Rural Sociology* 56, no. 2 (1991): 177–88.

Teaford, Jon. *The Rough Road to Renaissance: Urban Revitalization in America, 1940–1985.* Baltimore: John Hopkins Press, 1990.

Theoharis, Jeanne, and Komozi Woodard. *Freedom North: Black Freedom Struggles outside the South, 1940–1980.* New York: Palgrave McMillan, 2003.

Thornbrough, Emma Lou. *T. Thomas Fortune: Militant Journalist.* Chicago: University of Chicago Press, 1972.

Tolnay, Stewart E., and E. M. Beck. *Festival of Violence: An Analysis of Southern Lynchings, 1882–1930.* Chicago: University of Illinois Press, 1995.

Tomlinson, Gerald. *New Jersey? What Exit? 300 Questions and Answers about People, Places, and Events in the Garden State.* Lake Hopacong, NJ: Home Run Press, 1996.

Trotter, Joe William, Jr. *Black Milwaukee: The Making of an Industrial Proletariat, 1915–1940.* Urbana: University of Illinois Press, 1985.

———. *River Jordan: African American Urban Life in the Ohio Valley.* Lexington: University of Kentucky Press, 1998.

Troy, Leo. *Organized Labor in New Jersey.* Princeton, NJ: D. Van Nostrand Company, Inc., 1965.

Vecoli, Rudolph. *The People of New Jersey.* Princeton, NJ: Van Nostrand, 1965.

Venino, Richard O. *History of Sea Girt: Fiftieth Anniversary Celebration, 1917–1967.* Privately published, 1967.

Walker, Juliet E. K. *History of Black Business in America: Capitalism, Race, Entrepreneurship.* New York: Twayne Publishers, 1998.

Walling, Richard, and Middlesex County Vocational-Technical High School Students. *The African American Experience in Western Monmouth County, New Jersey: Two Historic Black Communities in Manalapan/Millstone and Freehold Townships.* Manalapan: Friends of Monmouth Battlefield, Inc., 1996.

Warner, Sam Bass. *Streetcar Suburbs: The Process of Growth in Boston, 1870–1990.* Cambridge, MA: Harvard University Press, 1962.

Watkins, Mel. *On the Real Side: A History of African American Comedy from Slavery to Chris Rock.* Chicago: Lawrence Hill Books, 1999.

Weems, Robert E., Jr. *Desegregating the Dollar: African American Consumerism in the Twentieth Century.* New York: New York University Press, 1998.

White, Wendell A. *Small Towns, Black Lives: African American Communities in Southern New Jersey.* Oceanville, NJ: Noyes Museum of Art, 2003.

Wiese, Andrew. "The Other Suburbanites: African American Suburbanization in the North before 1950." *Journal of American History* March 1999:1495–1524.

———. *Places of Their Own: African American Suburbanization in the Twentieth Century.* Chicago: University of Chicago Press, 2004.

Wilson, Harold, et al. *Outline History of New Jersey.* New Brunswick, NJ: Rutgers University Press, 1950.

Wilson, Leslie. "Dark Spaces: An Account of Afro-American Suburbanization." PhD diss., City University of New York, 1991.

Winch, Julie. *Philadelphia's Black Elite: Activism, Accommodation, and the Struggle for Autonomy, 1787–1848.* Philadelphia: Temple University Press, 1993.

Winner, Langdon. "Silicon Valley Mystery House." In *Variations on a Theme Park,* edited by Michael Sorkin. New York: Hill and Wang, 1994.

Winton, Stanley N., et al. *New Jersey, Past and Present.* New York: Hayden, 1964.

Wise, Tim. *White Like Me.* New York: Soft Skull Press, 2005.

Woodson, Carter G. *A Century of Negro Migration.* Washington, DC: Association for the Study of Negro Life and Culture, 1918.

Woodward, Carl B. *New Jersey Agriculture Past and Present.* New Brunswick, NJ: Rutgers University Press, 1933.

Wright, Giles R. *Afro-Americans in New Jersey: A Short History.* Trenton: New Jersey Historical Society, 1988.

Wright, Marion M. Thompson. *The Education of Negroes in New Jersey.* New York: privately published, 1941.

———. "Extending Civil Rights through the Division against Discrimination." *Journal of Negro History* 38, no. 1 (January 1953): 91–107.

Wright, William C. *Urban New Jersey since 1870.* Trenton: New Jersey Historical Commission, 1975.

Zilversmit, Arthur. *The First Emancipation: The Abolition of Slavery in the North.* Chicago: University of Chicago Press, 1967.

Index

About the Author

Dr. Walter David Greason is visiting professor of history at Monmouth University in West Long Branch, New Jersey. He is also the chief executive officer of the International Center for Metropolitan Growth. Dr. Greason is one of the world's foremost experts on race, housing, migration, and economic development.